NEW PENGUIN SHAKESPEARE

GENERAL EDITOR: T. J. B. SPENCER

ASSOCIATE EDITOR: STANLEY WELLS

WILLIAM SHAKESPEARE

✳

KING LEAR

EDITED BY
G. K. HUNTER

PENGUIN BOOKS

PENGUIN BOOKS

Published by the Penguin Group
Penguin Books Ltd, 80 Strand, London WC2R 0RL, England
Penguin Putnam Inc., 375 Hudson Street, New York, New York 10014, USA
Penguin Books Australia Ltd, Ringwood, Victoria, Australia
Penguin Books Canada Ltd, 10 Alcorn Avenue, Toronto, Ontario, Canada M4V 3B2
Penguin Books India (P) Ltd, 11 Community Centre, Panchsheel Park, New Delhi – 110 017, India
Penguin Books (NZ) Ltd, Cnr Rosedale and Airborne Roads, Albany, Auckland, New Zealand
Penguin Books (South Africa) (Pty) Ltd, 24 Sturdee Avenue, Rosebank 2196 South Africa

Penguin Books Ltd, Registered Offices: 80 Strand, London WC2R 0RL, England

www.penguin.com

This edition first published in Penguin Books 1972
Reprinted with revised Further Reading and Account of the Text 1996
42

Set in Monotype Ehrhardt
Printed in England by Clays Ltd, St Ives plc

CONTENTS

INTRODUCTION

King Lear is generally agreed today to be Shakespeare's 'greatest play', not only by the learned (who have long approved it) but also by the general public; and this latter approval is more recent. It seems to have been some time during the Second World War that the more grim and overwhelming work replaced *Hamlet* in popular esteem. But before we endorse this general approval too heartily we should consider a little what 'greatness' means in such a context. *King Lear* is certainly a play in which everything is at full stretch: extremes of cruelty and suffering face extremes of loyalty and self-sacrifice. The play as a whole gives an impression of a monolithic and rough-hewn grandeur, as if it were some Stonehenge of the mind. But not every work that claims these qualities justifies possession of them. André Gide, watching Laurence Olivier play King Lear in 1946, did not think of Beethoven and Michelangelo, but only of Victor Hugo. He found in the play nothing which was not 'forced, arbitrary, wished upon us. . . . Hugo himself could not have imagined anything more gigantically factitious, more false'.

Acquaintance with the play teaches us that these charges cannot be sustained. Lear's giant features do not lack humanity; they are impressive not simply because of the scope and sweep of the conception, but also because of the detail and accurate grain of experience. The imperious monarch is also the tedious father; the demonic energy he manifests – those who think of him as an enfeebled old man should read again – shows itself in 'pranks', in 'unsightly tricks', as his literal-minded daughters call them, in transformations of domestic trivia into the symbols of the Apocalypse. The world that his energy works upon is littered with the jumbled reality of common experience; it is the constantly asserted relationship between this and the gigantic vision that gives the play its integrity inside its power.

Alas, this is not what people usually talk about when they discuss the 'greatness' of *King Lear*. The modern popularity of the play is closely associated with a movement which uses as its touchstone the 'meaning' attributed to Shakespeare's plays, the spiritual messages they convey to us. Of course the idea that the work of art is a 'message' from the author is not new. Hazlitt tells us that '*King Lear* is the best of Shakespeare's plays, for it is the one in which he was most in earnest'. But modern critics are usually unable to stop at this point; they want to ask the next question: 'What is Shakespeare in earnest about?' One trouble with asking this question is that it produces answers of unbearable obviousness; it is a long way round about to learn only that Shakespeare felt love to be superior to hate or was strongly against sin. One aspect of the enormous energy of the play, of which I spoke above, is its perpetually renewed capacity for discovering life. Characters are all the time learning new and surprising truths, and we in the audience are learning with them. But this is quite different from supposing that the play is about learning a general lesson (for example, that love matters more than power) which can be stated in words other than the author's.

Those who attack the vague uplifting piety of such 'meanings' are not always, however, in a stronger position. Attacking mere moralizing they tend to substitute mere plot. The play, they tell us, cannot be about 'the salvation of Lear through the redeeming love of Cordelia' since the moments when redemption might seem to be asserted – in the reunion scene (IV.7) and the 'Come, let's away to prison' speech (V.3.8–25) – are discarded by a process which leads on to deprivation 'All dark and comfortless', indeed all the more dark and comfortless because of the hint of redemption that has preceded it. I cannot pretend that these points about the plot are untrue; but I note that it does the play a disservice to make them a limiting truth. What seems to be needed is a description of the play which relates plot to meaning in such a way that the two dimensions support each other. In this Introduction I seek to describe such a relationship, assuming that the play is not only a great work of art but also a successful one and that form and content are therefore totally compatible.

*

The first thing that we must notice about the plot of *King Lear* is its defectiveness by ordinary standards. To measure its weaknesses we need refer to no tradition outside that of the King Lear story itself. In all versions other than Shakespeare's there is a happy ending. Holinshed's *Chronicles*, Spenser's version in *The Faerie Queene*, that in *A Mirror for Magistrates*, the old play of *King Leir* (Shakespeare's main source), all restore Lear and Cordelia to power and happiness. Even though Cordelia may have killed herself later in history (as is reported by the first three), they all fulfil in terms of this particular story what Dr Johnson was to call 'the natural ideas of justice and the hope of the readers'. Not only Shakespeare's predecessors but also Nahum Tate, who refashioned the play in the form which was to hold the English stage from 1681 to 1834, give it a happy ending. The sense of moral logic and the sense of narrative logic seem to point naturally in only one direction.

But Shakespeare chose to divert both tradition and logic. If we ask why, and believe that the play is unified, we must seek our answer especially among those elements that are absent from the other versions of the story. Tate's version is like one of those modern miracles of steel rods and concrete piles with which engineers hold up tottering cathedrals; most of the fabric is preserved, but the weight is now carried by quite different systems, by believable or conventional characterization, by conflicts of personal loyalties, by unbroken lines of motivation. Shakespeare's Gothic structure distributes its weight in quite different places; and it is to these that we must pay particular attention.

The preceding versions of the King Lear story (and in many cases Tate's version) lack features that modern readers think of as central: there is no Fool, Lear does not go mad, there is no Poor Tom – indeed the addition of the parallel Gloucester plot is Shakespeare's largest single change – there is no powerfully generalizing and interrelating integument of verse. All these in various ways alter the nature of the story that is being told.

We may begin by thinking about the function of the madness (and the poetry which focuses it on our attention). Why does Shakespeare take us, in cardinal middle scenes of the play, into a world not only of social deprivation (as the story requires) but of mental deprivation as well, and not only in the case of the King but in the parallel and complementary cases of Edgar and the Fool? It is not that madness augments the pathos that the King's position already presents. Indeed the effect is opposite.

The pathos of the old *King Leir* play is almost wholly swallowed up in the terrifying maelstrom of words and images that express man's need to see himself as meaningful. And this is a depersonalizing process. In the scenes on the heath Lear joins Tom and the Fool in a world of fragmentary reactions to the present, a world without a connected past and therefore without personal purpose. They have become 'voices' rather than people, bound together by the orchestration of the scene rather than by anything that might be called social contact or individual expression.

The orchestration is skilfully and spaciously laid out: the three kinds of madness are carefully differentiated from one another. The Fool has a quality of savage innocence that the other two lack. The role is clearly designed for Robert Armin, the member of Shakespeare's company who also played Feste and Lavatch. Like these he is a professional Fool. His stock consists in the main of songs and riddles, nonsense-rhymes and a mock prophecy. These he deploys as oblique and self-protective comments on the real world. It is easy to sentimentalize him; too much is often made of a supposed relationship with Cordelia, based on the slender evidence of I.4.72–3 'Since my young lady's going into France, sir, the Fool hath much pined away'. This certainly indicates an intention to make fragility one of his characteristics; but literally it says no more than that the Fool feels keenly the pressures of the new world of Gonerill and Regan. Unlike Cordelia he has the destructive energy of innocence. We should remember also what Gonerill says of him, that he is 'more knave than fool' (I.4.311). He is a living manifestation of that world of irony and metaphor in which every experience can throw light on every other one, in which Lear too would 'make a good fool', and which the daughters seek to reduce to the literalism of appetite. In such a world, where bitterness and innocence, correction and irresponsibility effortlessly co-exist, it is pointless to ask if he is mad or sane. He knows as much as the next man; but he is exempted from the need to put his knowledge in logical order.

Edgar's Poor Tom is the possessed or demented man. Shakespeare had been reading about 'possession' (or pretended possession) in an anti-papist pamphlet of 1603, Samuel Harsnet's *Declaration of Egregious Popish Impostures*, and was obviously exercised by the idea of man in the grip of an identity he believes he can control but which assumes a reality in the world outside which he never anticipated. Poor Tom is in thrall to his obsessions, cold, hunger, lice and other incommodities, which he expresses as the local effects of 'the foul fiend', but which we (like Lear) may see as the basic features of unprotected humanity. In these terms we are all in danger of 'possession'. The Fool sees folly everywhere; Tom sees torment. His vision is of Hell; his song-snatches are free-wheeling phantasmagorias, not pointed social comments like the Fool's.

Lear's madness shares characteristics with both of these, but is different from each. He uses no songs or rhymes. His forms are the sermon, the prayer, the trial. His role is always a commanding one; though he may become a voice rather than a person, his is always the leading voice. It is he who directs our attention to circle round and round the obsessive centres of *need*, *nature*, *kind*, and the idea of identity. These, of course, are key ideas in sanity as well.

We may see how the two mental states relate by looking at *need* both in sanity and in terms of the madness which takes it up and develops it. 'But for true need', says Lear before rushing out into the storm, 'You heavens, give me that patience, patience I need'. Almost straight away his speech modulates from patience to anger and revenge (traditionally the opposite of patience). But the problem of *need* remains central in the mad scenes which follow and grow out of anger. Patience would be a way of expressing man's need, if it could in fact hold together the various passions – rage at injustice and hypocrisy, pity for the oppressed, disgust at human depravity, incomprehension at offences against that social solidarity of human beings that Shakespeare calls 'kind'. If patience could hold all these together then the need to understand oneself in relation to them could begin to be defined. But at the very end of this same speech an alternative to patience is declared:

> this heart
> *Shall break into a hundred thousand flaws. . . .*
> *O Fool, I shall go mad!*
> II.4.279–81

The madness is a bursting apart of the coherence which holds the hundred thousand flaws in a connected sequence. It does not involve any change in the nature of the obsessions. The need to find a respectable answer to the question

> *Who is it that can tell me who I am?*   I.4.22

moves into more radical questioning about the bonds of 'kind' which seem to guarantee identity. Lear asserts, in his sanity, that he cannot tell who he is, for the defining family relationship is denied by his daughters. In the mad scenes it is not only the relationship between a man and his family that he finds denied; it is the whole sequence of loyalties, duties, and respects that everywhere in Shakespeare describes the final good:

> *Piety and fear,*
> *Religion to the gods, peace, justice, truth,*
> *Domestic awe, night-rest, and neighbourhood,*
> *Instruction, manners, mysteries, and trades,*
> *Degrees, observances, customs, and laws.*
> *Timon of Athens*, IV.1.15–19

It is not only the individual Lear's identity that comes to be in question; it is the whole status of man. If humankind cannot satisfy the individual's need for a sense of himself, how then is man different from a beast? The relationship between man and beast, the potential for bestiality in man, is constantly referred to by the imagery. Man wears clothes, it is true. But he *need* not. Even the beggar's rags are *superfluous* (II.4.260). This is why it is the idea of Edgar's nakedness (however it was represented in the theatre of Shakespeare's day) that gives the final impulse to Lear's madness:

> *Thou art the thing itself! Unaccommodated man is*
> *no more but such a poor, bare, forked animal as thou*
> *art. Off, off, you lendings!* III.4.103–5

Here, when he tears off his own clothes, we have the point at which Lear's fear of madness becomes, unambiguously, the thing itself. The boundary separating his inner world from the outer 'reality' of things seems to dissolve. If Poor Tom 'out there' can fulfil so exactly the inner vision of man's deprivation, why should not a joint-stool be Regan (III.6.51) or Gloucester be 'Gonerill with a white beard' (IV.6.96)?

The external storm plays a preparatory part in this loosening of the baffle between inner and outer:

> *this tempest in my mind*
> *Doth from my senses take all feeling else*
> *Save what beats there.*   III.4.12–14

As the two worlds begin to dissolve into each other, it is the external world of duties and continuities, of business and homes and clothing that loses its shape. Its elements are reformed as part of an infernal Bosch-like landscape centred on

> *Poor Tom ... whom the foul fiend hath led through fire and through flame, through ford and whirlpool, o'er bog and quagmire, that hath laid knives under his pillow and halters in his pew, set ratsbane by his porridge, made him proud of heart, to ride on a bay trotting horse over four-inched bridges to course his own shadow for a traitor.*
>   III.4.49–55

In this unstructured and disparate world Lear comes to know things he (and we) could not know in sanity. The whirlpools of his obsession dredge up truths that are normally concealed. That there is any progression in these mad scenes (III.2, III.4, III.6, IV.6) is very doubtful. At the end of Act IV, scene 6, Lear's obsessions shift from the particular crimes of his own life-time to a more general vision of depravity in which the 'rascal beadle' whips the whore he lusts after, in which 'The usurer hangs the cozener' and the 'scurvy politician' seems to 'see the things' he does not. But the only real progression is towards the establishment of a vision which may stand in the play as one of the buttresses of its value-system. Lear's madness is a means of diverting our attention out

of the natural world of effects (where the other versions
of the story have their being) and into the metaphorical
world of causes. In the mad scenes nothing 'happens',
in the ordinary meaning of the word. But these scenes
convey that sense of an irreversible change of state which
an earlier dramaturgy (*The Spanish Tragedy*, *Titus Andro-
nicus*) derived from Ovid's horrific stories of metamor-
phosis – the sense of a world now frozen in the grotesque
forms of despair, and using the grotesque actions that
derive from this. In *King Lear* this world is focused, not
(as in the earlier plays) on public revenge, but on spiritual
change, and the actions reflect this. But as in *Titus Andron-
icus* and *The Spanish Tragedy*, so here we are given a new
vision of reality which the play must carry forward to
whatever resolutions its end can achieve. In this sense
Lear's recovery from madness cannot be regarded as more
than a personal emergence from a vision we can still see
everywhere around him. His own sense of coherence is
restored; but the paradisal calm of his reunion with
Cordelia is achieved, we must feel, by avoiding the irre-
ducibles. For the first time it is possible here to think of
Lear's age as enfeebling. The family pieties are restored,
but so muted and ironic are the restorations that they carry
with them almost the flavour of a loss.

*

The madness, I have suggested, translates the story into
a mode of vision that is absent from the other versions,
and it burdens the denouement with meanings which they
do not have. Other Shakespearian inventions operate in
the same direction. The history of King Lear belongs to
the sequence that Geoffrey of Monmouth invented to
bridge the gap between Aeneas and the coming of the
Romans to Britain. It is presented as history, but it is

fabulous history, closer to folk legend than to politics, and acceptable as part of the English royal story only because of the extreme remoteness of the time in which it is set – 'in the year of the world 3105, at what time Joas reigned in Judah', says Holinshed's *Chronicles*. The old play of *King Leir* conveys very well the sense of an antique (though Christian) life; but it gives no sense of the tension between the dreamy piety of that ancient time and the bustling modern world. Shakespeare on the other hand gives us a very clear sense of antique pieties dissolving under the impact of a modernism which is always around (raising the rational arguments for euthanasia, free love, etc.), but which in his day must have carried the particular stamp of Montaigne's scepticism and Machiavelli's cynical infidelity.

It seems clear that Shakespeare went to some pains to create the image of a society which had not yet received the Christian revelation. His art is usually quite happy to be anachronistic, and we must assume that his pains were designed to secure more than the establishment of Lear's antiquity. He seems to have wished to explore, with almost scientific thoroughness, the problem of Providence in a context which does not exact the Christian answer. In his picture of Gloucester's superstition, of Edmund's atheist determinism, of Lear's pagan piety and loss and recovery of faith, he raises the largest questions of man's relationship to destiny and leaves them unanswered, hanging like a cloud over the play. And this he could hardly do if he were writing about a Christian society.

The same effort to avoid dogmatic answers and to push the open hypothetical questions to the limit can be seen in more secular terms. One of the key ideas in the play is *nature*; set around this word are opposed and historically differentiated views of its meaning. For Gloucester as for

Lear the 'bias of nature' (I.2.111) requires children and parents to love and protect one another; the 'offices of nature' (II.4.173) cause the young to respect the old, the subordinate to yield to the superior, the passionate to bow to the rational, as female to male or human to divine. All this follows inevitably from an assumption that *nature* is a reflection of the *status quo*, of an order without which things could not hold together and meaning would not exist. And the *status quo* is thought of not simply as 'the way things happen to be' but rather as 'the way things must be', since God made them so, placing the king (as God's vicegerent) at the top of the hierarchy (like the father in a household) and giving every other creature a justified place in an explained and explaining total system. In Shakespeare's own day the noise of challenge to this view of *nature* was not hard to hear; perhaps it is never stifled. The 'generation gap', the sense of the child's need to outrage and replace the father (and his values) are not entirely strange to us today. The anarchic individual points to his own *nature* as wilful and wayward, owing no natural allegiance to 'the system'. And he points also at the system itself, noting that the *status quo* is held together by force and fraud, not by love and loyalty. What is *natural* may be quite other than what the system thinks is desirable; the individual may be able to defend his own nature only by 'illegal acts' against a system in bland possession of legality, by fighting it with the standards of another kind of nature – animal nature:

> *Thou, Nature, art my goddess ; to thy law*
> *My services are bound. Wherefore should I*
> *Stand in the plague of custom. . . .*
> *When my dimensions are as well-compact,*
> *My mind as generous, and my shape as true*

As honest madam's issue? Why brand they us
With 'base'? with 'baseness'? 'bastardy'? 'base, base'?
Who in the lusty stealth of nature take
More composition and fierce quality....   I.2.1–3, 7–12

What Shakespeare is doing here is rather interesting. He is taking a paradox on bastardy which first appeared in Ortensio Landi's *Paradossi* (1543), translated into French in 1553 and perhaps into English in the lost second part of Anthony Munday's *The Defence of Contraries* (1602). In Thomas Milles's *A Treasury of Ancient and Modern Times* (1613) it is headed 'A paradox in the defence of bastardy, approving that the bastard is more worthy to be esteemed than he that is lawfully born', and runs:

> *bastards generally are begot in more heat and vigour of*
> *love ... than the most part of our legitimate children.*
> *Consider withal that their conception is performed by*
> *stolen opportunities. ... Besides it seemeth as a certainty*
> *that Nature hath some peculiar respect of bastards. ...*

Such a 'paradox' was one of the smart 'new' literary forms of the turn of the seventeenth century, a favourite in advanced circles (such as those of John Donne), exploring the witty possibilities of infidelity without actually endorsing it. What Shakespeare does is to take it out of the merely theoretical context in which he found it. He dramatizes it as part of a world in which the structure of set beliefs (which kept the thought as a mere paradox) is weakened. 'What if the smart toy came alive; what if these entertaining propositions had to be accepted as part of our daily life?' he seems to be asking. 'What if the true Law of Nature were not the Christian Humanist one, centred on reason, but another, more red in tooth and claw, based on animal rapacity?' It may be that this is the 'kind' to which man belongs, and will always return:

> *It will come –*
> *Humanity must perforce prey on itself*
> *Like monsters of the deep.*   IV.2.48–50

In these terms Edmund stands for a whole class of anti-Establishment individualists, who, in every age, are thought to be finding it too easy to pull down the decencies of society.

The play dramatizes a crisis in the history of society. Shakespeare has chosen to widen the gap between opposites to its maximum, giving to the old a patriarchal Old Testament flavour (of 'what time Joas reigned in Judah') and to the young the newest cut of brash impiety:

> *I have heard him oft maintain it to be fit that, sons at perfect age and fathers declined, the father should be as ward to the son, and the son manage his revenue.*
>
> I.2.72–5

The Revolution fails, not for an absence of power in the revolutionaries but because its aims are (as in Kant's definition of evil) incapable of being universalized. The three revolutionary children are justifiably proud of their individual vigour, cunning, and determination. But one individual vigour only cancels another. Edmund comments when the deaths of Gonerill and Regan are announced:

> *I was contracted to them both. All three*
> *Now marry in an instant.*   V.3.226–7

This strange moment of concert is the most concerted the three have been able to achieve. It was easy for them to exploit and destroy the system they belonged to; but they have proved quite incapable of building another. The survivors, Edgar and Albany, in whom we have to repose such final confidence as remains in us, are characterized as men in whom the individual will has been completely subordinated to social duty.

The story that Shakespeare inherited showed the swing back to virtue at the end as an inevitable function of an unbreached moral system. In Shakespeare, the system with which the play began is, in effect, destroyed. The scything swing of assumptions throughout the play leaves the end desolated, hesitant, minimal, more certain of what has been lost than of what can survive:

> *we that are young*
> *Shall never see so much nor live so long.*

As I have said above, the most obvious modification of the source is the addition of the story of the Paphlagonian unkind king, found in Sidney's *Arcadia* (Book II, chapter 10) and turned into the Gloucester plot. The things that are usually said about this addition are undoubtedly true: the doubling of the fable of ingratitude, the paralleling of betrayals by a favoured child and rescue by one outcast and persecuted, direct our attention away from the particularities of either story and fasten it on a general image of a world where betrayal and monstrous ingratitude are customary laws. Of course it is important to notice that the overall effect is made by differences as well as similarities in the two plots. The active will to self-destruction in Lear is answered by daughters who take every advantage but only in response to a situation he creates. The more shallow and passive nature of Gloucester, happy to lay blame beyond his own reach – on the King or the stars – and pushed from compromise to compromise, is answered by the positive exploitations of Edmund. The two old men are joined to one another as if to exclude any further possibility of escape from the fate that catches both, for all their radical divergence of temper.

A. C. Bradley censured the sub-plot as one of the principal agents in what he takes to be the play's 'undramatic' quality:

'The number of essential characters is so large, their actions and movements are so complicated, and events towards the end crowd on one another so thickly that the reader's attention ... is overstrained.'

I believe this to be a misjudgement of the meaning of 'dramatic', deriving from too uncritical an acceptance of the realistic theatre of the nineteenth century as *the* theatre. It is difficult in *King Lear* to focus on single characters, single places, or single lines of development in action, and the double plot (the only one in Shakespeare's tragedies) undoubtedly contributes to these difficulties. But Shakespeare's vision in this play seems to have required a vagueness about place, a broadening and flattening of action and character. 'The reader's attention' is *meant* to be prised loose from individual motives and actions, I suspect, and attached to a different but equally dramatic sense of man's general status, rather than his individual destiny. Our attention is also, I suspect, meant to be detached from any sense of implausibility in the speed of plot development. The rapidity of the sub-plot (where the speed of Edmund's success is a function of his character) diverts our notice from the inexplicable speed of the Lear plot.

*

The madness and the questions it raises, the religious and social problems that rear up, the duplications of the double plot, all help to divert our attention from too narrow a focus in terms of cause and effect, motive and consequence. The effects of action are expressed in a variety of parallel symbolic and realistic channels. This does not imply that now we attend to the meaning and now follow the plot. The enlargements I have been speaking about are not departures from the story. It may be appropriate in this context to draw on the anthropologist Claude Lévi-Strauss's approach to myth – for 'the King Lear choice' is a recurrent folk-tale motif. Lévi-Strauss interprets myth in terms not only of its narrative (or 'diachronous') linear dimension but also of its recurrent (or 'synchronous') thematic elements, and finds meaning only by the relationship of these two (which co-exist like harmony and melody). It is interesting to observe that the addition of the Gloucester story to the Lear story produces precisely the same kind of dense synchronous dimension as Lévi-Strauss discovers in the repetitions and parallelisms of the Oedipus story. The vocabulary in which we focus the relationship between these two dimensions is unimportant; but it is important to notice the elaboration of attention which takes the emphases of the play away from the linear processes of motive and sequence. When Nahum Tate described the play as 'a heap of jewels, unstrung' he was of course referring to this weakness of linear connexion. The progress of the action is, in fact, extraordinarily elliptical. Albany's change of heart in Act IV, scene 2, the double love of the sisters for Edmund, the King of France's love for Cordelia, the death of Cornwall – all these come quite unprepared, as if being shown in pools of light surrounded by darkness. The battle is the most perfunctory of military actions, even in Shakespeare. On the other hand, the conflict between Albany and Cornwall, always being prepared for, never comes to anything.

There is another way of thinking about this lack of concern with motive and sequence. We may start from the point that the language of the play is not so much an imitation of the way people speak as an evocation of the realities *behind* what people say. The metaphors that characters use are not commonly chosen to represent their personal vocabulary or delineate their natures. They are more like trains of gunpowder laid across the play, capable of exploding into action when the poet requires it. Take the blinding of Gloucester. Why blinding? The most cogent answer to this question derives not from motive (Cornwall and Regan do have to be cruel, but not this way) nor from narrative convenience, but from the poetic vision of what man is doing to man. The blinding of Gloucester is a climax to the great series of comments on eyes and seeing that the play contains. When Gloucester says

> *I have no way and therefore want no eyes;*
> *I stumbled when I saw. . . .*
>
>   *O dear son Edgar . . .*
> *Might I but live to see thee in my touch*
> *I'd say I had eyes again*   IV.1.18–19, 21, 23–4

the relationship between Gloucester's physical eyeballs and his metaphorical insight does not clearly subordinate the latter to the former, even though we can see his physical eyelessness in front of us. On the other hand it would be wrong to think of Gloucester's blindness as simply a metaphor for his impercipience. He is a man, and not a walking allegory. The 'reality' of the blind Gloucester as a thinking and acting individual is great, but no greater than the 'reality' of the language in which the potential meanings of 'sight' have been explored. The effect of what Gloucester does and the meaning of what

Gloucester is are not divisible, for these are two dimensions of one and the same object.

Take as another example the many expressions of clothing and stripping that the play contains. In the light of these it can be seen that Lear's tearing off his own clothes is like the blinding of Gloucester – the climactic moment when the narrative and the language coalesce, giving the narrative event a force and density it could not have in another telling.

The use of ideas of number and of *nothing* reflects the same tendencies in the play. When the force of Lear's will is suddenly dammed up at Cordelia's 'Nothing' (I.1.87) it is clear that we are at a key moment. But it is not as yet clear what the moment means. That is the business of the play's language as a whole. We have to hear a repetition of Lear's 'Nothing will come of nothing' in the parallel history of Gloucester: 'The quality of nothing hath not such need to hide itself. Let's see! Come! If it be nothing I shall not need spectacles' (I.2.34–6). We have to learn that both Lear and Gloucester begin with an assurance that *nothing* is always at the empty end of the scale, far away from them. And we have to see the process of the play bringing them to *nothing* – by a plain system of arithmetic in Lear's case, reducing his train through a hundred, fifty, five-and-twenty, ten, five to the nothing that lies behind the final line of the sequence:

What need one?   II.4.258

It is at this moment when Lear returns to the *nothing* he had scorned in Cordelia that the arc of movement begun in the first scene comes to rest; and from the same moment springs the second span of the play, which is to carry Lear through the heath and the madness. In the great speech which marks the junction of the two spans ('O, reason not the need . . .') he rejects all numbers as superfluous and begins that exploration of *nothing* which is the substance of the central portion of the play. As often, it is the sub-plot that makes the more explicit statement: Edgar sinks through his own nothingness to take up another identity. On the other side of nothing he can survive as the 'horrible object' Poor Tom:

> *That's something yet; Edgar I nothing am.*
>
> II.3.21

More obliquely the Fool makes the same point to Lear:

> *Thou hast pared thy wit o'both sides and left nothing i'the middle. . . . Now thou art an O without a figure. I am better than thou art now; I am a fool; thou art nothing.*
>
> I.4.183-4, 188-90

Not until the end of the play, with its impassioned negatives, however, do we reach the end proposed for this pursuit of *nothing*. With Cordelia dead, Lear's passion turns to a rejection of a world full of unimportant somethings: 'No, no, no life', 'Thou'lt come no more', and then the climactic fivefold

> *Never, never, never, never, never.*
>
> V.3.306

The action of the play has reached the final *nothing*, not only of death, but of a world emptied of meaningful content. It has often been remarked that Lear's refusal to listen to Cordelia in Act I, scene 1, finds its mirror-image in Act V, scene 3, where her voice 'soft, | Gentle and low' is the only thing in the world he is listening for, and where her silence is his executioner. The choice of words, the metaphors in which the business of the play is expressed are here, as elsewhere, an indivisible part of the dramatic event, determining emphases and the focus of meaning in the action. We cannot separate the plot from the poetic pattern, the symbol from 'the picture of life'. A proper description of the play must not only encompass both of these; it must also reconcile them, or at least base itself on their inter-relation.

*

The ways in which developing action and poetic pattern grow out of one another can be described only in terms of detail. Here, the description of a single scene must suffice. Fortunately, Act I, scene 1, of *King Lear* is one of the great examples of Shakespeare's power of poetic fore-shortening, contraction of human motive into poetic motif, and incorporation of symbol into person. The old *King Leir* play gives an adequate motive for the love-contest, an unsubtle motive, but one that fits perfectly well into the nature of the play. Leir wishes to trick Cordella (Cordelia) into a profession of love so binding that he will be able to demand that she marry the Irish king – which he desires for political as well as personal reasons. Shakespeare removes this (understandably enough), but substitutes nothing else; in his play there is no motive at all, simply

Meantime we shall express our darker purpose.

Indeed, of all Shakespeare's plays this is the least concerned to explain the present by reference to the past. There is no 'exposition', though the traditional expository scene of two court gentlemen stands in front of the play (compare *Cymbeline*, Act I, scene 1) almost as if to say 'So you expect an explanation! Well, you're not going to get one.' Shakespeare seems to have wished to make Lear not so much the inheritor as the creator of the world of the play, acting at the start with total responsibility and total freedom. Our response must be a mixture of admiration for the creative energy of this godlike exercise and of dismay or terror at its exercise in terms of a merely human will. We are shown the conundrum of a complete confidence in will coupled to a complete indifference as to means or executive process. We wait for the indifference to catch up with and destroy the will.

I have spoken of the first span or arch of the play, which carries our attention from Act I, scene 1, to Act II, scene 4. The attention we give to this is not, of course, concerned only with forward movement. Our knowledge of the play comes to us also as a series of tableau-like discoveries of separate situations. We see the King divide his kingdom and disinherit his youngest daughter. We see this youngest daughter 'claimed' by the King of France. We see a true-speaking nobleman exiled for speaking true. We also learn how the wicked bastard Edmund tricks his brother out of his inheritance and his father's love; and how Lear comes to regret his abandonment of power to his two daughters, and how, driven frantic by their cruelties, he rushes out into the storm.

These are the bare facts of the case – the facts without their power. For it is not the facts, but the range of value-systems they incorporate that gives *King Lear* the power to be read again and again; and it is in these terms that we should look at the beginning of the first movement, at Act I, scene 1.

The opening dialogue of Kent and Gloucester is concerned with both national politics and domestic affairs. It is not chance, however, that brings these two men together. The father has two sons as the King has (we learn) two Dukes. The father's sons are, respectively, legitimate and bastard; these external distinctions make one 'no dearer in my account' than the other; yet one is to hear himself called a 'whoreson', and learns that 'there was good sport at his making'. He has 'been out nine years, and away he shall again'; I take this to mean that (like the by-blows of the Edwardian aristocracy) Edmund has been sent to distant parts where he can grow up without embarrassing his father – though in the clubman's morality of this dialogue there is not much evidence of embarrassment. In any case we can note that a sense of moral unease is generated in these opening lines, and already this attaches to Lear. The Dukes, like the sons, are weighed against one another in simple computation and found equal. Is the assertion of numerical equality in them as dubious as the similar assertion in respect of the sons? With this question, this unease, already in our minds, we move into the main part of the scene.

The King enters in full panoply of power. This is an abdication ritual. Lear is the medieval sovereign with his 'two bodies', one merely personal, and one belonging to the role. He proposes to divide them, and in his own natural body 'Unburdened crawl toward death'. Unlike the other abdication ritual in Shakespeare – that in *Richard II* – this one is supported by a widely diffused sense of the King's religious and even anthropological meaning. But another point of view is also present; and from that angle the whole ritual is a fake. The first words of the play tell us that the land is already divided. Marshall McLuhan has pointed out that the map denotes a degree of abstraction from the real land, and marks the separation of business (which has been completed) from ritual. Two divergent and incompatible views of what is going on are established. Lear represents both the terrifying and *mana*-laden god-king, whose verse has the sweep and majesty of one whose thoughts are laws:

> *We have this hour a constant will to publish*
> *Our daughters' several dowers, that future strife*
> *May be prevented now.*   I.1.43–5

And at the same time, behind the divine mask, he is the chief executive of a modern state, measuring worth and marking the map.

The land itself shares something of this duality. It can be abstracted into a map; but the terms in which Lear's words describe it are more physical:

> *Of all these bounds, even from this line to this,*
> *With shadowy forests and with champains riched,*
> *With plenteous rivers and wide-skirted meads,*
> *We make thee lady. To thine and Albany's issues*
> *Be this perpetual.*   I.1.63–7

The 'wide-skirted meads' here make explicit what is implied by the whole transaction, that the land is seen as a kind of extension from the physical life of the royal family. Its fertility (the point that is stressed, rather than the extent) is closely associated with Gonerill's own fertility. Fertility, as the form of the good that this part of the play is particularly anxious to stress, appears no less obviously in the first mention of Cordelia:

> *to whose young love*
> *The vines of France and milk of Burgundy*
> *Strive to be interested.*   I.1.83–5

The fertility of the land and the fertility of the daughters are held, it would seem, inside ritual as part of the blessing conferred by the existence and beneficence of a god-king closely associated with

> *the sacred radiance of the sun,*
> *The mysteries of Hecat and the night,*
> *... all the operation of the orbs*
> *From whom we do exist, and cease to be.*
>
> I.I.109–12

The full force of Lear's anthropological displeasure is not felt in this scene. The punishment for Cordelia and Kent is that they should be cut off from his life-giving beams. The full inversion of the anthropological gifts conferred in Act I, scene 1, is postponed till Act I, scene 4:

> *Hear, Nature, hear! Dear goddess, hear!*
> *Suspend thy purpose if thou didst intend*
> *To make this creature fruitful.*
> *Into her womb convey sterility,*
> *Dry up in her the organs of increase,*
> *And from her derogate body never spring*
> *A babe to honour her.*
>
> I.4.272–8

In rational terms it is a curious curse; but the continuity with which Lear calls on the gods to underwrite his role not as the arbiter of life and death but as the guarantor of fertility marks its central importance. In Lear's view it seems to be the power to promote or deny issue that holds his world together.

But his view of the king's role is not shared by his daughters. Gonerill and Regan reject it at the political level. They are willing to appear in the same ritual as Lear, but their language reveals that to them it is only a charade; the reality is the numerically assessed purchase they achieve by playing him along. As Regan says:

> *I am made of that self mettle as my sister*
> *And price me at her worth. In my true heart*
> *I find she names my very deed of love.*   I.1.69–71

As the chosen language exposes, the two sisters are alike in their concern for the metallic and legalistic aspects of the exchange, statement traded for land, or rather (more abstractly) power. Language for them is not the magical expression of continuity with and control over objects; it is a political expedient by which the individual secures temporary advantages which physical power will make actual.

Cordelia's rejection of Lear's strange conjunction of politics and magic is both similar to her sisters' and different. It is not so much towards a rejection of the political meaning that she moves; it is, rather, a refusal to allow personal relationships to be expressed in these terms. Her care is to insert some emotional realism into her personal situation:

> *Haply when I shall wed,*
> *That lord whose hand must take my plight shall carry*
> *Half my love with him, half my care and duty.*
> *Sure I shall never marry like my sisters,*
> *To love my father all.*   I.1.100–104

Computation is once again an enemy to Lear's demand that number be used to express relationship derived from love and affection. If it is number he demands then he must know that he can't have *all*, but only what is appropriate and 'According to my bond'.

What is this 'bond' that prescribes Cordelia's duty? It is basically, I suppose, the bond of nature which ties child to parent. The three other occasions when the word appears in *King Lear* (I.2.108; II.1.46; II.4.173) deal with this relationship. But I believe that 'bond' in the first scene carries a further meaning than this. *Bond* is also 'a uniting or cementing force' (*O.E.D.*7). It is that *bond* of natural sympathy which makes man-kind 'kind' in the modern sense of the word. This is why the family is (in this play and elsewhere) the model of the nation, and the nation the model of the 'kind' or species: at each level survival depends on 'kindness'. Cordelia acknowledges (as Gonerill and Regan do not) that she belongs to that blood-tied community her father describes:

> *You have begot me, bred me, loved me.*
> *I return those duties back as are right fit,*
> *Obey you, love you, and most honour you.*
>
> I.1.96–8

But she rejects the connexion between these feelings and the third of the kingdom which is to be their 'reward'. For her, as for Gonerill and Regan, the daughter's role is not the same as the inheritor's. They reject the daughter in order to enjoy power as inheritors. She rejects the inheritor in order to retain in its own idiom the role of daughter. All three are united in rejecting the combination of roles that Lear prepares for them, the equation of power and love, of rule with natural fertility. But again the choices differ. Gonerill and Regan choose the metallic barrenness of power; Cordelia remains close to the processes of nature:

> *All blest secrets,*
> *All you unpublished virtues of the earth,*
> *Spring with my tears.*   IV.4.15–17

Lear's recovery from madness, which these words lead up to, is expressed in terms of man's humble acceptance of

the healing powers of nature. The full madness is identi-
fied with high summer's choking riot of weeds:

> Crowned with rank fumiter and furrow-weeds,
> With hardokes, hemlock, nettles, cuckoo-flowers,
> Darnel, and all the idle weeds that grow
> In our sustaining corn.   IV.4.3–6

It is a context which prepares us for the re-entry of Cordelia into the action, part of nature but, like another Eve,
intent to 'Lop overgrown, or prune or prop or bind', well
adapted to recover the human garden from its 'natural'
rankness and promote its proper order.

In the first scene the Britain which is centred on Lear
flies apart into its constituent elements, as (in individual
terms) Lear's mind flies apart into its 'hundred thousand
flaws'. The opening establishes not only individual
characters but also a pattern of relationship between them,
and between a set of ideas and images which the play is to
change and rearrange and draw on throughout its length.
A world of competing values is established, and the values
are, on the whole, larger, more complex, and more
interesting than the people who profess them.

*

Any temptation to think Lear's character responsible for
what happens is in fact much limited by the absence of
any dimension of doubt or self-scrutiny in his nature; it
would be like assuming an interest in God's character. The
question he asks, 'Who is it that can tell me who I am?',
is to be answered in terms not of personal idiosyncrasy
but of function and role. The division of the kingdom
defines him; he does not explain it. In the sub-plot we
find that Edmund begins the action with a very similar

definition rather than explanation. 'I am a bastard' is enough to justify everything that follows. It is a kind of opening which is recurrent in *King Lear*. Edmund, Cordelia, Kent, all begin with powerful acts of self-definition, strong denials of their contexts. Gonerill and Regan begin by agreeing only in order to repudiate. But the strong context of settled beliefs and assumptions which allows and perhaps even encourages these acts of denial does not survive beyond the first few scenes. And as that collapses the power of the individual to define himself seems also to collapse. Exile and separation isolate one from another; disguise and madness lock away the individuals in their private worlds. The play seems to be intent on hunting down the man who thinks he knows what he believes or even who he is. This is a general drift of the plot, as I say; but it is probably easiest to see in the history of Edgar.

Edgar is the only character in the play who may be said to choose his own deprivation:

> *I will preserve myself. . . .*
> *And with presented nakedness outface*
> *The winds and persecutions of the sky.*
>
> II.3.6, 11–12

He outfaces persecution by becoming naked, by becoming as it were transparent, wholly unprotected. He abandons identity in favour of mere existence, mere survival:

> *That's something yet; Edgar I nothing am.*

But Edgar is not allowed to rest secure even as Poor Tom,

> *the basest and most poorest shape*
> *That ever penury, in contempt of man,*
> *Brought near to beast.*
>
> II.3.7–9

He constantly complains of the difficulty of keeping up
the role of Poor Tom, and in Act IV he abandons it – the
Tom role relates chiefly to Lear. With his father he
becomes 'A poor unfortunate beggar'; after the episode
at the supposed Dover Cliff he becomes someone else,
never defined, and then 'A most poor man made tame to
fortune's blows' (IV.6.221). But a minute after announcing
himself thus he turns into a Mummerset peasant, obviously
in antithesis to Oswald's Osric-like court dialect; then
when Oswald is dead he moves back to a neutral accent.
In the final scene he appears as a knight in shining armour,
unknown and treading the same isolated path as always,
talking chivalric jargon and achieving poetic justice.
Finally his wheel of identities can come full circle:

> *My name is Edgar, and thy father's son.*
>
> V.3.167

The context in which this anagnorisis or recognition occurs
defines and limits its meaning. The trumpets, the armour,
the stylized rhetoric, the too-neat morality, all serve to
place it in the world of art rather than in that bitterer
world which at the end of this play undercuts the traditional art-form. It is only in the dream of art that one
really recovers that which was lost. What Edgar can find
at the end of the play is only the debris of the world which
exploded in Act I. The only wisdom that is available to him
at the end is the knowledge of insufficiency:

> *we that are young*
> *Shall never see so much nor live so long.*

But it is not only in terms of identity that Edgar is hunted
throughout the play. His moral sense is equally subject to
challenge. He is much given to maxims and has an evident

capacity not only to endure but to moralize on his own endurance:

> Welcome, then,
> Thou unsubstantial air that I embrace!
>
> IV.1.6–7

But he has no sooner said this than he sees his blinded father being led towards him:

> O gods! Who is't can say 'I am at the worst'?
> I am worse than e'er I was. . . .
>   The worst is not,
> So long as we can say 'This is the worst'.
>
> IV.1.25–6, 27–8

Every security he reaches for turns out to be illusory. He has to learn that endurance is endless and without satisfaction.

This pattern of insecurity appears in lives other than Edgar's. Albany, late arriving at virtue, is always that minute too late to make it effective. The most reverberant irony in the play is given to him: 'The gods defend her' he says, hearing of Edmund's order on the life of Cordelia. He is immediately answered by '*Enter Lear with Cordelia in his arms*'. The gods seem to have defended her by killing her. But at least Albany has seen the wicked punished, and he proposes a distribution of rewards to the good who have survived:

> we will resign
> During the life of this old majesty
> To him our absolute power. . . .
>   All friends shall taste
> The wages of their virtue. . . .   V.3.296–8, 300–301

But Lear's only answer is 'No, no, no life'. The offer is hardly made before the recipient dies. The wages of virtue sound suspiciously like the wages of sin.

*

I began this Introduction by discussing the relationship between the plot and a meaning which is often spoken about in the form of 'what Lear learned'. I believe that it must now be obvious that the process of the play is one to which the idea of 'What have I learned?' is particularly inappropriate, since we see so many men setting up ideas of what they have learned and then see the play knocking them down.

Looked at from this angle the play can be seen to be a series of peripeteias, of oscillations between disappointment and relief. Gonerill and Regan deceive, but Cordelia speaks out; Lear tyrannizes, but Kent answers back; Cordelia is banished, but France takes up what is cast away; Kent is banished, but returns as Caius; Lear is forced out of civilization, but the only truly civilized people in the play follow him; he goes mad, but discovers hidden truths; Cornwall triumphs over Gloucester, but is killed for his cruelty; Gloucester loses his eyes, but gains insight; Gonerill bullies, but Albany wins. But the oscillations do not only work this way; they also move to disappointment. Edgar's rescue of his father is completed by his inability to tell him who he is; Kent can present himself to his master, but not make his message intelligible; Albany wins the battle but loses the purpose for which it is fought; Lear regains daughter, crown, and sanity, only to lose almost straight away daughter, crown, sanity, and life.

The process of the play see-saws between hope and disappointment; and any sense of values that the play is

supposed to affirm must be held against this background
of recurrent betrayal. Certainly no values held by the
characters themselves produce final positive affirmation.
We may, if we wish, follow A. C. Bradley and suppose that
Lear dies of joy, thinking that Cordelia is alive:

> Do you see this? Look on her! Look, her lips!
> Look there! Look there!

But in its context this can hardly be regarded as an affirmation of the conquering value of love. Both immediately
before – 'No, no, no life' – and immediately after –

> Vex not his ghost. O, let him pass. He hates him
> That would upon the rack of this tough world
> Stretch him out longer

– the negative is strongly asserted. The see-saw motion,
which has throughout the play been betraying, under-
cutting, and isolating the sense of achievement we share
with those who are steadfast in suffering, has not ceased to
operate. The only value left would seem to be the bare
fact of having survived.

One passage in the play points to some of the meaning
Shakespeare may initially have seen in such a process.
When Gloucester speaks to Edmund of 'These late eclipses'
he tells him that the effects fit with 'the prediction':

> love cools, friendship falls off, brothers divide. In cities,
> mutinies; in countries, discord; in palaces, treason; and
> the bond cracked 'twixt son and father.... son against
> father ... father against child.   I.2.106–11

Two passages are cited as very plausible sources of this;
and certainly they show the current context of such words
and of the events in the play to which they refer. One is

from the Elizabethan 'Homily against Wilful Rebellion', appointed to be read in all churches. This tells of

> the mischief and wickedness when the subjects unnaturally do rebel against their prince ... the brother to seek and often to work the death of his brother; the son of the father; the father to seek or procure the death of his sons, being at man's age, and by their faults to disinherit their innocent children and kinsmen.
>
> Certain Sermons or Homilies, 1817 edition, page 541

Probably behind both this and Gloucester's prediction lies a passage in Mark:

> Now the brother shall betray the brother to death and the father the son; and children shall rise up against their parents and shall cause them to be put to death ... but he that shall endure unto the end, the same shall be saved.
>
> 13.12-13

Had Shakespeare been given to epigraphs he might have used either of these passages, for each gives in some sense the substance of *King Lear*. But each gives it in a context that Shakespeare did not use in the play, though I believe he was aware of the pressure of these contexts. To see what Shakespeare chose not to embody is to glimpse something of the nature of his dramatic art.

The *Homilies* passage is set into a discussion of the sin of rebellion against proper authority. Lear's abdication and division of the kingdom – the opening premise of the play – obviously had for the Elizabethans a resonance it does not have for us. The old play of *Gorboduc* (1561) depends almost exclusively on the political meaning of such action, and of the chaos, the worst of worlds, that would ensue (so the Tudors said) if central authority were to be dissipated. The passage from the Gospels is larger in its view, but it does not necessarily contradict the assumptions of the *Homilies*. It comes from a series of verses dealing with the portents which will precede the Last Judgement, including the final chaos of the reign of Antichrist. The last Act of *King Lear* is studded with references to the Last Judgement. People in the play are conscious of the analogy, conscious that this is the direction in which their world seems to be heading. But the play does not end in the same mode of resolution as the Gospel passage ('but he that shall endure unto the end, the same shall be saved') and *could not do so*.

The *Homilies* passage and the Gospel one both see chaos as a horror that the individual is already guarded against. In the political terms of the *Homilies* we can say that the individual need not choose to rebel; good order and obedience are always there waiting to be gripped fast. In the eschatological world of Mark, salvation is an end and an answer available to all men. *King Lear* takes us through a version of the political and spiritual chaos of which these sources speak; but it cannot, as a play, mimic their answers. Endurance is certainly something the play is concerned with, but the endurance of Lear ('The wonder is he hath endured so long') is very different from that endurance in faith of which Christ speaks in the Gospels. The 'endurance' of *King Lear* is rather an endlessly adaptive acceptance of one's self and of the world in which one happens to exist, a process of struggle rather than achievement, a direction of the will rather than a knowledge of the Good, and is certainly far from the fixity of salvation.

Frank Kermode has expressed this quality of the play's ending very well:

'In *King Lear* everything tends towards a conclusion that does not occur.... The world may, as Gloucester supposes, exhibit all the symptoms of decay and change, all the terrors of an approaching end, but when the end comes it is not an end, and both suffering and the need for patience are perpetual.'

The Sense of an Ending (New York, 1967), page 82

In such a world the idea of 'the same shall be saved' can only exist as a potential, in the harmony but not the melody of the piece, as a perpetual hope in the perpetual disappointment.

What the play never allows is that any character should continue to hold a position of security. The role of plot in relation to character is to flatten self-assertion. I have already noted the tendency of people in this play to begin with strong self-definition. But the final scenes are full of statements that these individual lives do not matter. Edmund begins a career devoted to radical revaluation with

Thou, Nature, art my goddess.   I.2.1

But he ends it with the flat

The wheel is come full circle; I am here.   V.3.172

The only trajectory has been the self-defeating circle of his own individuality; the world has not moved for him. Gloucester dies, if not in a mist at least in a mystery – where contact with the mysterious truth of his fate bursts his heart with wonder. Kent's near-death, reported by Edgar immediately after Gloucester's, shows the same pattern. While he is telling 'the most piteous tale of Lear and him | That ever ear received', 'the strings of life | Began to crack. . . . And there I left him tranced' (V.3. 212–16). For all we know at this point, Kent has died (like Gloucester) at the moment of recognition. And even when

42

Kent appears, still alive, a few minutes later, he is still unable to secure recognition from his master. 'I'll see that straight' says Lear, and 'You are welcome hither'. But these vague courtesies have to be heard with Albany's comment attached:

> *He knows not what he sees, and vain is it*
> *That we present us to him.*   V.3.291–2

The Fool disappears in the middle of the play without any explanation. Edmund's death is 'but a trifle'; the deaths of Gonerill and Regan are matter for moralization, but not for personal response:

> *This judgement of the heavens that makes us tremble*
> *Touches us not with pity....*
>   *Cover their faces.*   V.3.229–30, 240

The 'gigantic' quality of *King Lear* might seem to be tied in with its lack of interest in the details of character which separate one person from another. Shakespeare certainly seems to be more interested in lining up the good against the bad than in discriminating the fine grain of one goodness from another. This is perhaps what Gide and others mean when they complain of the play's inhumanity. The play is true to the detail of our human experience, in fact, not in its characterization but only in the tracing of experiences by which we come to know the irrelevance of characterization. In a play where loss of identity is almost a prerequisite of survival (certainly so in the cases of Kent and Edgar) it is the way in which attitudes and assumptions distort, modify, disappear, under pressure that holds our continuous attention. The text is full of detailed perceptions, but they are all in motion or transformation; to stop the film and make any one perception 'the meaning' is to falsify. Those who wish to think of the whole work as a 'visionary statement' tend to suppose that the perceptions of Lear's madness are Shakespeare's central 'truth', and the process which diminishes these, as it diminishes all human effort, is somehow irrelevant. In fact the perception and the diminution are two sides to one coin.

In Act IV, scene 6, the climactic scene where plot and sub-plot merge, the mad Lear describes to the blind Gloucester a world of horror and anarchy; but it is also a world in which the individual is finally liberated from the pretences of social obligation:

> *Thorough tattered clothes great vices do appear;*
> *Robes and furred gowns hide all. Plate sins with gold,*
> *And the strong lance of justice hurtless breaks;*
> *Arm it in rags, a pygmy's straw does pierce it.*
> *None does offend, none, I say none.*   IV.6.165–9

The anarchic ultimate of the last line marks the furthest point in Lear's 'understanding'. But it is a perception so final that further movement can only back away from it. If 'None does offend' then there is no meaning in the discrimination between innocent and guilty, with which tragedy no less than law is centrally concerned. The play, to be a play (and it is a play), must disown such ideas. The action ends not with the perception of Lear but with the duty of Edgar:

> *The weight of this sad time we must obey.*

Those who carry the burden of time's imperfections are as necessary to the tragic vision as those who destroy the world in the flash of their understanding. Edgar's and Albany's patience with things as they are, with compromise and half-measures, does not rule out Lear's (and our) perception that ultimately 'None does offend'. Neither does Lear's perception obliterate the need for action at a level where some must seem to offend and be punished for it. The life that goes on beyond the end of the tragic process must depend on such good men, whose limitation is their virtue.

'KING LEAR' IN PERFORMANCE

The title-page of the Quarto (see below, page 313) tells us that *King Lear* was performed at court on 26 December; and we learn from another source that the year was 1606. Since the writing of the play is most likely to have taken place in 1605, one must suppose that the court performance was not the first. It was no doubt performed at the Globe, both earlier and later, as part of the normal repertory. We know that Richard Burbage was the original Lear, and may presume that Robert Armin played the Fool. Boys would have performed the parts of Gonerill, Regan, and Cordelia.

The text of the Quarto is unlikely, of course, to be the text of the play as performed in 1606. I argue below (page 315) that a great part of the Quarto text is based on Shakespeare's 'foul papers' or working draft. It follows that the actual court performance would not be recorded in this manuscript which the author handed over to the company for theatrical cutting and smoothing. The Folio text is our first unequivocal witness to what was involved in putting *King Lear* on to Shakespeare's stage. The cuts in the Folio show obvious ways in which the text can be shortened and simplified, comment, moralization, and indecisive action (the much-discussed wars between the Dukes) being reduced, but explicit action preserved. These cuts have an extraordinary persistence in the stage tradition; and one must presume that they preserve the theatrical fabric to the satisfaction of the stage, however abhorrent they are to literary connoisseurs.

I have argued above against the separation of poetry from action in *King Lear*. But I think it reasonable to assume that the play has always given peculiar difficulties to producers. Action in *King Lear* must be of a rather special kind if it is to convey the quality of its poetry. The title-role is demanding but not glamorous. The total effect depends on ensemble playing of chamber-music fidelity but of orchestral magnitude. There has to be a detailed control over the 'reality' projected, but without the usual naturalistic aids of defined place and time. The stage history gives an instructive account of the theatre's capacity to deal with these problems. Certainly it is more usefully seen from this point of view than, as usual, as a document of human perversity.

There is no evidence to suggest that *King Lear* made much impact during the seventeenth century. In the list of allusions to Shakespeare from 1591 to 1700 collected in *The Shakspere Allusion Book*, *King Lear* occupies a very lowly position, less mentioned than even *Pericles* or *The Merry Wives of Windsor*, and far outshone by *Julius Caesar*, *Hamlet*, and *Othello*. In the period after the Restoration, when theatrical records become significant in England, it is hardly mentioned. Downes, the prompter at the Theatre Royal, speaks of two performances by Davenant's company 'between 1662 and 1665'. We know from a surviving 'prompt-copy' that it was performed in Dublin, probably in the early 1680s. But in the main we may say that in this period *King Lear* was waiting for the great event in its theatrical history, Nahum Tate's rewriting in 1681.

Tate's *King Lear* is only one of the many Restoration 'improvements' of Shakespeare; but it is probably the most notorious, perhaps because of the stature of the play and the drastic turning of the ending from tragedy to reconciliation; or perhaps because of the hold Tate's version had in the theatre, and the difficulty experienced in re-establishing Shakespeare's text on the stage, even when the literary critics were united in denouncing Tate. *King Lear* demands a mode of action that is very different from the conventional intrigue-procedures of most drama. But intrigue is the stuff of the modern theatre, and is precisely what Tate supplied. Finding the play, as he says, 'a heap of jewels, unstrung and unpolished, yet dazzling in their disorder', he proceeded to restring them on the motive of Cordelia's love for Edgar – what he calls the 'one expedient to rectify what was wanting in the regularity and probability of the tale'. Cordelia's refusal to please her father in Act I, scene 1, is thus restrung on a motive (which Shakespeare had denied it), and, what is more, on a theatrically conventional motive. Sexual love becomes throughout a dominant motivation. Edmund's intrigue with Gonerill and Regan is amplified: Act IV, scene 1, discovers 'Edmund and Regan amorously seated, listening to music' in 'A Grotto':

EDMUND
> *Why were these beauties made another's right*
> *Which none can prize like me? Charming Queen,*
> *Take all my blooming youth; for ever fold me*
> *In these soft arms....*

Moreover, seeing Cordelia (who does not go to France) venturing on to the heath with only her confidante Arante, he sends two 'Ruffians' to detain her for the rape he intends. From this fate worse than death she is (of

course) rescued by Edgar. The battle in Act V is no longer
a foreign invasion, but a species of peasants' revolt, set
afoot by the taxations imposed by Gonerill and Regan,
and led by Kent and Edgar. The final scene takes us into
the prison with 'Lear asleep, with his head on Cordelia's
lap'. An exciting *coup de théâtre* is created by the struggle
to hang Cordelia, frustrated by Lear and stopped by
Edgar's entrance:

> *Death! Hell! Ye vultures, hold your impious hands*
> *Or take a speedier death than you would give.*

In a general reconciliation, Gloucester, Kent, Albany
(shrunk from his Shakespearian importance), and above
all Edgar and Cordelia restore order and justice. The last
words of the play leave 'this celestial pair' in possession
of the kingdom and of one another. Edgar says

> *Divine Cordelia, all the gods can witness*
> *How much thy love to empire I prefer!*
> *Thy bright example shall convince the world*
> *(Whatever storms of fortune are decreed)*
> *That truth and virtue shall at last succeed*

– a moral Shakespeare had been at some pains to deny.

Tate's version took immediate hold of the stage; and
the next 150 years of *King Lear* are a history of the tension
between Shakespeare's poetry and Tate's patent theatri-
cality. The scholarly and critical interest in Shakespeare as
a reading text produced (inevitably) an outcry against Tate.
As early as 1711 Addison was writing: '*King Lear* is an
admirable tragedy . . . as Shakespeare wrote it; but as it is
reformed according to the chimerical notion of poetical
justice, in my humble opinion it has lost half its beauties.'
On the other hand, Dr Johnson saw that 'in the present
case the public has decided, and Cordelia, from the time

of Tate, has always retired with victory and felicity'. Dr Johnson's pupil, David Garrick, the leading actor of the eighteenth century, had in King Lear perhaps his most celebrated role, but it was Tate's *Lear* that he played. Inevitably, given the cultural pressure, he had a guilty conscience about this. He tampered with the text, introducing Shakespearian lines and phrases where he could without damaging the Tate framework.

One of the curiosities of the movement against Tate is that it often implies attitudes to *King Lear* which are more remote from Shakespeare than is the 1681 version. George Colman the elder produced in 1768 a text of (for its date) startlingly anti-Tate character. He removed the love story and even thought of restoring the Fool (but decided that in performance this part could only 'sink into burlesque'). On the other hand, we should note, he removes the fall over 'Dover Cliff' which Tate retained. He also initiates the nineteenth-century habit of ending Acts with big climactic 'curtain' speeches. Thus Act I ends with 'Hear, Nature, hear ...' (I.4.272–86), which had already been moved to a more prominent (though not final) position by Tate. Likewise, Act II now ends with 'O, reason not the need ...' (II.4.259–81). This marks a notable distortion of Shakespearian dramaturgy. Shakespeare characteristically ends his scenes (and his plays) on diminuendos – movements in which ordinary people try to digest or accept what has happened, or to reduce great events to individual or domestic terms. The stage is cleared and re-entered in the trough of the dramatic wave.

The nineteenth century inherits and develops this complex set of contradictory attitudes to *King Lear*. There is a crescendo of literary protest against Tate, but this is often coupled to a sense that Shakespeare's play is, in any case, unactable, and is his greatest play precisely because it is unactable. Charles Lamb has the most famous expression of this:

> To see Lear acted, to see an old man tottering about the stage with a walking stick, turned out of doors by his daughters in a rainy night, has nothing in it but what is painful and disgusting. . . . But the Lear of Shakespeare cannot be acted . . . they might more easily propose to personate the Satan of Milton upon a stage, or one of Michelangelo's terrible figures . . . . But the play is beyond all art, as the tamperings with it show: it is too hard and stony; it must have love scenes and a happy ending. It is not enough that Cordelia is a daughter; she must shine as a lover too. Tate has put his hook in the nostrils of this Leviathan for Garrick and his followers, the showmen of the scene, to draw the mighty beast about more easily. . . . Lear is essentially impossible to be represented on a stage.

At the same time there are theatrical and social developments – gigantic theatres, dominant and isolated actor-managers, a sentimental middle-class audience, a deference to female taste – all of which militated against both Tate, on the one hand, and the real Shakespeare on the other. Given all this, it is not surprising that the Fool was the last Shakespeare character to return to the play (1838). As constructed by Shakespeare the play sets Lear in counterpoint against a series of other important roles, Gloucester, Kent, and above all the Fool, who reflect what he himself does not know; and meaning emerges from the pattern of these quite unnaturalistic relationships. It was only when Macready hit on the expedient of a young lady (Miss Horton) playing the (heavily cut) Fool's role as one of innocent pathos rather than bitter bawdry that the character could be brought back.

With the return of the Fool in 1838 it is often thought

that the history of *King Lear* has reached a happy ending: all the elements in Shakespeare are restored and all the Tate additions removed. What this version of the history does not notice is that Macready's *King Lear* – and, even more, Charles Kean's (first performed in 1858) – omit large portions of the play: twelve hundred lines are missing in Charles Kean's. The Tate–Garrick–Kemble–Edmund Kean conflation of III.4 and III.6 is preserved; III.5, III.7, IV.3, and V.2 have disappeared; and restructuring to end every scene with a big 'curtain' effect is carried through with great resolution.

The bowdlerizing of passages is (as one might expect at this date) a fertile source of omission. The blinding of Gloucester was handed over to servants by Tate (such is the progress of civilization); Garrick pushed it into the wings; now it is omitted altogether. The 'Dover Cliff' leap is prevented by the entry of Lear (as in the Kemble and Edmund Kean versions).

The cuts are, inevitably (given the number), widespread. But they tend to curtail parts other than Lear's own, and leave the King's role in greater isolation. The effect of a star part set against a fairly undifferentiated background had earlier been promoted by the omission of the Fool. Now, by judicious cutting, it is confirmed and even developed though the Fool is present.

The effects that Shakespeare had been at some pains to secure by the structure of the double plot and the flattening of character are patiently undone; indeed it is likely that 'Shakespeare' could not have replaced Tate if they had not been undone. Irving's version of the play, the last of the great nineteenth-century impersonations, was also heavily cut. Bernard Shaw's remark that Irving 'does not merely cut plays: he disembowels them' seems to have been amply demonstrated in his 'fearfully mutilated acting version of *King Lear*'. It is likely that Bradley (for example) could not have seen on the stage anything approximating to the play that Shakespeare wrote.

The twentieth-century *King Lear* has been more faithful to the text than the nineteenth-century one. One should note, of course, that the modern director's control of lighting and production allows him to impose 'interpretation' without changing the text. The modern popularity of the play among readers has its obvious counterpart in the theatrical movement which stresses the theatre's social role to shock and distress. If the later nineteenth century stressed the pathetic side of the play and highlighted the healing role of Cordelia, the twentieth century's special contribution has been to stress the inhumanity and impersonality of the processes which crush Lear. The 1962 production by Peter Brook is the most famous expression of this view, by which the play became parallel to the *Waiting for Godot* or *Endgame* of Samuel Beckett. For this purpose Lear had to be made an overbearing belching boor, and his knights shown as in fact a 'deboshed' company of bullies who break up the furniture when their dinner is late. The servants who bind up Gloucester's eyes and prophesy the downfall of wickedness (III.7.98–106) were omitted as providing too sugary an image. The fall over 'Dover Cliff', aimed at a grotesque and nihilistic comedy, was thought to be the central image of the whole structure. The production was enormously successful, for it answered many modern feelings about the play; but it made these powerful contemporary effects largely by turning the play into a contemporary document – which is what the theatre has always done.

FURTHER READING

Editions and Editorial Problems

The New Variorum edition of H. H. Furness (1880), though now mainly a monument to past interpretations, is still useful for the historically pertinent material it contains (particularly from German sources). A replacement for it, designed on the same comprehensive scale, is being edited by Richard Knowles. Kenneth Muir's Arden edition (1952, revised 1972) has long remained standard. R. A. Foakes is re-editing the play for the latest version of the Arden series. The most recent single-volume editions (printed and projected) follow the 'two text' theory of *King Lear* (see below). Jay L. Halio has produced an edition of the Folio text (1992) in the New Cambridge Shakespeare series and an unannotated edition of the First Quarto (1994). Michael Warren has issued a *Complete King Lear* (1989), consisting of photographic facsimiles of the First and Second Quartos and the Folio and a volume setting out Q1 and F texts in parallel. The latter has been issued separately as *The Parallel King Lear, 1608–1623* (1989). The one-volume Riverside Shakespeare prints a traditional single text (1974). The Oxford Shakespeare Complete Works (1986) prints two texts in both the modernized- and original-spelling volumes.

The basic documents for the earlier view of the text of *King Lear* are W. W. Greg, *The Variants in the First Quarto of 'King Lear'* (1940), G. I. Duthie's *Elizabethan Shorthand and the First Quarto of 'King Lear'* (1949), Alice Walker's *Textual Problems of the First Folio* (1953). The later view can be found in E. A. J. Honigmann's *The Stability of Shakespeare's Text* (1965), *The Division of the Kingdoms*, ed. Taylor and Warren (1983), and in the editorial material contained in the Oxford Shakespeare's *A Textual Companion* (1987).

Sources

The old *King Leir* play is available as a Malone Society Reprint (1907; 1956). It is reprinted, along with other relevant material, in Geoffrey Bullough's *Narrative and Dramatic Sources of Shakespeare*, vol. VII (1973). The standard sources are also available (in part) in Muir's and other editions. The development of the traditional story of Lear is set out in Wilfrid Perrett's *The Story of King Lear from Geoffrey of Monmouth to Shakespeare* (1904). For further information on Samuel Harsnett's *Declaration of Egregious Popish Impostures*, see F. W. Brownlow, *Shakespeare, Harsnett and the Devils of Denham* (1993).

Criticism

Critical responses from 1623 to 1801 are presented in Brian Vickers, *Shakespeare: the Cultural Heritage*, 6 vols. (1974–81) and touched on in Harold Bloom's Major Author series, vol. II (1986). A. C. Bradley's essays on *King Lear* in *Shakespearean Tragedy* (1904) provide a bridge between Victorian and modern attitudes to the play. He deals with the Romantic notion of the play's 'unactability' (see Charles Lamb, 'On the Tragedies of Shakespeare, considered with reference to their fitness for stage representation', 1811) as part of an integrating dialectic between the 'poetic' and the 'dramatic'. The 'poetic' is the aspect that has, until recently, sparked most criticism, but the pendulum now seems to be swinging the other way. G. Wilson Knight's essay in *The Wheel of Fire* (1930) marks the first full expression of a 'thematic' interpretation that reached its most elaborated expression in R. B. Heilman's *This Great Stage: Image and Structure in 'King Lear'* (1948). J. F. Danby, *Shakespeare's Doctrine of Nature* (1949), by the same methods invokes a more explicitly Christian meaning, and the debate between Christian or spiritualizing understanding and a nihilistic reading of the play has been the main critical issue for the last fifty years. This has been all the more intense because of the growing assumption that *King Lear* is the great play of Western Civilization (see R. A. Foakes, *Hamlet Versus King Lear*, 1993). The Christianizing and allegorical movement was attacked by Barbara Everett in 'The New King Lear', *Critical Quarterly* II (1960), 325–9. A more purely documentary examination of the play's Christianity appears in William Elton's *King Lear and the Gods* (1966). From a different angle, Jan Kott's *Shakespeare Our Contemporary* (1964) finds the play nihilistic in the manner of Samuel Beckett's *End Game*. Maynard Mack's *King Lear in Our Time* (1966) defends the play's humanism against Kott and against the Peter Brook production that derived from it. 'Cultural materialists' such as Jonathan Dollimore (*Radical Tragedy*, 1984) argue that the play is not about forgiveness but about 'power, property, and inheritance' and therefore points us towards political activism. Collections of critical essays on *King Lear* have been edited by Frank Kermode (1969) and Kenneth Muir (1984). Surveys of *King Lear* criticism can be found in *Aspects of 'King Lear'*, ed. Muir and Wells (1982), and in the relevant chapter of *Shakespeare: A Bibliographical Guide*, ed. Stanley Wells (1990). There is an annotated bibliography by Larry Champion (1980).

Performance

Nahum Tate's version of the play is discussed in Hazelton Spencer's *Shakespeare Improved* (1927) and is printed in Christopher Spencer's *Five Restoration Adaptations of Shakespeare* (1965). Tate's and other theatrical adaptations (Colman's, Garrick's, Elliston's, Charles Kean's) are reprinted in facsimile in the Cornmarket Press series, 'Acting Versions of Shakespeare'. Marvin Rosenberg's *The Masks of King Lear* (1972) gives a moment-by-moment account of the various theatrical realizations of the action. Grigori Kosintsev's *King Lear: the Space of Tragedy* (1977) provides an illuminating account of the perceptions that lie behind his film version

(1971). Kurosawa's 1985 samurai film, *Ran* (war, revolt), gives great physical power to the action by turning the daughters into sons.

Laurence Olivier's remarkable performance for TV (with magnificent supporting cast) is available on video.

KING LEAR

THE CHARACTERS IN THE PLAY

LEAR, King of Britain
GONERILL, Lear's eldest daughter
REGAN, Lear's second daughter
CORDELIA, Lear's youngest daughter
DUKE OF ALBANY, husband of Gonerill
DUKE OF CORNWALL, husband of Regan
KING OF FRANCE
DUKE OF BURGUNDY

EARL OF KENT, later disguised as Caius
EARL OF GLOUCESTER
EDGAR, son of Gloucester, later disguised as Poor Tom
EDMUND, bastard son of Gloucester

OSWALD, Gonerill's steward
Lear's FOOL
Three KNIGHTS
CURAN, gentleman of Gloucester's household
GENTLEMEN
Three SERVANTS
OLD MAN, a tenant of Gloucester
Two MESSENGERS
DOCTOR, attendant on Cordelia
A CAPTAIN, follower of Edmund
HERALD
Two OFFICERS

Knights of Lear's train, servants, soldiers, attendants, gentlemen

KENT I thought the King had more affected the Duke of
Albany than Cornwall.

GLOUCESTER It did always seem so to us. But now in the
division of the kingdom it appears not which of the
Dukes he values most, for qualities are so weighed that
curiosity in neither can make choice of either's moiety.

KENT Is not this your son, my lord?

GLOUCESTER His breeding, sir, hath been at my charge.
I have so often blushed to acknowledge him that now I
am brazed to it. 10

KENT I cannot conceive you.

GLOUCESTER Sir, this young fellow's mother could;
whereupon she grew round-wombed, and had indeed,
sir, a son for her cradle ere she had a husband for her
bed. Do you smell a fault?

KENT I cannot wish the fault undone, the issue of it being
so proper.

GLOUCESTER But I have a son, sir, by order of law, some
year elder than this, who yet is no dearer in my account.
Though this knave came something saucily to the world, 20
before he was sent for, yet was his mother fair; there
was good sport at his making, and the whoreson must be
acknowledged. Do you know this noble gentleman,
Edmund?

EDMUND No, my lord.

GLOUCESTER My lord of Kent. Remember him hereafter
as my honourable friend.

EDMUND My services to your lordship.

KENT I must love you and sue to know you better.

30 EDMUND Sir, I shall study deserving.

GLOUCESTER He hath been out nine years, and away he
shall again. The King is coming.

> *Sound a sennet. Enter one bearing a coronet*
> *Enter King Lear, Cornwall, Albany, Gonerill, Regan,*
> *Cordelia, and attendants*

LEAR Attend the lords of France and Burgundy, Gloucester.

GLOUCESTER I shall, my liege.

> *Exeunt Gloucester and Edmund*

LEAR

Meantime we shall express our darker purpose.
Give me the map there. Know that we have divided
In three our kingdom; and 'tis our fast intent
To shake all cares and business from our age,
40 Conferring them on younger strengths, while we
Unburdened crawl toward death. Our son of Cornwall –
And you, our no less loving son of Albany –
We have this hour a constant will to publish
Our daughters' several dowers, that future strife
May be prevented now. The princes, France and
      Burgundy,
Great rivals in our youngest daughter's love,
Long in our court have made their amorous sojourn,
And here are to be answered. Tell me, my daughters,
Since now we will divest us both of rule,
50 Interest of territory, cares of state,
Which of you shall we say doth love us most,
That we our largest bounty may extend
Where nature doth with merit challenge. Gonerill,
Our eldest born, speak first.

GONERILL

Sir, I love you more than word can wield the matter,
Dearer than eyesight, space, and liberty,
Beyond what can be valued rich or rare,
No less than life, with grace, health, beauty, honour,
As much as child e'er loved or father found;
A love that makes breath poor and speech unable;   60
Beyond all manner of 'so much' I love you.

CORDELIA (aside)

What shall Cordelia speak? Love, and be silent.

LEAR

Of all these bounds, even from this line to this,
With shadowy forests and with champains riched,
With plenteous rivers and wide-skirted meads,
We make thee lady. To thine and Albany's issues
Be this perpetual. – What says our second daughter,
Our dearest Regan, wife of Cornwall?

REGAN

I am made of that self mettle as my sister
And price me at her worth. In my true heart   70
I find she names my very deed of love;
Only she comes too short, that I profess
Myself an enemy to all other joys
Which the most precious square of sense possesses,
And find I am alone felicitate
In your dear highness' love.

CORDELIA (aside)   Then poor Cordelia!

And yet not so, since I am sure my love's
More ponderous than my tongue.

LEAR

To thee and thine hereditary ever
Remain this ample third of our fair kingdom,   80
No less in space, validity, and pleasure

Than that conferred on Gonerill. – Now, our joy,
Although our last and least, to whose young love
The vines of France and milk of Burgundy
Strive to be interessed: what can you say to draw
A third more opulent than your sisters'? Speak!

CORDELIA Nothing, my lord.

LEAR Nothing?

CORDELIA Nothing.

LEAR

90 Nothing will come of nothing. Speak again.

CORDELIA
Unhappy that I am, I cannot heave
My heart into my mouth. I love your majesty
According to my bond, no more nor less.

LEAR
How, how, Cordelia! Mend your speech a little
Lest you may mar your fortunes.

CORDELIA   Good my lord,
You have begot me, bred me, loved me.
I return those duties back as are right fit,
Obey you, love you, and most honour you.
Why have my sisters husbands, if they say

100 They love you all? Haply when I shall wed,
That lord whose hand must take my plight shall carry
Half my love with him, half my care and duty.
Sure I shall never marry like my sisters,
To love my father all.

LEAR
But goes thy heart with this?

CORDELIA   Ay, my good lord.

LEAR So young, and so untender?

CORDELIA So young, my lord, and true.

LEAR
Let it be so! Thy truth then be thy dower!

64

For by the sacred radiance of the sun,
The mysteries of Hecat and the night,   110
By all the operation of the orbs
From whom we do exist, and cease to be,
Here I disclaim all my paternal care,
Propinquity and property of blood,
And as a stranger to my heart and me
Hold thee from this for ever. The barbarous Scythian,
Or he that makes his generation messes
To gorge his appetite, shall to my bosom
Be as well neighboured, pitied, and relieved
As thou my sometime daughter.

KENT   Good my liege –   120
LEAR Peace, Kent!
Come not between the dragon and his wrath.
I loved her most, and thought to set my rest
On her kind nursery. (*To Cordelia*) Hence and avoid
      my sight! –
So be my grave my peace as here I give
Her father's heart from her. Call France! Who stirs?
Call Burgundy! Cornwall and Albany,
With my two daughters' dowers digest the third.
Let pride, which she calls plainness, marry her.
I do invest you jointly with my power,   130
Pre-eminence, and all the large effects
That troop with majesty. Ourself by monthly course,
With reservation of an hundred knights,
By you to be sustained, shall our abode
Make with you by due turn. Only we shall retain
The name and all th'addition to a king; the sway,
Revenue, execution of the rest,
Beloved sons, be yours; which to confirm,
This coronet part between you.

KENT   Royal Lear,

140 Whom I have ever honoured as my king,
Loved as my father, as my master followed,
As my great patron thought on in my prayers –

LEAR
The bow is bent and drawn; make from the shaft.

KENT
Let it fall rather, though the fork invade
The region of my heart. Be Kent unmannerly
When Lear is mad. What wouldst thou do, old man?
Think'st thou that duty shall have dread to speak
When power to flattery bows? To plainness honour's
          bound
When majesty stoops to folly. Reserve thy state,
150 And in thy best consideration check
This hideous rashness. Answer my life my judgement,
Thy youngest daughter does not love thee least,
Nor are those empty-hearted whose low sounds
Reverb no hollowness.

LEAR   Kent, on thy life, no more!

KENT
My life I never held but as a pawn
To wage against thine enemies; nor fear to lose it,
Thy safety being motive.

LEAR   Out of my sight!

KENT
See better, Lear, and let me still remain
The true blank of thine eye.

LEAR
160 Now by Apollo –

KENT   Now by Apollo, King,
Thou swear'st thy gods in vain.

LEAR   O vassal, miscreant!
          He makes to strike him
ALBANY *and* CORNWALL Dear sir, forbear!

KENT

    Kill thy physician and thy fee bestow
    Upon the foul disease. Revoke thy gift,
    Or whilst I can vent clamour from my throat
    I'll tell thee thou dost evil.

LEAR   Hear me, recreant,
    On thine allegiance hear me!
    That thou hast sought to make us break our vow,
    Which we durst never yet, and, with strained pride,
    To come betwixt our sentence and our power,   170
    Which nor our nature nor our place can bear,
    Our potency made good, take thy reward.
    Five days we do allot thee for provision
    To shield thee from disasters of the world,
    And on the sixth to turn thy hated back
    Upon our kingdom. If on the tenth day following
    Thy banished trunk be found in our dominions
    The moment is thy death. Away! By Jupiter,
    This shall not be revoked!

KENT

    Fare thee well, King, sith thus thou wilt appear,   180
    Freedom lives hence and banishment is here.
    (*To Cordelia*)
    The gods to their dear shelter take thee, maid,
    That justly think'st and hast most rightly said.
    (*To Gonerill and Regan*)
    And your large speeches may your deeds approve
    That good effects may spring from words of love. –
    Thus Kent, O princes, bids you all adieu;
    He'll shape his old course in a country new.   *Exit*
        Flourish. Enter Gloucester with France and Bur-
        gundy, and attendants

GLOUCESTER

    Here's France and Burgundy, my noble lord.

LEAR My lord of Burgundy,

190 We first address toward you, who with this king
Hath rivalled for our daughter: what in the least
Will you require in present dower with her
Or cease your quest of love?

BURGUNDY   Most royal majesty,
I crave no more than hath your highness offered,
Nor will you tender less.

LEAR   Right noble Burgundy,
When she was dear to us we did hold her so;
But now her price is fallen. Sir, there she stands;
If aught within that little-seeming substance,
Or all of it, with our displeasure pieced,

200 And nothing more, may fitly like your grace,
She's there and she is yours.

BURGUNDY   I know no answer.

LEAR

Will you with those infirmities she owes,
Unfriended, new-adopted to our hate,
Dowered with our curse and strangered with our oath,
Take her or leave her?

BURGUNDY   Pardon me, royal sir,
Election makes not up in such conditions.

LEAR

Then leave her, sir, for, by the power that made me,
I tell you all her wealth. (*To France*) For you, great
    king,
I would not from your love make such a stray

210 To match you where I hate; therefore beseech you
T'avert your liking a more worthier way
Than on a wretch whom Nature is ashamed
Almost t'acknowledge hers.

FRANCE   This is most strange,
That she whom even but now was your best object,

The argument of your praise, balm of your age,
The best, the dearest, should in this trice of time
Commit a thing so monstrous to dismantle
So many folds of favour. Sure her offence
Must be of such unnatural degree
That monsters it; or your fore-vouched affection   220
Fall into taint; which to believe of her
Must be a faith that reason without miracle
Should never plant in me.

CORDELIA   I yet beseech your majesty –
If for I want that glib and oily art
To speak and purpose not, since what I well intend
I'll do't before I speak – that you make known
It is no vicious blot, murder or foulness,
No unchaste action or dishonoured step
That hath deprived me of your grace and favour,
But even for want of that for which I am richer: 230
A still-soliciting eye and such a tongue
That I am glad I have not, though not to have it
Hath lost me in your liking.

LEAR   Better thou
Hadst not been born than not t'have pleased me better.

FRANCE
Is it but this, a tardiness in nature
Which often leaves the history unspoke
That it intends to do? My lord of Burgundy,
What say you to the lady? Love's not love
When it is mingled with regards that stands
Aloof from th'entire point. Will you have her?   240
She is herself a dowry.

BURGUNDY   Royal Lear,
Give but that portion which yourself proposed
And here I take Cordelia by the hand,
Duchess of Burgundy.

LEAR

Nothing! I have sworn; I am firm.

BURGUNDY (*to Cordelia*)

I am sorry then you have so lost a father

That you must lose a husband.

CORDELIA   Peace be with Burgundy!

Since that respect and fortunes are his love,

I shall not be his wife.

FRANCE

250 Fairest Cordelia, that art most rich, being poor,

Most choice, forsaken, and most loved, despised,

Thee and thy virtues here I seize upon.

Be it lawful I take up what's cast away.

Gods, gods! 'Tis strange that from their cold'st neglect

My love should kindle to inflamed respect.

Thy dowerless daughter, King, thrown to my chance,

Is queen of us, of ours, and our fair France.

Not all the dukes of waterish Burgundy

Can buy this unprized-precious maid of me.

260 Bid them farewell, Cordelia, though unkind.

Thou losest here, a better where to find.

LEAR

Thou hast her, France; let her be thine, for we

Have no such daughter, nor shall ever see

That face of hers again. Therefore begone,

Without our grace, our love, our benison!

Come, noble Burgundy.

> *Flourish. Exeunt Lear, Burgundy, Cornwall, Albany,*
> *Gloucester, and attendants*

FRANCE Bid farewell to your sisters.

CORDELIA

The jewels of our father, with washed eyes

Cordelia leaves you. I know you what you are;

270 And, like a sister, am most loath to call

Your faults as they are named. Love well our father!
To your professèd bosoms I commit him.
But yet, alas, stood I within his grace,
I would prefer him to a better place.
So farewell to you both.

REGAN
Prescribe not us our duty.

GONERILL   Let your study
Be to content your lord, who hath received you
At Fortune's alms. You have obedience scanted,
And well are worth the want that you have wanted.

CORDELIA
Time shall unfold what plighted cunning hides;   280
Who covers faults, at last with shame derides.
Well may you prosper!

FRANCE   Come, my fair Cordelia.

Exeunt France and Cordelia

GONERILL Sister, it is not little I have to say of what most
nearly appertains to us both. I think our father will
hence tonight.

REGAN That's most certain, and with you; next month
with us.

GONERILL You see how full of changes his age is. The
observation we have made of it hath not been little. He
always loved our sister most; and with what poor judge-   290
ment he hath now cast her off appears too grossly.

REGAN 'Tis the infirmity of his age. Yet he hath ever but
slenderly known himself.

GONERILL The best and soundest of his time hath been
but rash. Then must we look from his age to receive not
alone the imperfections of long-ingraffed condition, but
therewithal the unruly waywardness that infirm and
choleric years bring with them.

REGAN Such unconstant starts are we like to have from

300   him as this of Kent's banishment.

GONERILL There is further compliment of leave-taking
between France and him. Pray you, let us hit together.
If our father carry authority with such disposition as he
bears, this last surrender of his will but offend us.

REGAN We shall further think of it.

GONERILL We must do something, and i'th'heat.

Exeunt

I.2   *Enter Edmund*

EDMUND

Thou, Nature, art my goddess; to thy law
My services are bound. Wherefore should I
Stand in the plague of custom and permit
The curiosity of nations to deprive me,
For that I am some twelve or fourteen moonshines
Lag of a brother? Why bastard? Wherefore base?
When my dimensions are as well-compact,
My mind as generous, and my shape as true
As honest madam's issue? Why brand they us

10   With 'base'? with 'baseness'? 'bastardy'? 'base, base'?
Who in the lusty stealth of nature take
More composition and fierce quality
Than doth within a dull, stale, tired bed
Go to the creating a whole tribe of fops
Got 'tween asleep and wake? Well then,
Legitimate Edgar, I must have your land.
Our father's love is to the bastard Edmund
As to the legitimate. Fine word 'legitimate'!
Well, my 'legitimate', if this letter speed

20   And my invention thrive, Edmund the base
Shall top the legitimate. I grow. I prosper.
Now gods stand up for bastards!

Enter Gloucester

GLOUCESTER
Kent banished thus? and France in choler parted?
And the King gone tonight? prescribed his power?
Confined to exhibition? All this done
Upon the gad? Edmund, how now? What news?

EDMUND So please your lordship, none.

GLOUCESTER Why so earnestly seek you to put up that
letter?

EDMUND I know no news, my lord.   30

GLOUCESTER What paper were you reading?

EDMUND Nothing, my lord.

GLOUCESTER No? What needed then that terrible dispatch of it into your pocket? The quality of nothing
hath not such need to hide itself. Let's see! Come! If it
be nothing I shall not need spectacles.

EDMUND I beseech you, sir, pardon me. It is a letter from
my brother that I have not all o'er-read; and for so much
as I have perused, I find it not fit for your o'erlooking.

GLOUCESTER Give me the letter, sir.   40

EDMUND I shall offend either to detain or give it. The
contents, as in part I understand them, are to blame.

GLOUCESTER Let's see, let's see!

EDMUND I hope for my brother's justification he wrote
this but as an essay or taste of my virtue.

GLOUCESTER (*reading*) *This policy and reverence of age
makes the world bitter to the best of our times, keeps our
fortunes from us till our oldness cannot relish them. I begin
to find an idle and fond bondage in the oppression of aged
tyranny, who sways not as it hath power but as it is*   50
*suffered. Come to me that of this I may speak more. If our
father would sleep till I waked him, you should enjoy half
his revenue for ever, and live the beloved of your brother,*
                                                Edgar.

73

Hum! Conspiracy! 'Sleep till I waked him, you should
enjoy half his revenue'. My son Edgar, had he a hand to
write this? a heart and brain to breed it in? When came
you to this? Who brought it?

EDMUND It was not brought me, my lord. There's the
60 cunning of it. I found it thrown in at the casement of my
closet.

GLOUCESTER You know the character to be your
brother's?

EDMUND If the matter were good, my lord, I durst swear
it were his; but in respect of that I would fain think it
were not.

GLOUCESTER It is his!

EDMUND It is his hand, my lord; but I hope his heart is
not in the contents.

70 GLOUCESTER Has he never before sounded you in this
business?

EDMUND Never, my lord. But I have heard him oft maintain it to be fit that, sons at perfect age and fathers
declined, the father should be as ward to the son, and
the son manage his revenue.

GLOUCESTER O villain, villain! His very opinion in the
letter! Abhorred villain! Unnatural, detested, brutish
villain! worse than brutish! Go, sirrah, seek him. I'll
apprehend him. Abominable villain! Where is he?

80 EDMUND I do not well know, my lord. If it shall please
you to suspend your indignation against my brother till
you can derive from him better testimony of his intent,
you should run a certain course; where, if you violently
proceed against him, mistaking his purpose, it would
make a great gap in your own honour and shake in
pieces the heart of his obedience. I dare pawn down my
life for him that he hath writ this to feel my affection to
your honour and to no other pretence of danger.

GLOUCESTER Think you so?

EDMUND If your honour judge it meet I will place you 90
where you shall hear us confer of this and by an
auricular assurance have your satisfaction, and that
without any further delay than this very evening.

GLOUCESTER He cannot be such a monster –

EDMUND Nor is not, sure.

GLOUCESTER To his father that so tenderly and entirely
loves him. Heaven and earth! Edmund, seek him out.
Wind me into him, I pray you. Frame the business after
your own wisdom. I would unstate myself to be in a due
resolution. 100

EDMUND I will seek him, sir, presently, convey the business as I shall find means, and acquaint you withal.

GLOUCESTER These late eclipses in the sun and moon
portend no good to us. Though the wisdom of nature
can reason it thus and thus, yet nature finds itself
scourged by the sequent effects: love cools, friendship
falls off, brothers divide. In cities, mutinies; in countries,
discord; in palaces, treason; and the bond cracked 'twixt
son and father. This villain of mine comes under the
prediction: there's son against father; the King falls 110
from bias of nature: there's father against child. We
have seen the best of our time. Machinations, hollowness, treachery, and all ruinous disorders follow us dis-
quietly to our graves – find out this villain, Edmund;
it shall lose thee nothing; do it carefully – and the noble
and true-hearted Kent banished! His offence, honesty!
'Tis strange. *Exit*

EDMUND This is the excellent foppery of the world, that
when we are sick in fortune – often the surfeits of our
own behaviour – we make guilty of our disasters the sun, 120
the moon, and stars, as if we were villains on necessity,
fools by heavenly compulsion, knaves, thieves, and

treachers by spherical predominance, drunkards, liars,
and adulterers by an enforced obedience of planetary
influence; and all that we are evil in by a divine
thrusting-on. An admirable evasion of whoremaster
man, to lay his goatish disposition to the charge of a
star. My father compounded with my mother under the
Dragon's tail, and my nativity was under Ursa Major, so
130 that it follows I am rough and lecherous. Fut! I should
have been that I am had the maidenliest star in the
firmament twinkled on my bastardizing. Edgar –
    (*Enter Edgar*)
pat he comes, like the catastrophe of the old comedy.
My cue is villainous melancholy, with a sigh like Tom
o'Bedlam. (*Aloud*) O these eclipses do portend these
divisions: (*he sings*) Fa, sol, la, mi.

EDGAR How now, brother Edmund! What serious con-
templation are you in?

EDMUND I am thinking, brother, of a prediction I read
140 this other day, what should follow these eclipses.

EDGAR Do you busy yourself with that?

EDMUND I promise you, the effects he writes of succeed
unhappily, as of unnaturalness between the child and the
parent, death, dearth, dissolutions of ancient amities,
divisions in state, menaces and maledictions against king
and nobles, needless diffidences, banishment of friends,
dissipation of cohorts, nuptial breaches, and I know not
what.

EDGAR How long have you been a sectary astronomical?
150 EDMUND When saw you my father last?

EDGAR The night gone by.

EDMUND Spake you with him?

EDGAR Ay, two hours together.

EDMUND Parted you in good terms? Found you no displeasure in him by word nor countenance?

EDGAR None at all.

EDMUND Bethink yourself wherein you may have offended him, and at my entreaty forbear his presence until some little time hath qualified the heat of his displeasure, which at this instant so rageth in him that with 160 the mischief of your person it would scarcely allay.

EDGAR Some villain hath done me wrong.

EDMUND That's my fear. I pray you have a continent forbearance till the speed of his rage goes slower; and, as I say, retire with me to my lodging, from whence I will fitly bring you to hear my lord speak. Pray ye, go! There's my key. If you do stir abroad, go armed.

EDGAR Armed, brother?

EDMUND Brother, I advise you to the best. I am no honest man if there be any good meaning toward you. I have 170 told you what I have seen and heard but faintly, nothing like the image and horror of it. Pray you, away!

EDGAR Shall I hear from you anon?

EDMUND I do serve you in this business.

Exit Edgar

A credulous father and a brother noble,
Whose nature is so far from doing harms
That he suspects none; on whose foolish honesty
My practices ride easy – I see the business:
Let me, if not by birth, have lands by wit;
All with me's meet that I can fashion fit. *Exit* 180

Enter Gonerill and Oswald, her steward I.3

GONERILL Did my father strike my gentleman for chiding of his Fool?

OSWALD Ay, Madam.

GONERILL
By day and night he wrongs me; every hour

He flashes into one gross crime or other
That sets us all at odds. I'll not endure it!
His knights grow riotous, and himself upbraids us
On every trifle. When he returns from hunting
I will not speak with him. Say I am sick.
10   If you come slack of former services
You shall do well; the fault of it I'll answer.

OSWALD He's coming, madam; I hear him.

GONERILL

Put on what weary negligence you please,
You and your fellows. I'd have it come to question.
If he distaste it let him to my sister,
Whose mind and mine I know in that are one,
Not to be overruled. Idle old man,
That still would manage those authorities
That he hath given away! Now, by my life,
20   Old fools are babes again, and must be used
With checks, as flatteries, when they are seen abused.
Remember what I have said.

OSWALD   Well, madam.

GONERILL

And let his knights have colder looks among you.
What grows of it, no matter. Advise your fellows so.
I would breed from hence occasions, and I shall,
That I may speak. I'll write straight to my sister
To hold my very course. Prepare for dinner.   *Exeunt*

I.4   *Enter Kent in disguise*

KENT

If but as well I other accents borrow
That can my speech diffuse, my good intent
May carry through itself to that full issue
For which I razed my likeness. Now, banished Kent,

If thou canst serve where thou dost stand condemned,
So may it come thy master whom thou lovest
Shall find thee full of labours.

Horns within. Enter Lear and Knights

LEAR Let me not stay a jot for dinner! Go, get it ready!

Exit First Knight

How now? What art thou?

KENT A man, sir.

LEAR What dost thou profess? What wouldst thou with us?

KENT I do profess to be no less than I seem: to serve him truly that will put me in trust, to love him that is honest, to converse with him that is wise and says little, to fear judgement, to fight when I cannot choose, and to eat no fish.

LEAR What art thou?

KENT A very honest-hearted fellow, and as poor as the King.

LEAR If thou be'st as poor for a subject as he's for a king thou art poor enough. What wouldst thou?

KENT Service.

LEAR Who wouldst thou serve?

KENT You.

LEAR Dost thou know me, fellow?

KENT No, sir; but you have that in your countenance which I would fain call master.

LEAR What's that?

KENT Authority.

LEAR What services canst thou do?

KENT I can keep honest counsel, ride, run, mar a curious tale in telling it, and deliver a plain message bluntly. That which ordinary men are fit for I am qualified in, and the best of me is diligence.

LEAR How old art thou?

KENT Not so young, sir, to love a woman for singing, nor
so old to dote on her for anything. I have years on my
back forty-eight.

40 LEAR Follow me; thou shalt serve me if I like thee no
worse after dinner. I will not part from thee yet. Dinner,
ho, dinner! Where's my knave, my Fool? Go you and
call my Fool hither.   *Exit Second Knight*
        Enter Oswald
You! You, sirrah! Where's my daughter?

OSWALD So please you –   *Exit*

LEAR What says the fellow there? Call the clotpoll back.
                                    Exit Third Knight
Where's my Fool? Ho, I think the world's asleep.
        Enter Third Knight
How now? Where's that mongrel?

THIRD KNIGHT He says, my lord, your daughter is not
50 well.

LEAR Why came not the slave back to me when I called
him?

THIRD KNIGHT Sir, he answered me in the roundest
manner he would not.

LEAR He would not!

THIRD KNIGHT My lord, I know not what the matter is,
but to my judgement your highness is not entertained
with that ceremonious affection as you were wont.
There's a great abatement of kindness appears as well
60 in the general dependants as in the Duke himself also
and your daughter.

LEAR Ha! Sayest thou so?

THIRD KNIGHT I beseech you pardon me, my lord, if I
be mistaken; for my duty cannot be silent when I think
your highness wronged.

LEAR Thou but rememberest me of mine own conception. I have perceived a most faint neglect of late,

which I have rather blamed as mine own jealous
curiosity than as a very pretence and purpose of unkindness. I will look further into't. But where's my 70
Fool? I have not seen him this two days.

THIRD KNIGHT Since my young lady's going into
France, sir, the Fool hath much pined away.

LEAR No more of that! I have noted it well. Go you and
tell my daughter I would speak with her.

        Exit Third Knight

Go you, call hither my Fool.   *Exit another Knight*
  Enter Oswald

O, you, sir, you! Come you hither, sir. Who am I, sir?

OSWALD My lady's father.

LEAR 'My lady's father', my lord's knave! You whoreson
dog! You slave! You cur!   80

OSWALD I am none of these, my lord, I beseech your
pardon.

LEAR Do you bandy looks with me, you rascal?
  He strikes him

OSWALD I'll not be strucken, my lord.

KENT Nor tripped neither, you base football-player?
  He trips him

LEAR I thank thee, fellow. Thou servest me and I'll love
thee.

KENT (*to Oswald*) Come, sir, arise, away! I'll teach you
differences. Away, away! If you will measure your
lubber's length again, tarry; but away, go to! Have you 90
wisdom?
  He pushes Oswald out
So.

LEAR Now, my friendly knave, I thank thee. There's
earnest of thy service.
  He gives him money
  Enter the Fool

FOOL Let me hire him too. Here's my coxcomb.

LEAR How now, my pretty knave! How dost thou?

FOOL Sirrah, you were best take my coxcomb.

KENT Why, Fool?

FOOL Why? For taking one's part that's out of favour.
100 Nay, and thou canst not smile as the wind sits, thou'lt
catch cold shortly. There, take my coxcomb! Why, this
fellow has banished two on's daughters, and did the
third a blessing against his will. If thou follow him, thou
must needs wear my coxcomb. How now, nuncle!
Would I had two coxcombs and two daughters!

LEAR Why, my boy?

FOOL If I gave them all my living, I'd keep my coxcombs
myself. There's mine. Beg another of thy daughters.

LEAR Take heed, sirrah, the whip!

110 FOOL Truth's a dog must to kennel; he must be whipped
out when the Lady Brach may stand by the fire and
stink.

LEAR A pestilent gall to me!

FOOL Sirrah, I'll teach thee a speech.

LEAR Do.

FOOL Mark it, nuncle:
    Have more than thou showest,
    Speak less than thou knowest,
    Lend less than thou owest,
120   Ride more than thou goest,
    Learn more than thou trowest,
    Set less than thou throwest;
    Leave thy drink and thy whore
    And keep in-a-door,
    And thou shalt have more
    Than two tens to a score.

KENT This is nothing, Fool.

FOOL Then 'tis like the breath of an unfee'd lawyer: you

gave me nothing for't. Can you make no use of nothing, nuncle?   130

LEAR Why, no, boy. Nothing can be made out of nothing.

FOOL (*to Kent*) Prithee tell him; so much the rent of his land comes to. He will not believe a fool.

LEAR A bitter fool!

FOOL Dost thou know the difference, my boy, between a bitter fool and a sweet one?

LEAR No, lad; teach me.

FOOL

   That lord that counselled thee
     To give away thy land,
   Come place him here by me;   140
     Do thou for him stand.
   The sweet and bitter fool
     Will presently appear:
   The one in motley here,
     The other found out – there.

LEAR Dost thou call me fool, boy?

FOOL All thy other titles thou hast given away; that thou wast born with.

KENT This is not altogether fool, my lord.

FOOL No, faith; lords and great men will not let me. If I   150 had a monopoly out they would have part on't; and ladies too – they will not let me have all the fool to my-self; they'll be snatching. Nuncle, give me an egg and I'll give thee two crowns.

LEAR What two crowns shall they be?

FOOL Why, after I have cut the egg i'the middle and eat up the meat, the two crowns of the egg. When thou clovest thy crown i'the middle, and gavest away both parts, thou borest thine ass on thy back o'er the dirt. Thou hadst little wit in thy bald crown when thou   160 gavest thy golden one away. If I speak like myself in this, let him be whipped that first finds it so.

Fools had ne'er less grace in a year,
For wise men are grown foppish
And know not how their wits to wear,
Their manners are so apish.

LEAR When were you wont to be so full of songs, sirrah?

FOOL I have used it, nuncle, e'er since thou madest thy
daughters thy mothers; for when thou gavest them the
170 rod and puttest down thine own breeches,
(*sings*)
Then they for sudden joy did weep,
And I for sorrow sung,
That such a king should play bo-peep
And go the fools among.

Prithee, nuncle, keep a schoolmaster that can teach thy
fool to lie; I would fain learn to lie.

LEAR And you lie, sirrah, we'll have you whipped.

FOOL I marvel what kin thou and thy daughters are.
They'll have me whipped for speaking true; thou'lt
180 have me whipped for lying; and sometimes I am
whipped for holding my peace. I had rather be any kind
o'thing than a fool. And yet I would not be thee, nuncle.
Thou hast pared thy wit o'both sides and left nothing
i'the middle. Here comes one o'the parings.
Enter Gonerill

LEAR How now, daughter! What makes that frontlet on?
You are too much of late i'the frown.

FOOL Thou wast a pretty fellow when thou hadst no need
to care for her frowning. Now thou art an 0 without a
figure. I am better than thou art now; I am a fool; thou
190 art nothing. (*To Gonerill*) Yes, forsooth, I will hold my
tongue. So your face bids me, though you say nothing.
Mum, mum!
He that keeps nor crust nor crumb,

Weary of all, shall want some.
>   *He points to Lear*

That's a shelled peascod.

GONERILL

Not only, sir, this your all-licensed fool
But other of your insolent retinue
Do hourly carp and quarrel, breaking forth
In rank and not-to-be-endurèd riots. Sir,
I had thought by making this well known unto you   200
To have found a safe redress; but now grow fearful
By what yourself too late have spoke and done
That you protect this course and put it on
By your allowance; which if you should, the fault
Would not 'scape censure, nor the redresses sleep;
Which in the tender of a wholesome weal
Might in their working do you that offence
Which else were shame, that then necessity
Will call discreet proceeding.

FOOL For you know, nuncle,   210
>   The hedge-sparrow fed the cuckoo so long
>   That it's had it head bit off by it young.

So out went the candle and we were left darkling.

LEAR Are you our daughter?

GONERILL

I would you would make use of your good wisdom,
Whereof I know you are fraught, and put away
These dispositions which of late transport you
From what you rightly are.

FOOL May not an ass know when the cart draws the
horse?   220
>   Whoop, Jug, I love thee!

LEAR

Does any here know me? This is not Lear.
Does Lear walk thus, speak thus? Where are his eyes?

Either his notion weakens, his discernings
Are lethargied – Ha! Waking? 'Tis not so!
Who is it that can tell me who I am?

FOOL Lear's shadow.

LEAR I would learn that; for by the marks of sovereignty,
knowledge, and reason, I should be false persuaded I
230 had daughters.

FOOL Which they will make an obedient father.

LEAR Your name, fair gentlewoman?

GONERILL
This admiration, sir, is much o'the savour
Of other your new pranks. I do beseech you
To understand my purposes aright:
As you are old and reverend, should be wise.
Here do you keep a hundred knights and squires,
Men so disordered, so deboshed and bold,
That this our court, infected with their manners,
240 Shows like a riotous inn; epicurism and lust
Makes it more like a tavern or a brothel
Than a graced palace. The shame itself doth speak
For instant remedy. Be then desired,
By her that else will take the thing she begs,
A little to disquantity your train,
And the remainders that shall still depend
To be such men as may besort your age,
Which know themselves and you.

LEAR   Darkness and devils!
Saddle my horses! Call my train together!
250 Degenerate bastard, I'll not trouble thee.
Yet have I left a daughter.

GONERILL
You strike my people, and your disordered rabble
Make servants of their betters.
          Enter Albany

LEAR

  Woe that too late repents! – O, sir, are you come?
Is it your will? Speak, sir! – Prepare my horses.
Ingratitude, thou marble-hearted fiend,
More hideous when thou showest thee in a child
Than the sea-monster!

ALBANY   Pray, sir, be patient.

LEAR (*to Gonerill*)

  Detested kite, thou liest!
My train are men of choice and rarest parts,   260
That all particulars of duty know
And in the most exact regard support
The worships of their name. O most small fault,
How ugly didst thou in Cordelia show!
Which, like an engine, wrenched my frame of nature
From the fixed place, drew from my heart all love,
And added to the gall. O Lear, Lear, Lear!
Beat at this gate that let thy folly in
    (*he strikes his head*)
And thy dear judgement out! Go, go, my people.

                      Exeunt Kent and Knights

ALBANY

  My lord, I am guiltless as I am ignorant   270
Of what hath moved you.

LEAR   It may be so, my lord.

    He kneels

Hear, Nature, hear! Dear goddess, hear!
Suspend thy purpose if thou didst intend
To make this creature fruitful.
Into her womb convey sterility,
Dry up in her the organs of increase,
And from her derogate body never spring
A babe to honour her. If she must teem,
Create her child of spleen, that it may live

280 And be a thwart disnatured torment to her.
Let it stamp wrinkles in her brow of youth,
With cadent tears fret channels in her cheeks,
Turn all her mother's pains and benefits
To laughter and contempt, that she may feel
How sharper than a serpent's tooth it is
To have a thankless child! Away, away!   *Exit*

ALBANY
Now gods that we adore, whereof comes this?

GONERILL
Never afflict yourself to know more of it;
But let his disposition have that scope
290 As dotage gives it.
             Enter Lear

LEAR
What, fifty of my followers at a clap?
Within a fortnight?

ALBANY   What's the matter, sir?

LEAR
I'll tell thee – (*to Gonerill*) life and death! I am
             ashamed
That thou hast power to shake my manhood thus,
That these hot tears which break from me perforce
Should make thee worth them. Blasts and fogs upon
             thee!
Th'untented woundings of a father's curse
Pierce every sense about thee! – Old fond eyes,
Beweep this cause again, I'll pluck ye out
300 And cast you with the waters that you loose
To temper clay. Yea, is't come to this?
Let it be so. I have another daughter,
Who, I am sure, is kind and comfortable.
When she shall hear this of thee, with her nails
She'll flay thy wolvish visage. Thou shalt find

That I'll resume the shape which thou dost think
I have cast off for ever.   *Exit*

GONERILL   Do you mark that?

ALBANY
I cannot be so partial, Gonerill,
To the great love I bear you –

GONERILL
Pray you, content – What, Oswald, ho!   310
(*To the Fool*) You, sir, more knave than fool, after your
        master!

FOOL Nuncle Lear, nuncle Lear, tarry! Take the Fool
with thee.
    A fox, when one has caught her,
    And such a daughter
    Should sure to the slaughter,
    If my cap would buy a halter –
    So the fool follows after.   *Exit*

GONERILL
This man hath had good counsel! A hundred knights!
'Tis politic and safe to let him keep   320
At point a hundred knights! Yes, that on every dream,
Each buzz, each fancy, each complaint, dislike,
He may enguard his dotage with their powers
And hold our lives in mercy. – Oswald, I say!

ALBANY
Well, you may fear too far.

GONERILL   Safer than trust too far.
Let me still take away the harms I fear,
Not fear still to be taken. I know his heart.
What he hath uttered I have writ my sister;
If she sustain him and his hundred knights
When I have showed th'unfitness –
        Enter Oswald

                                How now, Oswald! 330

What, have you writ that letter to my sister?

OSWALD Ay, madam.

GONERILL

Take you some company and away to horse.
Inform her full of my particular fear,
And thereto add such reasons of your own
As may compact it more. Get you gone,
And hasten your return.   *Exit Oswald*

              No, no, my lord,
This milky gentleness and course of yours,
Though I condemn not, yet, under pardon,
340 You are much more a-taxed for want of wisdom
Than praised for harmful mildness.

ALBANY

How far your eyes may pierce I cannot tell;
Striving to better, oft we mar what's well.

GONERILL Nay then –

ALBANY Well, well – th'event!   *Exeunt*

I.5   *Enter Lear, Kent, Knight, and the Fool*

LEAR (*to Kent*) Go you before to Gloucester with these
letters. Acquaint my daughter no further with anything
you know than comes from her demand out of the letter.
If your diligence be not speedy I shall be there afore
you.

KENT I will not sleep, my lord, till I have delivered your
letter.   *Exit*

FOOL If a man's brains were in's heels, were't not in
danger of kibes?

10 LEAR Ay, boy.

FOOL Then I prithee be merry. Thy wit shall not go slipshod.

LEAR Ha, ha, ha!

FOOL Shalt see thy other daughter will use thee kindly; for though she's as like this as a crab's like an apple, yet I can tell what I can tell.

LEAR What canst tell, boy?

FOOL She will taste as like this as a crab does to a crab. Thou canst tell why one's nose stands i'the middle on's face? 20

LEAR No.

FOOL Why, to keep one's eyes of either side's nose; that what a man cannot smell out he may spy into.

LEAR I did her wrong.

FOOL Canst tell how an oyster makes his shell?

LEAR No.

FOOL Nor I neither. But I can tell why a snail has a house.

LEAR Why?

FOOL Why, to put's head in; not to give it away to his daughters, and leave his horns without a case. 30

LEAR I will forget my nature. So kind a father! – Be my horses ready?

FOOL Thy asses are gone about 'em. The reason why the seven stars are no more than seven is a pretty reason.

LEAR Because they are not eight?

FOOL Yes, indeed. Thou wouldst make a good fool.

LEAR To take't again perforce! Monster ingratitude!

FOOL If thou wert my fool, nuncle, I'd have thee beaten for being old before thy time.

LEAR How's that? 40

FOOL Thou shouldst not have been old till thou hadst been wise.

LEAR
O let me not be mad, not mad, sweet heaven!
Keep me in temper; I would not be mad!
How now! Are the horses ready?

KNIGHT Ready, my lord.

LEAR Come, boy. *Exeunt all except the Fool*

FOOL

 She that's a maid now, and laughs at my departure,
 Shall not be a maid long, unless things be cut shorter.

Exit

*

II.1 *Enter Edmund and Curan by opposite doors*

EDMUND Save thee, Curan.

CURAN And you, sir. I have been with your father and
 given him notice that the Duke of Cornwall and Regan
 his Duchess will be here with him this night.

EDMUND How comes that?

CURAN Nay, I know not. You have heard of the news
 abroad – I mean the whispered ones, for they are yet but
 ear-kissing arguments?

EDMUND Not I. Pray you what are they?

10 CURAN Have you heard of no likely wars toward 'twixt
 the Dukes of Cornwall and Albany?

EDMUND Not a word.

CURAN You may do, then, in time. Fare you well, sir. *Exit*

EDMUND

 The Duke be here tonight! The better! best!
 This weaves itself perforce into my business.
 My father hath set guard to take my brother,
 And I have one thing of a queasy question
 Which I must act. Briefness and fortune work! –
 Brother, a word! Descend! Brother, I say!
  Enter Edgar

20 My father watches. O, sir, fly this place;
 Intelligence is given where you are hid.
 You have now the good advantage of the night.

Have you not spoken 'gainst the Duke of Cornwall?
He's coming hither now i'the night, i'th'haste,
And Regan with him. Have you nothing said
Upon his party 'gainst the Duke of Albany?
Advise yourself.

EDGAR   I am sure on't, not a word.

EDMUND

I hear my father coming. Pardon me;
In cunning I must draw my sword upon you.
Draw! Seem to defend yourself! Now quit you well.   30
(*Aloud*) Yield! Come before my father! Light, ho, here!
(*Aside*) Fly, brother! (*Aloud*) Torches, torches! (*Aside*)
      So farewell.   *Exit Edgar*
Some blood drawn on me would beget opinion
Of my more fierce endeavour. I have seen drunkards
Do more than this in sport.
            He wounds himself in the arm
                  (*Aloud*) Father, father! –
Stop, stop! – No help?
            Enter Gloucester and servants with torches

GLOUCESTER   Now, Edmund, where's the villain?

EDMUND

Here stood he in the dark, his sharp sword out,
Mumbling of wicked charms, conjuring the moon
To stand auspicious mistress.

GLOUCESTER   But where is he?

EDMUND

Look, sir, I bleed.

GLOUCESTER   Where is the villain, Edmund?   40

EDMUND

Fled this way, sir, when by no means he could –

GLOUCESTER

Pursue him, ho! Go after.   *Exeunt some servants*
                  'By no means' what?

93

EDMUND

Persuade me to the murder of your lordship;
But that I told him the revenging gods
'Gainst parricides did all the thunder bend,
Spoke with how manifold and strong a bond
The child was bound to the father – sir, in fine,
Seeing how loathly opposite I stood
To his unnatural purpose, in fell motion
50 With his preparèd sword he charges home
My unprovided body, latched mine arm;
But when he saw my best alarumed spirits
Bold in the quarrel's right, roused to th'encounter,
Or whether gasted by the noise I made,
Full suddenly he fled.

GLOUCESTER   Let him fly far,
Not in this land shall he remain uncaught;
And found – dispatch. The noble Duke, my master,
My worthy arch and patron, comes tonight.
By his authority I will proclaim it
60 That he which finds him shall deserve our thanks,
Bringing the murderous coward to the stake;
He that conceals him, death.

EDMUND

When I dissuaded him from his intent,
And found him pight to do it, with curst speech
I threatened to discover him. He replied,
'Thou unpossessing bastard, dost thou think,
If I would stand against thee, would the reposal
Of any trust, virtue, or worth in thee
Make thy words faithed? No, what I should deny –
70 As this I would; ay, though thou didst produce
My very character – I'd turn it all
To thy suggestion, plot, and damnèd practice;
And thou must make a dullard of the world

94

If they not thought the profits of my death
Were very pregnant and potential spurs
To make thee seek it.'

GLOUCESTER   O strange and fastened villain!
Would he deny his letter, said he? I never got him.

    Tucket within

Hark, the Duke's trumpets! I know not why he comes. –
All ports I'll bar; the villain shall not 'scape.
The Duke must grant me that. Besides, his picture   80
I will send far and near, that all the kingdom
May have due note of him; and of my land,
Loyal and natural boy, I'll work the means
To make thee capable.

    Enter Cornwall, Regan, and attendants

CORNWALL
How now, my noble friend? Since I came hither –
Which I can call but now – I have heard strange news.

REGAN
If it be true, all vengeance comes too short
Which can pursue th'offender. How dost, my lord?

GLOUCESTER
O madam, my old heart is cracked; it's cracked.

REGAN
What, did my father's godson seek your life?   90
He whom my father named? your Edgar?

GLOUCESTER
O lady, lady, shame would have it hid!

REGAN
Was he not companion with the riotous knights
That tended upon my father?

GLOUCESTER
I know not, madam. 'Tis too bad, too bad!

EDMUND
Yes, madam, he was of that consort.

REGAN
No marvel then though he were ill affected.
'Tis they have put him on the old man's death,
To have th'expense and waste of his revenues.
100 I have this present evening from my sister
Been well informed of them, and with such cautions
That if they come to sojourn at my house
I'll not be there.
CORNWALL   Nor I, assure thee, Regan.
Edmund, I hear that you have shown your father
A child-like office.
EDMUND   It was my duty, sir.
GLOUCESTER
He did bewray his practice, and received
This hurt you see, striving to apprehend him.
CORNWALL
Is he pursued?
GLOUCESTER   Ay, my good lord.
CORNWALL
If he be taken he shall never more
110 Be feared of doing harm. Make your own purpose
How in my strength you please. For you, Edmund,
Whose virtue and obedience doth this instant
So much commend itself, you shall be ours.
Natures of such deep trust we shall much need;
You we first seize on.
EDMUND   I shall serve you, sir,
Truly, however else.
GLOUCESTER   For him I thank your grace.
CORNWALL
You know not why we came to visit you –
REGAN
Thus out of season, threading dark-eyed night –
Occasions, noble Gloucester, of some price,

Wherein we must have use of your advice. 120
Our father he hath writ, so hath our sister,
Of differences, which I best thought it fit
To answer from our home. The several messengers
From hence attend dispatch. Our good old friend,
Lay comforts to your bosom, and bestow
Your needful counsel to our businesses,
Which craves the instant use.

GLOUCESTER   I serve you, madam.
Your graces are right welcome.   *Exeunt. Flourish*

Enter Kent and Oswald by opposite doors   II.2

OSWALD
Good dawning to thee, friend. Art of this house?

KENT Ay.

OSWALD Where may we set our horses?

KENT I'the mire.

OSWALD Prithee, if thou lovest me, tell me.

KENT I love thee not.

OSWALD Why then, I care not for thee.

KENT If I had thee in Lipsbury pinfold I would make thee
care for me.

OSWALD Why dost thou use me thus? I know thee not. 10

KENT Fellow, I know thee.

OSWALD What dost thou know me for?

KENT A knave, a rascal, an eater of broken meats, a base,
proud, shallow, beggarly, three-suited, hundred-pound,
filthy-worsted-stocking knave; a lily-livered, action-
taking, whoreson glass-gazing super-serviceable finical
rogue, one-trunk-inheriting slave; one that wouldst be a
bawd in way of good service, and art nothing but the
composition of a knave, beggar, coward, pander, and
the son and heir of a mongrel bitch; one whom I will 20

97

    beat into clamorous whining if thou deniest the least
syllable of thy addition.

OSWALD Why, what a monstrous fellow art thou thus to
rail on one that is neither known of thee nor knows thee!

KENT What a brazen-faced varlet art thou, to deny thou
knowest me! Is it two days since I tripped up thy heels
and beat thee before the King? Draw, you rogue! For
though it be night, yet the moon shines. I'll make a sop
o'the moonshine of you, you whoreson cullionly barber-

30   monger! Draw!

    He brandishes his sword

OSWALD Away! I have nothing to do with thee.

KENT Draw, you rascal! You come with letters against the
King, and take Vanity the puppet's part against the
royalty of her father. Draw, you rogue! or I'll so
carbonado your shanks – Draw, you rascal! Come your
ways!

OSWALD Help, ho! Murder! Help!

KENT Strike, you slave!

    Oswald tries to escape

    Stand, rogue! Stand, you neat slave! Strike!

    He beats him

40 OSWALD Help, ho! Murder! Murder!

    *Enter Edmund, Cornwall, Regan, Gloucester, and
    servants*

EDMUND How now! What's the matter? Part!

KENT With you, goodman boy, and you please! Come, I'll
flesh ye; come on, young master.

GLOUCESTER Weapons? Arms? What's the matter here?

CORNWALL

    Keep peace, upon your lives!

    He dies that strikes again. What is the matter?

REGAN

    The messengers from our sister and the King –

CORNWALL What is your difference? Speak.

OSWALD I am scarce in breath, my lord.

KENT No marvel, you have so bestirred your valour. You 50
cowardly rascal, nature disclaims in thee; a tailor made
thee.

CORNWALL Thou art a strange fellow. A tailor make a
man?

KENT A tailor, sir. A stone-cutter or a painter could not
have made him so ill, though they had been but two
years o'the trade.

CORNWALL (to Oswald) Speak yet, how grew your
quarrel?

OSWALD This ancient ruffian, sir, whose life I have 60
spared at suit of his grey beard –

KENT Thou whoreson zed, thou unnecessary letter! My
lord, if you will give me leave, I will tread this unbolted
villain into mortar and daub the wall of a jakes with him.
'Spare my grey beard', you wagtail!

CORNWALL Peace, sirrah!
You beastly knave, know you no reverence?

KENT
Yes, sir; but anger hath a privilege.

CORNWALL Why art thou angry?

KENT
That such a slave as this should wear a sword 70
Who wears no honesty. Such smiling rogues as these,
Like rats, oft bite the holy cords atwain,
Which are t' intrinse t'unloose; smooth every passion
That in the natures of their lords rebel,
Being oil to fire, snow to the colder moods,
Renege, affirm, and turn their halcyon beaks
With every gale and vary of their masters,
Knowing naught – like dogs – but following. –
A plague upon your epileptic visage!

80   Smile you my speeches as I were a fool?
    Goose, if I had you upon Sarum Plain,
    I'd drive ye cackling home to Camelot.

CORNWALL What, art thou mad, old fellow?

GLOUCESTER How fell you out? Say that.

KENT
    No contraries hold more antipathy
    Than I and such a knave.

CORNWALL
    Why dost thou call him knave? What is his fault?

KENT His countenance likes me not.

CORNWALL
    No more perchance does mine, nor his, nor hers.

KENT
90   Sir, 'tis my occupation to be plain.
    I have seen better faces in my time
    Than stands on any shoulder that I see
    Before me at this instant.

CORNWALL   This is some fellow
    Who, having been praised for bluntness, doth affect
    A saucy roughness, and constrains the garb
    Quite from his nature. He cannot flatter, he!
    An honest mind and plain – he must speak truth!
    And they will take it, so; if not, he's plain.
    These kind of knaves I know, which in this plainness
100   Harbour more craft and more corrupter ends
    Than twenty silly-ducking observants
    That stretch their duties nicely.

KENT
    Sir, in good faith, in sincere verity,
    Under th'allowance of your great aspect
    Whose influence like the wreath of radiant fire
    On flickering Phoebus' front –

CORNWALL   What mean'st by this?

KENT To go out of my dialect which you discommend so
much. I know, sir, I am no flatterer. He that beguiled
you in a plain accent was a plain knave; which, for my
part, I will not be, though I should win your displeasure 110
to entreat me to't.

CORNWALL What was th'offence you gave him?

OSWALD I never gave him any.
It pleased the King his master very late
To strike at me upon his misconstruction,
When he, compact, and flattering his displeasure,
Tripped me behind; being down, insulted, railed,
And put upon him such a deal of man
That worthied him, got praises of the King
For him attempting who was self-subdued;   120
And in the fleshment of this dread exploit
Drew on me here again.

KENT   None of these rogues and cowards
But Ajax is their fool.

CORNWALL   Fetch forth the stocks!
You stubborn ancient knave, you reverend braggart,
We'll teach you –

KENT   Sir, I am too old to learn.
Call not your stocks for me. I serve the King,
On whose employment I was sent to you.
You shall do small respect, show too bold malice
Against the grace and person of my master,
Stocking his messenger.   130

CORNWALL
Fetch forth the stocks! As I have life and honour,
There shall he sit till noon.

REGAN
Till noon? Till night, my lord, and all night too.

KENT
Why, madam, if I were your father's dog

You should not use me so.

REGAN   Sir, being his knave, I will.

CORNWALL

This is a fellow of the selfsame colour

Our sister speaks of. Come, bring away the stocks.

Stocks brought out

GLOUCESTER

Let me beseech your grace not to do so.

His fault is much, and the good King, his master,

140   Will check him for't. Your purposed low correction

Is such as basest and contemned'st wretches

For pilferings and most common trespasses

Are punished with. The King must take it ill

That he, so slightly valued in his messenger,

Should have him thus restrained.

CORNWALL   I'll answer that.

REGAN

My sister may receive it much more worse

To have her gentleman abused, assaulted,

For following her affairs. – Put in his legs.

Kent is put in the stocks

Come, my lord, away.

Exeunt all but Gloucester and Kent

GLOUCESTER

150   I am sorry for thee, friend. 'Tis the Duke's pleasure,

Whose disposition all the world well knows

Will not be rubbed nor stopped. I'll entreat for thee.

KENT

Pray do not, sir. I have watched and travelled hard.

Some time I shall sleep out, the rest I'll whistle.

A good man's fortune may grow out at heels.

Give you good morrow!

GLOUCESTER   The Duke's to blame in this.

'Twill be ill taken.   *Exit*

KENT

    Good King, that must approve the common saw,
    Thou out of Heaven's benediction comest
    To the warm sun.   160
    Approach, thou beacon to this under globe,
    That by thy comfortable beams I may
    Peruse this letter. Nothing almost sees miracles
    But misery. I know 'tis from Cordelia,
    Who hath most fortunately been informed
    Of my obscurèd course, and (*reading*) 'shall find time
    From this enormous state, seeking to give
    Losses their remedies'. All weary and o'erwatched,
    Take vantage, heavy eyes, not to behold
    This shameful lodging.   170
    Fortune, good night; smile once more; turn thy wheel.
       He sleeps

      Enter Edgar   II.3

EDGAR

    I heard myself proclaimed,
    And by the happy hollow of a tree
    Escaped the hunt. No port is free, no place
    That guard and most unusual vigilance
    Does not attend my taking. Whiles I may 'scape
    I will preserve myself; and am bethought
    To take the basest and most poorest shape
    That ever penury, in contempt of man,
    Brought near to beast. My face I'll grime with filth,
    Blanket my loins, elf all my hairs in knots,   10
    And with presented nakedness outface
    The winds and persecutions of the sky.
    The country gives me proof and precedent
    Of Bedlam beggars, who, with roaring voices,

Strike in their numbed and mortified bare arms
Pins, wooden pricks, nails, sprigs of rosemary;
And with this horrible object, from low farms,
Poor pelting villages, sheepcotes, and mills
Sometimes with lunatic bans, sometime with prayers,
20   Enforce their charity: 'Poor Turlygod! Poor Tom!'
That's something yet; Edgar I nothing am.   *Exit*

II.4   *Kent still in the stocks*
          Enter Lear, the Fool, and a Gentleman

LEAR
'Tis strange that they should so depart from home
And not send back my messengers.

GENTLEMAN   As I learned,
The night before there was no purpose in them
Of this remove.

KENT   Hail to thee, noble master!

LEAR
Ha!
Makest thou this shame thy pastime?

KENT   No, my lord.

FOOL Ha, ha! He wears cruel garters. Horses are tied by
the heads, dogs and bears by the neck, monkeys by the
loins, and men by the legs. When a man's over-lusty at
10   legs, then he wears wooden nether-stocks.

LEAR
What's he that hath so much thy place mistook
To set thee here?

KENT   It is both he and she;
Your son and daughter.

LEAR No.

KENT Yes.

LEAR No, I say.

KENT I say yea.

LEAR No, no, they would not.

KENT Yes, they have.

LEAR By Jupiter, I swear no!   20

KENT
　By Juno, I swear ay!

LEAR　　　　　　　　They durst not do't;
　They could not, would not do't; 'tis worse than murder
　To do upon respect such violent outrage.
　Resolve me with all modest haste which way
　Thou mightst deserve or they impose this usage,
　Coming from us.

KENT　　　　　　　My lord, when at their home
　I did commend your highness' letters to them,
　Ere I was risen from the place that showed
　My duty kneeling, came there a reeking post,
　Stewed in his haste, half breathless, panting forth   30
　From Gonerill his mistress salutations;
　Delivered letters, spite of intermission,
　Which presently they read; on whose contents
　They summoned up their meiny, straight took horse,
　Commanded me to follow and attend
　The leisure of their answer, gave me cold looks;
　And meeting here the other messenger,
　Whose welcome I perceived had poisoned mine –
　Being the very fellow which of late
　Displayed so saucily against your highness –   40
　Having more man than wit about me, drew.
　He raised the house with loud and coward cries.
　Your son and daughter found this trespass worth
　The shame which here it suffers.

FOOL Winter's not gone yet if the wild geese fly that way.
　Fathers that wear rags
　　Do make their children blind,

But fathers that bear bags
　　Shall see their children kind.
50　Fortune, that arrant whore,
　　Ne'er turns the key to the poor.
But for all this thou shalt have as many dolours for thy
daughters as thou canst tell in a year.

LEAR

O, how this mother swells up toward my heart!
Hysterica passio, down, thou climbing sorrow!
Thy element's below. Where is this daughter?

KENT With the Earl, sir, here within.

LEAR Follow me not; stay here. 　　　　　　　　　　　*Exit*

GENTLEMAN

Made you no more offence but what you speak of?

60　**KENT** None.

How chance the King comes with so small a number?

FOOL And thou hadst been set i'the stocks for that question, thou'dst well deserved it.

KENT Why, Fool?

FOOL We'll set thee to school to an ant to teach thee
there's no labouring i'the winter. All that follow their
noses are led by their eyes, but blind men; and there's
not a nose among twenty but can smell him that's
stinking. Let go thy hold when a great wheel runs down
70　a hill, lest it break thy neck with following. But the great
one that goes upward, let him draw thee after. When a
wise man gives thee better counsel, give me mine again;
I would ha' none but knaves use it, since a fool gives it.
　　That sir which serves and seeks for gain,
　　　　And follows but for form,
　　Will pack when it begins to rain,
　　　　And leave thee in the storm;
　　But I will tarry, the fool will stay,
　　　　And let the wise man fly.

 The knave turns fool that runs away;   80
 The fool no knave, perdy.
KENT Where learned you this, Fool?
FOOL Not i'the stocks, fool.
 Enter Lear and Gloucester

LEAR
 Deny to speak with me? They are sick; they are weary?
 They have travelled all the night? Mere fetches,
 The images of revolt and flying-off.
 Fetch me a better answer.

GLOUCESTER   My dear lord,
 You know the fiery quality of the Duke,
 How unremovable and fixed he is
 In his own course.

LEAR   Vengeance, plague, death, confusion! 90
 'Fiery'? What 'quality'? Why, Gloucester, Gloucester,
 I'd speak with the Duke of Cornwall and his wife.

GLOUCESTER
 Well, my good lord, I have informed them so.

LEAR
 'Informed them'! Dost thou understand me, man?

GLOUCESTER Ay, my good lord.

LEAR
 The King would speak with Cornwall, the dear father
 Would with his daughter speak, commands, tends,
   service.
 Are they 'informed' of this? My breath and blood!
 'Fiery'? The 'fiery' Duke? Tell the hot Duke that –
 No, but not yet! Maybe he is not well. 100
 Infirmity doth still neglect all office
 Whereto our health is bound; we are not ourselves
 When nature, being oppressed, commands the mind
 To suffer with the body. I'll forbear;
 And am fallen out with my more headier will

To take the indisposed and sickly fit
For the sound man. – Death on my state! Wherefore
Should he sit here? This act persuades me
That this remotion of the Duke and her
110   Is practice only. Give me my servant forth.
Go tell the Duke and's wife I'd speak with them –
Now presently! Bid them come forth and hear me,
Or at their chamber door I'll beat the drum
Till it cry sleep to death.

GLOUCESTER I would have all well betwixt you.   *Exit*

LEAR
O me, my heart, my rising heart! But down!

FOOL Cry to it, nuncle, as the cockney did to the eels
when she put 'em i'the paste alive. She knapped 'em
o'the coxcombs with a stick and cried 'Down, wantons,
120   down!' 'Twas her brother that in pure kindness to his
horse buttered his hay.

    Enter Cornwall, Regan, Gloucester, and servants

LEAR
Good morrow to you both.

CORNWALL   Hail to your grace.
    Kent is here set at liberty

REGAN
I am glad to see your highness.

LEAR
Regan, I think you are. I know what reason
I have to think so. If thou shouldst not be glad,
I would divorce me from thy mother's tomb,
Sepulchring an adult'ress. (*To Kent*) O, are you free?
Some other time for that. – Beloved Regan,
Thy sister's naught. O Regan, she hath tied
130   Sharp-toothed unkindness like a vulture here –
    (*laying his hand on his heart*)
I can scarce speak to thee – thou'lt not believe

With how depraved a quality – O Regan!

REGAN

I pray you, sir, take patience. I have hope
You less know how to value her desert
Than she to scant her duty.

LEAR   Say? How is that?

REGAN

I cannot think my sister in the least
Would fail her obligation. If, sir, perchance,
She have restrained the riots of your followers,
'Tis on such ground and to such wholesome end
As clears her from all blame.   140

LEAR

My curses on her.

REGAN   O sir, you are old.
Nature in you stands on the very verge
Of his confine. You should be ruled and led
By some discretion that discerns your state
Better than you yourself. Therefore I pray you
That to our sister you do make return.
Say you have wronged her.

LEAR   Ask her forgiveness?
Do you but mark how this becomes the house:
     (*he kneels*)
'Dear daughter, I confess that I am old;
Age is unnecessary; on my knees I beg   150
That you'll vouchsafe me raiment, bed, and food.'

REGAN

Good sir, no more! These are unsightly tricks.
Return you to my sister.

LEAR (*rising*)   Never, Regan.
She hath abated me of half my train,
Looked black upon me, struck me with her tongue,
Most serpent-like, upon the very heart.

All the stored vengeances of heaven fall
On her ingrateful top! Strike her young bones,
You taking airs, with lameness!

CORNWALL   Fie, sir, fie!

LEAR
160 You nimble lightnings, dart your blinding flames
Into her scornful eyes! Infect her beauty,
You fen-sucked fogs drawn by the powerful sun,
To fall and blister.

REGAN   O the blest gods!
So will you wish on me when the rash mood is on.

LEAR
No, Regan, thou shalt never have my curse.
Thy tender-hefted nature shall not give
Thee o'er to harshness. Her eyes are fierce; but thine
Do comfort, and not burn. 'Tis not in thee
To grudge my pleasures, to cut off my train,
170 To bandy hasty words, to scant my sizes,
And, in conclusion, to oppose the bolt
Against my coming in. Thou better knowest
The offices of nature, bond of childhood,
Effects of courtesy, dues of gratitude.
Thy half o'the kingdom hast thou not forgot,
Wherein I thee endowed.

REGAN   Good sir, to the purpose.

LEAR
Who put my man i'the stocks?
          Tucket within

CORNWALL   What trumpet's that?

REGAN
I know't – my sister's. This approves her letter
That she would soon be here.
          Enter Oswald

                    Is your lady come?

LEAR

    This is a slave whose easy-borrowed pride   180
    Dwells in the fickle grace of her he follows.
    Out, varlet, from my sight!

CORNWALL   What means your grace?

LEAR

    Who stocked my servant? Regan, I have good hope
    Thou didst not know on't.

      Enter Gonerill

                      Who comes here? O heavens!
    If you do love old men, if your sweet sway
    Allow obedience, if you yourselves are old,
    Make it your cause! Send down and take my part!
    (*To Gonerill*) Art not ashamed to look upon this beard?
    O Regan, will you take her by the hand?

GONERILL

    Why not by th'hand, sir? How have I offended?   190
    All's not offence that indiscretion finds
    And dotage terms so.

LEAR   O sides, you are too tough!
    Will you yet hold? – How came my man i'the stocks?

CORNWALL

    I set him there, sir; but his own disorders
    Deserved much less advancement.

LEAR   You? Did you?

REGAN

    I pray you, father, being weak, seem so.
    If till the expiration of your month
    You will return and sojourn with my sister,
    Dismissing half your train, come then to me.
    I am now from home and out of that provision   200
    Which shall be needful for your entertainment.

LEAR

    Return to her, and fifty men dismissed!

No, rather I abjure all roofs and choose
To wage against the enmity o'th'air,
To be a comrade with the wolf and owl –
Necessity's sharp pinch! Return with her?
Why, the hot-blooded France that dowerless took
Our youngest born, I could as well be brought
To knee his throne and, squire-like, pension beg
210 To keep base life afoot. Return with her!
Persuade me rather to be slave and sumpter
To this detested groom.

He points to Oswald

GONERILL   At your choice, sir.

LEAR
I prithee, daughter, do not make me mad.
I will not trouble thee, my child. Farewell.
We'll no more meet, no more see one another.
But yet thou art my flesh, my blood, my daughter –
Or rather a disease that's in my flesh,
Which I must needs call mine. Thou art a boil,
A plague-sore, or embossed carbuncle,
220 In my corrupted blood. But I'll not chide thee.
Let shame come when it will, I do not call it.
I do not bid the thunder-bearer shoot,
Nor tell tales of thee to high-judging Jove.
Mend when thou canst, be better at thy leisure;
I can be patient, I can stay with Regan,
I and my hundred knights.

REGAN   Not altogether so.
I looked not for you yet, nor am provided
For your fit welcome. Give ear, sir, to my sister;
For those that mingle reason with your passion
230 Must be content to think you old, and so –
But she knows what she does.

LEAR   Is this well spoken?

REGAN

   I dare avouch it, sir. What, fifty followers?
   Is it not well? What should you need of more?
   Yea, or so many, sith that both charge and danger
   Speak 'gainst so great a number? How in one house
   Should many people under two commands
   Hold amity? 'Tis hard, almost impossible.

GONERILL

   Why might not you, my lord, receive attendance
   From those that she calls servants, or from mine?

REGAN

   Why not, my lord? If then they chanced to slack ye,   240
   We could control them. If you will come to me,
   For now I spy a danger, I entreat you
   To bring but five-and-twenty; to no more
   Will I give place or notice.

LEAR

   I gave you all –

REGAN   And in good time you gave it.

LEAR

   Made you my guardians, my depositaries;
   But kept a reservation to be followed
   With such a number. What, must I come to you
   With five-and-twenty – Regan, said you so?

REGAN

   And speak't again, my lord. No more with me.   250

LEAR

   Those wicked creatures yet do look well-favoured
   When others are more wicked. Not being the worst
   Stands in some rank of praise. (*To Gonerill*) I'll go
      with thee.
   Thy fifty yet doth double five-and-twenty,
   And thou art twice her love.

GONERILL   Hear me, my lord;

    What need you five-and-twenty, ten, or five
    To follow, in a house where twice so many
    Have a command to tend you?

REGAN   What need one?

LEAR

    O, reason not the need! Our basest beggars
260 Are in the poorest thing superfluous.
    Allow not nature more than nature needs –
    Man's life is cheap as beast's. Thou art a lady;
    If only to go warm were gorgeous,
    Why, nature needs not what thou gorgeous wear'st,
    Which scarcely keeps thee warm. But for true need –
    You heavens, give me that patience, patience I need!
    You see me here, you gods, a poor old man,
    As full of grief as age, wretched in both;
    If it be you that stirs these daughters' hearts
270 Against their father, fool me not so much
    To bear it tamely; touch me with noble anger,
    And let not women's weapons, water drops,
    Stain my man's cheeks. No, you unnatural hags,
    I will have such revenges on you both
    That all the world shall – I will do such things –
    What they are yet I know not; but they shall be
    The terrors of the earth. You think I'll weep.
    No, I'll not weep.
    I have full cause of weeping;

        (*storm and tempest*)

                           but this heart
280 Shall break into a hundred thousand flaws
    Or ere I'll weep. O Fool, I shall go mad!
    Exeunt Lear, Gloucester, Kent, the Fool, and Gentleman

CORNWALL Let us withdraw; 'twill be a storm.

REGAN

    This house is little; the old man and's people

Cannot be well bestowed.

GONERILL

'Tis his own blame; hath put himself from rest
And must needs taste his folly.

REGAN

For his particular, I'll receive him gladly,
But not one follower.

GONERILL   So am I purposed.
Where is my lord of Gloucester?

CORNWALL

Followed the old man forth. He is returned.   290

    Enter Gloucester

GLOUCESTER

The King is in high rage.

CORNWALL   Whither is he going?

GLOUCESTER

He calls to horse; but will I know not whither.

CORNWALL

'Tis best to give him way. He leads himself.

GONERILL

My lord, entreat him by no means to stay.

GLOUCESTER

Alack, the night comes on and the bleak winds
Do sorely ruffle. For many miles about
There's scarce a bush.

REGAN   O sir, to wilful men
The injuries that they themselves procure
Must be their schoolmasters. Shut up your doors.
He is attended with a desperate train,   300
And what they may incense him to, being apt
To have his ear abused, wisdom bids fear.

CORNWALL

Shut up your doors, my lord; 'tis a wild night.
My Regan counsels well. Come out o'the storm. *Exeunt*

Storm still. Enter Kent and a Gentleman by opposite
              doors

KENT Who's there besides foul weather?

GENTLEMAN
  One minded like the weather, most unquietly.

KENT I know you. Where's the King?

GENTLEMAN
  Contending with the fretful elements:
  Bids the wind blow the earth into the sea,
  Or swell the curlèd waters 'bove the main,
  That things might change or cease; tears his white hair,
  Which the impetuous blasts with eyeless rage
  Catch in their fury and make nothing of;
10 Strives in his little world of man to out-storm
  The to-and-fro conflicting wind and rain.
  This night, wherein the cub-drawn bear would couch,
  The lion and the belly-pinchèd wolf
  Keep their fur dry, unbonneted he runs
  And bids what will take all.

KENT   But who is with him?

GENTLEMAN
  None but the Fool, who labours to out-jest
  His heart-struck injuries.

KENT   Sir, I do know you,
  And dare upon the warrant of my note
  Commend a dear thing to you. There is division –
20 Although as yet the face of it is covered
  With mutual cunning – 'twixt Albany and Cornwall;
  Who have – as who have not that their great stars
  Throned and set high – servants, who seem no less,
  Which are to France the spies and speculations
  Intelligent of our state. What hath been seen,
  Either in snuffs and packings of the Dukes,
  Or the hard rein which both of them hath borne

Against the old kind King, or something deeper,
Whereof, perchance, these are but furnishings –
But true it is, from France there comes a power 30
Into this scattered kingdom, who already,
Wise in our negligence, have secret feet
In some of our best ports and are at point
To show their open banner. Now to you:
If on my credit you dare build so far
To make your speed to Dover, you shall find
Some that will thank you making just report
Of how unnatural and bemadding sorrow
The King hath cause to plain.
I am a gentleman of blood and breeding, 40
And from some knowledge and assurance offer
This office to you.

GENTLEMAN
I will talk further with you.

KENT   No, do not.
For confirmation that I am much more
Than my out-wall, open this purse and take
What it contains. If you shall see Cordelia –
As fear not but you shall – show her this ring,
And she will tell you who that fellow is
That yet you do not know. Fie on this storm!
I will go seek the King. 50

GENTLEMAN
Give me your hand. Have you no more to say?

KENT
Few words, but to effect more than all yet:
That when we have found the King – in which your pain
That way, I'll this – he that first lights on him
Holla the other.   *Exeunt by opposite doors*

117

LEAR

> Blow, winds, and crack your cheeks! Rage! Blow!
> You cataracts and hurricanoes, spout
> Till you have drenched our steeples, drowned the cocks!
> You sulphurous and thought-executing fires,
> Vaunt-curriers of oak-cleaving thunderbolts,
> Singe my white head! And thou all-shaking thunder,
> Strike flat the thick rotundity o'the world,
> Crack Nature's moulds, all germens spill at once
> That makes ingrateful man!

10 FOOL O nuncle, court holy-water in a dry house is better than this rain-water out o'door. Good nuncle, in; ask thy daughters' blessing. Here's a night pities neither wise men nor fools.

LEAR

> Rumble thy bellyful! Spit, fire! Spout, rain!
> Nor rain, wind, thunder, fire are my daughters.
> I tax not you, you elements, with unkindness;
> I never gave you kingdom, called you children.
> You owe me no subscription; then let fall
> Your horrible pleasure. Here I stand, your slave,
20 A poor, infirm, weak, and despised old man.
> But yet I call you servile ministers,
> That will with two pernicious daughters join
> Your high-engendered battles 'gainst a head
> So old and white as this. O, ho! 'Tis foul!

FOOL He that has a house to put's head in has a good head-piece:

> > The cod-piece that will house
> > Before the head has any,
> > The head and he shall louse;
30 > > So beggars marry many.
> > The man that makes his toe

What he his heart should make,
  Shall of a corn cry woe,
    And turn his sleep to wake.
For there was never yet fair woman but she made mouths
in a glass.

Enter Kent

LEAR
No, I will be the pattern of all patience.
I will say nothing.

KENT Who's there?

FOOL Marry, here's grace and a cod-piece – that's a wise 40
man and a fool.

KENT
Alas, sir, are you here? Things that love night
Love not such nights as these. The wrathful skies
Gallow the very wanderers of the dark
And make them keep their caves. Since I was man,
Such sheets of fire, such bursts of horrid thunder,
Such groans of roaring wind and rain I never
Remember to have heard. Man's nature cannot carry
Th'affliction nor the fear.

LEAR   Let the great gods
That keep this dreadful pudder o'er our heads   50
Find out their enemies now. Tremble, thou wretch
That hast within thee undivulgèd crimes
Unwhipped of justice. Hide thee, thou bloody hand,
Thou perjured, and thou simular of virtue
That art incestuous. Caitiff, to pieces shake,
That under covert and convenient seeming
Has practised on man's life. Close pent-up guilts,
Rive your concealing continents, and cry
These dreadful summoners grace. I am a man
More sinned against than sinning.

KENT   Alack, bare-headed? 60

Gracious my lord, hard by here is a hovel;
Some friendship will it lend you 'gainst the tempest.
Repose you there while I to this hard house –
More harder than the stones whereof 'tis raised;
Which even but now, demanding after you,
Denied me to come in – return and force
Their scanted courtesy.

LEAR   My wits begin to turn.
Come on, my boy. How dost my boy? Art cold?
I am cold myself. Where is this straw, my fellow?
70 The art of our necessities is strange
And can make vile things precious. Come, your hovel.
Poor fool and knave, I have one part in my heart
That's sorry yet for thee.

FOOL (*sings*)
        He that has and a little tiny wit,
        With heigh-ho, the wind and the rain,
        Must make content with his fortunes fit,
        Though the rain it raineth every day.

LEAR True, boy. Come, bring us to this hovel.
                                        Exeunt Lear and Kent

FOOL This is a brave night to cool a courtesan. I'll speak
80 a prophecy ere I go:
        When priests are more in word than matter,
        When brewers mar their malt with water,
        When nobles are their tailors' tutors,
        No heretics burned but wenches' suitors –
        Then shall the realm of Albion
        Come to great confusion.

        When every case in law is right,
        No squire in debt nor no poor knight,
        When slanders do not live in tongues,
90   Nor cutpurses come not to throngs,

When usurers tell their gold i'the field,
And bawds and whores do churches build –
Then comes the time, who lives to see't,
That going shall be used with feet.
This prophecy Merlin shall make; for I live before his
time.   *Exit*

Enter Gloucester and Edmund with lights   III.3

GLOUCESTER Alack, alack, Edmund, I like not this unnatural dealing. When I desired their leave that I might
pity him, they took from me the use of mine own house,
charged me on pain of perpetual displeasure neither to
speak of him, entreat for him, or any way sustain him.
EDMUND Most savage and unnatural!
GLOUCESTER Go to. Say you nothing. There is division
between the Dukes; and a worse matter than that. I
have received a letter this night; 'tis dangerous to be
spoken; I have locked the letter in my closet. These in- 10
juries the King now bears will be revenged home. There
is part of a power already footed. We must incline to the
King. I will look him and privily relieve him. Go you
and maintain talk with the Duke, that my charity be not
of him perceived. If he ask for me, I am ill and gone to
bed. If I die for it, as no less is threatened me, the King
my old master must be relieved. There is strange things
toward, Edmund. Pray you, be careful.   *Exit*
EDMUND
This courtesy forbid thee shall the Duke
Instantly know, and of that letter too.   20
This seems a fair deserving, and must draw me
That which my father loses – no less than all.
The younger rises when the old doth fall.   *Exit*

Enter Lear, Kent, and the Fool

KENT

Here is the place, my lord; good my lord, enter.
The tyranny of the open night's too rough
For nature to endure.

Storm still

LEAR   Let me alone.

KENT

Good my lord, enter here.

LEAR   Wilt break my heart?

KENT

I had rather break mine own. Good my lord, enter.

LEAR

Thou think'st 'tis much that this contentious storm
Invades us to the skin; so 'tis to thee.
But where the greater malady is fixed
The lesser is scarce felt. Thou'dst shun a bear;
10 But if thy flight lay toward the roaring sea
Thou'dst meet the bear i'the mouth. When the mind's free
The body's delicate; this tempest in my mind
Doth from my senses take all feeling else
Save what beats there. – Filial ingratitude!
Is it not as this mouth should tear this hand
For lifting food to't? But I will punish home.
No, I will weep no more! In such a night
To shut me out! Pour on; I will endure.
In such a night as this! O Regan, Gonerill!
20 Your old kind father, whose frank heart gave all!
O, that way madness lies; let me shun that;
No more of that!

KENT   Good my lord, enter here.

LEAR

Prithee go in thyself; seek thine own ease.

This tempest will not give me leave to ponder
On things would hurt me more; but I'll go in.
(*To the Fool*) In, boy, go first. – You houseless
    poverty –
Nay, get thee in. I'll pray and then I'll sleep.

Exit the Fool

Poor naked wretches, wheresoe'er you are,
That bide the pelting of this pitiless storm,
How shall your houseless heads and unfed sides,   30
Your looped and windowed raggedness, defend you
From seasons such as these? O, I have ta'en
Too little care of this! Take physic, pomp;
Expose thyself to feel what wretches feel,
That thou mayst shake the superflux to them
And show the heavens more just.

EDGAR (*within*)
    Fathom and half, fathom and half! Poor Tom!

Enter the Fool from the hovel

FOOL Come not in here, nuncle; here's a spirit. Help me,
help me!

KENT Give me thy hand. Who's there?   40

FOOL A spirit, a spirit! He says his name's Poor Tom.

KENT What art thou that dost grumble there i'the straw?
Come forth.

Enter Edgar disguised as Poor Tom

EDGAR Away! The foul fiend follows me.
    Through the sharp hawthorn blow the cold winds.
Humh! Go to thy bed and warm thee.

LEAR Didst thou give all to thy daughters? And art thou
come to this?

EDGAR Who gives anything to Poor Tom? whom the foul
fiend hath led through fire and through flame, through   50
ford and whirlpool, o'er bog and quagmire, that hath
laid knives under his pillow and halters in his pew, set

ratsbane by his porridge, made him proud of heart, to
ride on a bay trotting horse over four-inched bridges to
course his own shadow for a traitor. Bless thy five wits!
Tom's a-cold. O do, de, do, de, do, de. Bless thee from
whirlwinds, star-blasting, and taking! Do Poor Tom
some charity, whom the foul fiend vexes. There could I
have him now, and there, and there again, and there.

Storm still

LEAR

60   What, has his daughters brought him to this pass?
Couldst thou save nothing? Wouldst thou give 'em all?

FOOL Nay, he reserved a blanket; else we had been all
shamed.

LEAR

Now all the plagues that in the pendulous air
Hang fated o'er men's faults light on thy daughters!

KENT He hath no daughters, sir.

LEAR

Death, traitor! Nothing could have subdued nature
To such a lowness but his unkind daughters.
Is it the fashion that discarded fathers
70   Should have thus little mercy on their flesh?
Judicious punishment! 'Twas this flesh begot
Those pelican daughters.

EDGAR

Pillicock sat on Pillicock Hill.
Alow, alow, loo, loo!

FOOL This cold night will turn us all to fools and madmen.

EDGAR Take heed o'the foul fiend, obey thy parents, keep
thy word's justice, swear not, commit not with man's
sworn spouse, set not thy sweet heart on proud array.
80   Tom's a-cold.

LEAR What hast thou been?

EDGAR A servingman, proud in heart and mind, that curled my hair, wore gloves in my cap, served the lust of my mistress' heart and did the act of darkness with her, swore as many oaths as I spake words and broke them in the sweet face of heaven; one that slept in the contriving of lust and waked to do it. Wine loved I deeply, dice dearly, and in woman out-paramoured the Turk – false of heart, light of ear, bloody of hand; hog in sloth, fox in stealth, wolf in greediness, dog in madness, lion in prey. 90 Let not the creaking of shoes nor the rustling of silks betray thy poor heart to woman. Keep thy foot out of brothels, thy hand out of plackets, thy pen from lenders' books, and defy the foul fiend.

Still through the hawthorn blows the cold wind,
Says suum, mun, nonny.
Dolphin, my boy, boy, sesey! Let him trot by.
Storm still

LEAR Thou wert better in a grave than to answer with thy uncovered body this extremity of the skies. Is man no more than this? Consider him well. Thou owest the 100 worm no silk, the beast no hide, the sheep no wool, the cat no perfume. Ha! Here's three on's are sophisticated. Thou art the thing itself! Unaccommodated man is no more but such a poor, bare, forked animal as thou art. Off, off, you lendings! Come, unbutton here.
He tears off his clothes

FOOL Prithee, nuncle, be contented; 'tis a naughty night to swim in. Now a little fire in a wild field were like an old lecher's heart – a small spark, all the rest on's body cold. Look, here comes a walking fire.
Enter Gloucester with a torch

EDGAR This is the foul fiend Flibberdigibbet. He begins 110 at curfew and walks till the first cock. He gives the web and the pin, squenies the eye and makes the harelip, mildews the white wheat, and hurts the poor creature of earth.

> S'Withold footed thrice the 'old;
> He met the nightmare and her nine-fold,
> Bid her alight and her troth plight –
> And aroint thee, witch, aroint thee!

KENT How fares your grace?

120 LEAR What's he?

KENT (*to Gloucester*) Who's there? What is't you seek?

GLOUCESTER What are you there? Your names?

EDGAR Poor Tom, that eats the swimming frog, the toad, the todpole, the wall-newt and the water; that in the fury of his heart, when the foul fiend rages, eats cow-dung for sallets, swallows the old rat and the ditch-dog, drinks the green mantle of the standing pool; who is whipped from tithing to tithing and stock-punished and imprisoned; who hath had three suits to his back, six

130 shirts to his body,

> Horse to ride and weapon to wear –
> But mice and rats and such small deer
> Have been Tom's food for seven long year.

Beware my follower! Peace, Smulkin! Peace, thou fiend!

GLOUCESTER What, hath your grace no better company?

EDGAR The prince of darkness is a gentleman; Modo he's called and Mahu.

GLOUCESTER
Our flesh and blood, my lord, is grown so vile
That it doth hate what gets it.

140 EDGAR Poor Tom's a-cold.

GLOUCESTER
Go in with me. My duty cannot suffer
T'obey in all your daughters' hard commands;
Though their injunction be to bar my doors
And let this tyrannous night take hold upon you,

Yet have I ventured to come seek you out
And bring you where both fire and food is ready.

LEAR
First let me talk with this philosopher.
(*To Edgar*) What is the cause of thunder?

KENT   Good my lord,
Take his offer, go into the house.

LEAR
I'll talk a word with this same learnèd Theban.   150
(*To Edgar*) What is your study?

EDGAR How to prevent the fiend and to kill vermin.

LEAR Let me ask you one word in private.
        Lear and Edgar talk apart

KENT
Importune him once more to go, my lord.
His wits begin t'unsettle.

GLOUCESTER   Canst thou blame him? —
        (*storm still*)
His daughters seek his death. Ah, that good Kent,
He said it would be thus, poor banished man!
Thou sayest the King grows mad; I'll tell thee, friend,
I am almost mad myself. I had a son,
Now outlawed from my blood; he sought my life   160
But lately, very late. I loved him, friend,
No father his son dearer. True to tell thee,
The grief hath crazed my wits. What a night's this! —
I do beseech your grace —

LEAR   O, cry you mercy, sir.
(*To Edgar*) Noble philosopher, your company.

EDGAR Tom's a-cold.

GLOUCESTER In, fellow, there, into th'hovel; keep thee
warm.

LEAR
Come, let's in all.

KENT   This way, my lord.
LEAR   With him!
170   I will keep still with my philosopher.
KENT Good my lord, soothe him: let him take the fellow.
GLOUCESTER Take him you on.
KENT Sirrah, come on. Go along with us.
LEAR Come, good Athenian.
GLOUCESTER No words, no words! Hush!
EDGAR

> Child Roland to the dark tower came;
> His word was still 'Fie, foh, and fum,
> I smell the blood of a British man.'   *Exeunt*

III.5   *Enter Cornwall and Edmund*

CORNWALL I will have my revenge ere I depart his house.
EDMUND How, my lord, I may be censured that nature
    thus gives way to loyalty, something fears me to think of.
CORNWALL I now perceive it was not altogether your
    brother's evil disposition made him seek his death; but
    a provoking merit set a-work by a reprovable badness in
    himself.
EDMUND How malicious is my fortune that I must repent
    to be just! This is the letter he spoke of, which approves
10   him an intelligent party to the advantages of France. O
    heavens! that this treason were not, or not I the de-
    tector.
CORNWALL Go with me to the Duchess.
EDMUND If the matter of this paper be certain, you have
    mighty business in hand.
CORNWALL True or false, it hath made thee Earl of
    Gloucester. Seek out where thy father is, that he may be
    ready for our apprehension.
EDMUND (*aside*) If I find him comforting the King it will

stuff his suspicion more fully. (*Aloud*) I will persever in 20
my course of loyalty, though the conflict be sore between that and my blood.
CORNWALL I will lay trust upon thee, and thou shalt find
a dearer father in my love.   *Exeunt*

Enter Kent and Gloucester   III.6

GLOUCESTER Here is better than the open air. Take it
thankfully; I will piece out the comfort with what
addition I can. I will not be long from you.
KENT All the power of his wits have given way to his im-
patience. The gods reward your kindness!
                                         Exit Gloucester
Enter Lear, Edgar, and the Fool

EDGAR Fraterretto calls me and tells me Nero is an angler
in the lake of darkness. Pray, innocent, and beware the
foul fiend.
FOOL Prithee, nuncle, tell me whether a madman be a
gentleman or a yeoman.   10
LEAR A king, a king!
FOOL No! He's a yeoman that has a gentleman to his son;
for he's a mad yeoman that sees his son a gentleman
before him.
LEAR
To have a thousand with red burning spits
Come hissing in upon 'em!
EDGAR The foul fiend bites my back.
FOOL He's mad that trusts in the tameness of a wolf, a
horse's health, a boy's love, or a whore's oath.
LEAR
It shall be done; I will arraign them straight.   20
(*To Edgar*)
Come, sit thou here, most learnèd justicer.

(*To the Fool*)
Thou sapient sir, sit here. No, you she-foxes –

EDGAR Look where he stands and glares! Want'st thou
eyes at trial, madam?
(*sings*)
Come o'er the burn, Bessy, to me.

FOOL (*sings*) Her boat hath a leak
And she must not speak
Why she dares not come over to thee.

EDGAR The foul fiend haunts Poor Tom in the voice of a
30 nightingale. Hoppedance cries in Tom's belly for two
white herring. Croak not, black angel! I have no food for
thee.

KENT
How do you, sir? Stand you not so amazed.
Will you lie down and rest upon the cushings?

LEAR
I'll see their trial first; bring in their evidence.
(*To Edgar*)
Thou robed man of justice, take thy place.
(*To the Fool*)
And thou, his yokefellow of equity,
Bench by his side. (*To Kent*) You are o'the commission;
Sit you too.

40 EDGAR Let us deal justly.
Sleepest or wakest thou, jolly shepherd?
Thy sheep be in the corn,
And for one blast of thy minikin mouth
Thy sheep shall take no harm.
Pur, the cat is grey.

LEAR Arraign her first. 'Tis Gonerill! I here take my oath
before this honourable assembly she kicked the poor
King her father.

FOOL Come hither, mistress. Is your name Gonerill?

LEAR She cannot deny it. 50

FOOL Cry you mercy, I took you for a joint-stool.

LEAR

And here's another whose warped looks proclaim
What store her heart is made on. Stop her there!
Arms, arms, sword, fire! Corruption in the place!
False justicer, why hast thou let her 'scape?

EDGAR Bless thy five wits!

KENT

O pity! Sir, where is the patience now
That you so oft have boasted to retain?

EDGAR (*aside*)

My tears begin to take his part so much
They mar my counterfeiting. 60

LEAR

The little dogs and all –
Trey, Blanch, and Sweetheart – see, they bark at me.

EDGAR Tom will throw his head at them. Avaunt, you
curs!

Be thy mouth or black or white,
Tooth that poisons if it bite,
Mastiff, greyhound, mongrel grim,
Hound or spaniel, brach or lym,
Or bobtail tike, or trundle-tail,
Tom will make him weep and wail; 70
For, with throwing thus my head,
Dogs leapt the hatch and all are fled.

Do, de, de, de. Sese! Come, march to wakes and fairs
and market-towns. Poor Tom, thy horn is dry.

LEAR Then let them anatomize Regan, see what breeds
about her heart. Is there any cause in nature that makes
these hard hearts? You, sir, I entertain for one of my hundred. Only I do not like the fashion of your garments.
You will say they are Persian; but let them be changed.

KENT
80   Now, good my lord, lie here and rest awhile.

LEAR Make no noise, make no noise; draw the curtains.
So, so. We'll go to supper i'the morning.

FOOL And I'll go to bed at noon.

Enter Gloucester

GLOUCESTER
Come hither, friend. Where is the King my master?

KENT
Here, sir; but trouble him not; his wits are gone.

GLOUCESTER
Good friend, I prithee take him in thy arms;
I have o'erheard a plot of death upon him.
There is a litter ready; lay him in't
And drive toward Dover, friend, where thou shalt meet
90   Both welcome and protection. Take up thy master;
If thou shouldst dally half an hour, his life,
With thine and all that offer to defend him,
Stand in assurèd loss. Take up, take up,
And follow me, that will to some provision
Give thee quick conduct.

KENT   Oppressèd nature sleeps.
This rest might yet have balmed thy broken sinews
Which, if convenience will not allow,
Stand in hard cure. (*To the Fool*) Come, help to bear
thy master.
Thou must not stay behind.

GLOUCESTER   Come, come, away!
*Exeunt Kent, Gloucester, and the Fool,
bearing off the King*

EDGAR
100   When we our betters see bearing our woes,
We scarcely think our miseries our foes.
Who alone suffers, suffers most i'the mind,

Leaving free things and happy shows behind;
But then the mind much sufferance doth o'erskip
When grief hath mates, and bearing fellowship.
How light and portable my pain seems now,
When that which makes me bend makes the King bow –
He childed as I fathered. Tom, away!
Mark the high noises, and thyself bewray
When false opinion, whose wrong thoughts defile thee,   110
In thy just proof repeals and reconciles thee.
What will hap more tonight, safe 'scape the King!
Lurk, lurk!   *Exit*

Enter Cornwall, Regan, Gonerill, Edmund, and   III.7
servants

CORNWALL (*to Gonerill*) Post speedily to my lord your
husband, show him this letter. The army of France is
landed. – Seek out the traitor Gloucester.
                              Exeunt some servants

REGAN Hang him instantly!

GONERILL Pluck out his eyes!

CORNWALL Leave him to my displeasure. Edmund, keep
you our sister company; the revenges we are bound to
take upon your traitorous father are not fit for your be-
holding. Advise the Duke where you are going to a most
festinate preparation; we are bound to the like. Our   10
posts shall be swift and intelligent betwixt us. Farewell,
dear sister. Farewell, my lord of Gloucester.

      Enter Oswald

How now? Where's the King?

OSWALD
My lord of Gloucester hath conveyed him hence.
Some five- or six-and-thirty of his knights,
Hot questrists after him, met him at gate,

Who with some other of the lord's dependants
Are gone with him toward Dover, where they boast
To have well-armèd friends.

20 CORNWALL Get horses for your mistress.   *Exit Oswald*

GONERILL Farewell, sweet lord, and sister.

CORNWALL
Edmund, farewell.

> *Exeunt Gonerill and Edmund*

Go seek the traitor Gloucester.
Pinion him like a thief; bring him before us.

> *Exeunt servants*

Though well we may not pass upon his life
Without the form of justice, yet our power
Shall do a curtsy to our wrath, which men
May blame but not control.

> *Enter Gloucester, brought in by two or three servants*

Who's there? The traitor?

REGAN Ingrateful fox, 'tis he!

CORNWALL Bind fast his corky arms.

GLOUCESTER

30   What means your graces? Good my friends, consider
You are my guests. Do me no foul play, friends.

CORNWALL
Bind him, I say.

> *Servants tie his hands*

REGAN   Hard, hard! O filthy traitor!

GLOUCESTER
Unmerciful lady as you are, I'm none.

CORNWALL
To this chair bind him. Villain, thou shalt find –

> *Regan plucks his beard*

GLOUCESTER
By the kind gods, 'tis most ignobly done
To pluck me by the beard.

REGAN
  So white, and such a traitor!
GLOUCESTER   Naughty lady,
  These hairs which thou dost ravish from my chin
  Will quicken and accuse thee. I am your host;
  With robbers' hands my hospitable favours   40
  You should not ruffle thus. What will you do?
CORNWALL
  Come, sir; what letters had you late from France?
REGAN
  Be simple-answered, for we know the truth.
CORNWALL
  And what confederacy have you with the traitors
  Late footed in the kingdom –
REGAN
  To whose hands you have sent the lunatic King? Speak!
GLOUCESTER
  I have a letter guessingly set down
  Which came from one that's of a neutral heart
  And not from one opposed.
CORNWALL   Cunning.
REGAN   And false.
CORNWALL
  Where hast thou sent the King?
GLOUCESTER   To Dover.   50
REGAN
  Wherefore to Dover? Wast thou not charged at peril –
CORNWALL
  Wherefore to Dover? Let him answer that.
GLOUCESTER
  I am tied to the stake, and I must stand the course.
REGAN Wherefore to Dover?
GLOUCESTER
  Because I would not see thy cruel nails

Pluck out his poor old eyes; nor thy fierce sister
In his anointed flesh rash boarish fangs.
The sea, with such a storm as his bare head
In hell-black night endured, would have buoyed up
60 And quenched the stellèd fires;
Yet, poor old heart, he holp the heavens to rain.
If wolves had at thy gate howled that dern time
Thou shouldst have said, 'Good porter, turn the key;
All cruels else subscribe'. But I shall see
The wingèd Vengeance overtake such children.

CORNWALL
See't shalt thou never. Fellows, hold the chair.
Upon these eyes of thine I'll set my foot.

GLOUCESTER
He that will think to live till he be old
Give me some help! – O, cruel! O, you gods!

REGAN
70 One side will mock another. Th'other too!

CORNWALL
If you see Vengeance –

FIRST SERVANT   Hold your hand, my lord!
I have served you ever since I was a child;
But better service have I never done you
Than now to bid you hold.

REGAN   How now, you dog!

FIRST SERVANT
If you did wear a beard upon your chin
I'd shake it on this quarrel.
     (*Cornwall draws his sword*)
                              What do you mean?

CORNWALL My villain!
     He lunges at him

FIRST SERVANT (*drawing his sword*)
Nay then, come on, and take the chance of anger.

He wounds Cornwall

REGAN

Give me thy sword. A peasant stand up thus!
She takes a sword and runs at him behind

FIRST SERVANT

O, I am slain! My lord, you have one eye left   80
To see some mischief on him. O!   *He dies*

CORNWALL

Lest it see more, prevent it. Out, vile jelly!
Where is thy lustre now?

GLOUCESTER

All dark and comfortless. Where's my son Edmund?
Edmund, enkindle all the sparks of nature
To quit this horrid act.

REGAN   Out, treacherous villain!
Thou call'st on him that hates thee. It was he
That made the overture of thy treasons to us;
Who is too good to pity thee.

GLOUCESTER

O my follies! Then Edgar was abused.   90
Kind gods, forgive me that and prosper him.

REGAN

Go thrust him out at gates and let him smell
His way to Dover.   *Exit a servant with Gloucester*
How is't, my lord? How look you?

CORNWALL

I have received a hurt. Follow me, lady.
Turn out that eyeless villain. Throw this slave
Upon the dunghill. Regan, I bleed apace.
Untimely comes this hurt. Give me your arm.
Exit Cornwall, supported by Regan

SECOND SERVANT

I'll never care what wickedness I do
If this man come to good.

THIRD SERVANT   If she live long,
100 And in the end meet the old course of death,
    Women will all turn monsters.
SECOND SERVANT
    Let's follow the old Earl, and get the Bedlam
    To lead him where he would; his roguish madness
    Allows itself to anything.
THIRD SERVANT
    Go thou. I'll fetch some flax and whites of eggs
    To apply to his bleeding face. Now heaven help him!
                              Exeunt by opposite doors

*

IV.1   *Enter Edgar*
    EDGAR
        Yet better thus, and known to be contemned,
        Than still contemned and flattered. To be worst,
        The lowest and most dejected thing of fortune,
        Stands still in esperance, lives not in fear.
        The lamentable change is from the best;
        The worst returns to laughter. Welcome, then,
        Thou unsubstantial air that I embrace!
        The wretch that thou hast blown unto the worst
        Owes nothing to thy blasts.
                Enter Gloucester, led by an Old Man
                              But who comes here?
10   My father, parti-eyed! World, world, O world!
        But that thy strange mutations make us hate thee
        Life would not yield to age.
    OLD MAN   O my good lord,
        I have been your tenant and your father's tenant
        These fourscore years!

GLOUCESTER

   Away! Get thee away! Good friend, be gone.

   Thy comforts can do me no good at all;

   Thee they may hurt.

OLD MAN   You cannot see your way.

GLOUCESTER

   I have no way and therefore want no eyes;

   I stumbled when I saw. Full oft 'tis seen

   Our means secure us, and our mere defects   20

   Prove our commodities. O dear son Edgar,

   The food of thy abusèd father's wrath!

   Might I but live to see thee in my touch

   I'd say I had eyes again.

OLD MAN   How now? Who's there?

EDGAR (*aside*)

   O gods! Who is't can say 'I am at the worst'?

   I am worse than e'er I was.

OLD MAN   'Tis poor mad Tom.

EDGAR (*aside*)

   And worse I may be yet. The worst is not,

   So long as we can say 'This is the worst'.

OLD MAN

   Fellow, where goest?

GLOUCESTER   Is it a beggar-man?

OLD MAN Madman and beggar too.   30

GLOUCESTER

   He has some reason, else he could not beg.

   I'the last night's storm I such a fellow saw

   Which made me think a man a worm. My son

   Came then into my mind; and yet my mind

   Was then scarce friends with him. I have heard more

         since.

   As flies to wanton boys are we to the gods;

   They kill us for their sport.

EDGAR (*aside*)   How should this be?
Bad is the trade that must play fool to sorrow,
Angering itself and others. (*Aloud*) Bless thee, master!

GLOUCESTER

40 Is that the naked fellow?

OLD MAN   Ay, my lord.

GLOUCESTER
Then prithee get thee away. If for my sake
Thou wilt o'ertake us hence a mile or twain
I'the way toward Dover, do it for ancient love,
And bring some covering for this naked soul,
Which I'll entreat to lead me.

OLD MAN   Alack, sir, he is mad.

GLOUCESTER
'Tis the time's plague when madmen lead the blind.
Do as I bid thee, or rather do thy pleasure.
Above the rest, begone.

OLD MAN
I'll bring him the best 'parel that I have,
50 Come on't what will.   *Exit*

GLOUCESTER   Sirrah naked fellow!

EDGAR
Poor Tom's a-cold. (*Aside*) I cannot daub it further.

GLOUCESTER Come hither, fellow.

EDGAR (*aside*)
And yet I must. (*Aloud*) Bless thy sweet eyes, they bleed.

GLOUCESTER Knowest thou the way to Dover?

EDGAR Both stile and gate, horse-way and footpath, Poor
Tom hath been scared out of his good wits. Bless thee,
good man's son, from the foul fiend. Five fiends have
been in Poor Tom at once: of lust, as Obidicut; Hobbididence, prince of dumbness; Mahu, of stealing;
60 Modo, of murder; Flibberdigibbet, of mopping and
mowing, who since possesses chambermaids and

waiting-women. So bless thee, master!

GLOUCESTER

Here, take this purse, thou whom the heavens' plagues
Have humbled to all strokes. That I am wretched
Makes thee the happier. Heavens deal so still!
Let the superfluous and lust-dieted man
That slaves your ordinance, that will not see
Because he does not feel, feel your power quickly!
So distribution should undo excess
And each man have enough. Dost thou know Dover?   70

EDGAR Ay, master.

GLOUCESTER

There is a cliff whose high and bending head
Looks fearfully in the confinèd deep;
Bring me but to the very brim of it
And I'll repair the misery thou dost bear
With something rich about me. From that place
I shall no leading need.

EDGAR   Give me thy arm;
Poor Tom shall lead thee.   *Exeunt*

Enter Gonerill and Edmund   IV.2

GONERILL

Welcome, my lord. I marvel our mild husband
Not met us on the way.

    Enter Oswald

               Now, where's your master?

OSWALD

Madam, within; but never man so changed.
I told him of the army that was landed.
He smiled at it. I told him you were coming.
His answer was 'The worse'. Of Gloucester's treachery
And of the loyal service of his son

141

When I informed him, then he called me sot
And told me I had turned the wrong side out.
10 What most he should dislike seems pleasant to him;
What like, offensive.

GONERILL (*to Edmund*) Then shall you go no further.
It is the cowish terror of his spirit
That dares not undertake. He'll not feel wrongs
Which tie him to an answer. Our wishes on the way
May prove effects. Back, Edmund, to my brother!
Hasten his musters and conduct his powers.
I must change arms at home and give the distaff
Into my husband's hands. This trusty servant
Shall pass between us; ere long you are like to hear,
20 If you dare venture in your own behalf,
A mistress's command. Wear this;
    (*giving a favour*)   spare speech.
Decline your head; this kiss, if it durst speak,
Would stretch thy spirits up into the air.
Conceive; and fare thee well.

EDMUND
Yours in the ranks of death.

GONERILL   My most dear Gloucester!
                             Exit Edmund

O, the difference of man and man!
To thee a woman's services are due;
A fool usurps my bed.

OSWALD   Madam, here comes my lord.
                                 Exit

   Enter Albany

GONERILL
I have been worth the whistling.

ALBANY   O Gonerill,
30 You are not worth the dust which the rude wind
Blows in your face. I fear your disposition:

That nature which contemns its origin
Cannot be bordered certain in itself.
She that herself will sliver and disbranch
From her material sap perforce must wither
And come to deadly use.

GONERILL No more; the text is foolish.

ALBANY
Wisdom and goodness to the vile seem vile;
Filths savour but themselves. What have you done,
Tigers not daughters, what have you performed?   40
A father, and a gracious agèd man,
Whose reverence even the head-lugged bear would lick,
Most barbarous, most degenerate, have you madded.
Could my good brother suffer you to do it?
A man, a prince, by him so benefited?
If that the heavens do not their visible spirits
Send quickly down to tame these vile offences,
It will come –
Humanity must perforce prey on itself
Like monsters of the deep.

GONERILL   Milk-livered man!   50
That bear'st a cheek for blows, a head for wrongs!
Who hast not in thy brows an eye discerning
Thine honour from thy suffering, that not knowest
Fools do those villains pity who are punished
Ere they have done their mischief. Where's thy drum?
France spreads his banners in our noiseless land,
With plumèd helm thy state begins to threat,
Whilst thou, a moral fool, sits still and cries
'Alack, why does he so?'

ALBANY   See thyself, devil!
Proper deformity shows not in the fiend   60
So horrid as in woman.

GONERILL   O vain fool!

143

ALBANY

Thou changèd and self-covered thing, for shame,
Be-monster not thy feature. Were't my fitness
To let these hands obey my blood,
They are apt enough to dislocate and tear
Thy flesh and bones. Howe'er thou art a fiend,
A woman's shape doth shield thee.

GONERILL Marry, your manhood! Mew!

Enter a Messenger

ALBANY What news?

MESSENGER

70   O, my good lord, the Duke of Cornwall's dead,
Slain by his servant, going to put out
The other eye of Gloucester.

ALBANY   Gloucester's eyes?

MESSENGER

A servant that he bred, thrilled with remorse,
Opposed against the act, bending his sword
To his great master; who, thereat enraged,
Flew on him and amongst them felled him dead,
But not without that harmful stroke which since
Hath plucked him after.

ALBANY   This shows you are above,
You justicers, that these our nether crimes
80   So speedily can venge! But, O, poor Gloucester!
Lost he his other eye?

MESSENGER   Both, both, my lord.
This letter, madam, craves a speedy answer.
'Tis from your sister.

GONERILL (*aside*)   One way I like this well.
But being widow, and my Gloucester with her,
May all the building in my fancy pluck
Upon my hateful life. Another way

The news is not so tart. – (*Aloud*) I'll read and
    answer.   *Exit*

ALBANY
Where was his son when they did take his eyes?

MESSENGER
Come with my lady hither.

ALBANY   He is not here.

MESSENGER
No, my good lord; I met him back again.   90

ALBANY Knows he the wickedness?

MESSENGER
Ay, my good lord. 'Twas he informed against him,
And quit the house on purpose that their punishment
Might have the freer course.

ALBANY   Gloucester, I live
To thank thee for the love thou show'dst the King
And to revenge thine eyes. Come hither, friend;
Tell me what more thou knowest.   *Exeunt*

Enter Kent and a Gentleman   IV.3

KENT Why the King of France is so suddenly gone back
know you no reason?

GENTLEMAN Something he left imperfect in the state,
which since his coming forth is thought of, which im-
ports to the kingdom so much fear and danger that his
personal return was most required and necessary.

KENT Who hath he left behind him general?

GENTLEMAN The Marshal of France, Monsieur La Far.

KENT Did your letters pierce the Queen to any demon-
stration of grief?   10

GENTLEMAN
Ay, sir; she took them, read them in my presence,

And now and then an ample tear trilled down
Her delicate cheek. It seemed she was a queen
Over her passion who, most rebel-like,
Sought to be king o'er her.

KENT   O, then it moved her?

GENTLEMAN
Not to a rage; patience and sorrow strove
Who should express her goodliest. You have seen
Sunshine and rain at once; her smiles and tears
Were like a better way; those happy smilets

20 That played on her ripe lip seem not to know
What guests were in her eyes, which parted thence
As pearls from diamonds dropped. In brief,
Sorrow would be a rarity most beloved
If all could so become it.

KENT   Made she no verbal question?

GENTLEMAN
Faith, once or twice she heaved the name of father
Pantingly forth, as if it pressed her heart,
Cried 'Sisters! Sisters! Shame of ladies! Sisters!
Kent! Father! Sisters! – What, i'the storm? i'the night?
Let pity not be believed!' There she shook

30 The holy water from her heavenly eyes,
And clamour moistened; then away she started
To deal with grief alone.

KENT   It is the stars,
The stars above us govern our conditions.
Else one self mate and make could not beget
Such different issues. You spoke not with her since?

GENTLEMAN No.

KENT
Was this before the King returned?

GENTLEMAN   No, since.

KENT

  Well, sir, the poor distressèd Lear's i'the town,
  Who sometime in his better tune remembers
  What we are come about, and by no means   40
  Will yield to see his daughter.

GENTLEMAN   Why, good sir?

KENT

  A sovereign shame so elbows him: his own unkindness
  That stripped her from his benediction, turned her
  To foreign casualties, gave her dear rights
  To his dog-hearted daughters – these things sting
  His mind so venomously that burning shame
  Detains him from Cordelia.

GENTLEMAN   Alack, poor gentleman!

KENT

  Of Albany's and Cornwall's powers you heard not?

GENTLEMAN 'Tis so. They are afoot.

KENT

  Well, sir, I'll bring you to our master Lear   50
  And leave you to attend him. Some dear cause
  Will in concealment wrap me up awhile.
  When I am known aright you shall not grieve
  Lending me this acquaintance. I pray you
  Go along with me.   *Exeunt*

    Enter, with drum and colours, Cordelia, Doctor, and **IV.4**
    soldiers

CORDELIA

  Alack, 'tis he! Why, he was met even now
  As mad as the vexed sea, singing aloud,
  Crowned with rank fumiter and furrow-weeds,
  With hardokes, hemlock, nettles, cuckoo-flowers,

Darnel, and all the idle weeds that grow
In our sustaining corn. (*To soldiers*) A century send
    forth;
Search every acre in the high-grown field
And bring him to our eye.   *Exeunt soldiers*
(*To Doctor*)   What can man's wisdom
In the restoring his bereavèd sense?

10 He that helps him, take all my outward worth.

DOCTOR

There is means, madam.
Our foster-nurse of nature is repose,
The which he lacks; that to provoke in him
Are many simples operative, whose power
Will close the eye of anguish.

CORDELIA   All blest secrets,
All you unpublished virtues of the earth,
Spring with my tears! Be aidant and remediate
In the good man's distress. Seek, seek for him,
Lest his ungoverned rage dissolve the life

20 That wants the means to lead it.

    Enter a Messenger

MESSENGER   News, madam:
The British powers are marching hitherward.

CORDELIA

'Tis known before. Our preparation stands
In expectation of them. O dear father,
It is thy business that I go about.
Therefore great France
My mourning and importuned tears hath pitied.
No blown ambition doth our arms incite
But love, dear love, and our aged father's right.
Soon may I hear and see him!   *Exeunt*

REGAN

But are my brother's powers set forth?

OSWALD   Ay, madam.

REGAN

Himself in person there?

OSWALD   Madam, with much ado.
Your sister is the better soldier.

REGAN

Lord Edmund spake not with your lord at home?

OSWALD No, madam.

REGAN

What might import my sister's letter to him?

OSWALD I know not, lady.

REGAN

Faith, he is posted hence on serious matter.
It was great ignorance, Gloucester's eyes being out,
To let him live. Where he arrives he moves   10
All hearts against us. Edmund, I think, is gone,
In pity of his misery, to dispatch
His nighted life – moreover to descry
The strength o'th'enemy.

OSWALD

I must needs after him, madam, with my letter.

REGAN

Our troops set forth tomorrow; stay with us.
The ways are dangerous.

OSWALD   I may not, madam.
My lady charged my duty in this business.

REGAN

Why should she write to Edmund? Might not you
Transport her purposes by word? Belike –   20
Some things – I know not what – I'll love thee much –
Let me unseal the letter.

149

OSWALD   Madam, I had rather –

REGAN

  I know your lady does not love her husband –
  I am sure of that – and at her late being here
  She gave strange œillades and most speaking looks
  To noble Edmund. I know you are of her bosom.

OSWALD I, madam?

REGAN

  I speak in understanding. Y'are; I know't.
  Therefore I do advise you take this note:

30   My lord is dead; Edmund and I have talked,
  And more convenient is he for my hand
  Than for your lady's. You may gather more.
  If you do find him, pray you give him this;
  And when your mistress hears thus much from you,
  I pray desire her call her wisdom to her.
  So fare you well.
  If you do chance to hear of that blind traitor,
  Preferment falls on him that cuts him off.

OSWALD

  Would I could meet him, madam! I should show

40   What party I do follow.

REGAN   Fare thee well.   *Exeunt*

IV.6   *Enter Gloucester and Edgar in peasant's clothes*

GLOUCESTER

  When shall I come to the top of that same hill?

EDGAR

  You do climb up it now. Look how we labour.

GLOUCESTER

  Methinks the ground is even.

EDGAR   Horrible steep.
  Hark, do you hear the sea?

GLOUCESTER   No, truly.

EDGAR

Why then your other senses grow imperfect
By your eyes' anguish.

GLOUCESTER   So may it be indeed.

Methinks thy voice is altered, and thou speak'st
In better phrase and matter than thou didst.

EDGAR

Y'are much deceived. In nothing am I changed
But in my garments.

GLOUCESTER   Methinks y'are better spoken.   10

EDGAR

Come on, sir; here's the place. Stand still! How fearful
And dizzy 'tis to cast one's eyes so low!
The crows and choughs that wing the midway air
Show scarce so gross as beetles. Halfway down
Hangs one that gathers sampire – dreadful trade!
Methinks he seems no bigger than his head.
The fishermen that walk upon the beach
Appear like mice, and yon tall anchoring bark
Diminished to her cock; her cock, a buoy
Almost too small for sight. The murmuring surge   20
That on th'unnumbered idle pebble chafes
Cannot be heard so high. I'll look no more,
Lest my brain turn, and the deficient sight
Topple down headlong.

GLOUCESTER   Set me where you stand.

EDGAR

Give me your hand. You are now within a foot
Of th'extreme verge. For all beneath the moon
Would I not leap upright.

GLOUCESTER   Let go my hand.

Here, friend, 's another purse; in it a jewel
Well worth a poor man's taking. Fairies and gods

30 Prosper it with thee! Go thou further off.
    Bid me farewell; and let me hear thee going.

EDGAR

    Now fare ye well, good sir.

GLOUCESTER   With all my heart.

EDGAR (*aside*)

    Why I do trifle thus with his despair
    Is done to cure it.

GLOUCESTER (*kneeling*) O you mighty gods!
    This world I do renounce, and in your sights
    Shake patiently my great affliction off.
    If I could bear it longer and not fall
    To quarrel with your great opposeless wills,
    My snuff and loathèd part of nature should
40 Burn itself out. If Edgar live, O bless him!
    Now, fellow, fare thee well.

EDGAR   Gone, sir. Farewell.
        Gloucester throws himself forward
    And yet I know not how conceit may rob
    The treasury of life, when life itself
    Yields to the theft. Had he been where he thought,
    By this had thought been past. – Alive or dead?
    Ho, you, sir! Friend! Hear you, sir? Speak! –
    Thus might he pass indeed. Yet he revives –
    What are you, sir?

GLOUCESTER   Away, and let me die.

EDGAR

    Hadst thou been aught but gossamer, feathers, air,
50 So many fathom down precipitating,
    Thou'dst shivered like an egg; but thou dost breathe,
    Hast heavy substance, bleed'st not, speak'st, art sound.
    Ten masts at each make not the altitude
    Which thou hast perpendicularly fell.
    Thy life's a miracle. Speak yet again.

GLOUCESTER But have I fallen or no?

EDGAR

From the dread summit of this chalky bourn.
Look up a-height. The shrill-gorged lark so far
Cannot be seen or heard. Do but look up.

GLOUCESTER Alack, I have no eyes. 60
Is wretchedness deprived that benefit
To end itself by death? 'Twas yet some comfort
When misery could beguile the tyrant's rage
And frustrate his proud will.

EDGAR   Give me your arm.
Up – so. How is't? Feel you your legs? You stand.

GLOUCESTER

Too well, too well.

EDGAR   This is above all strangeness.
Upon the crown o'the cliff what thing was that
Which parted from you?

GLOUCESTER   A poor unfortunate beggar.

EDGAR

As I stood here below methought his eyes
Were two full moons; he had a thousand noses, 70
Horns welked and waved like the enridgèd sea.
It was some fiend. Therefore, thou happy father,
Think that the clearest gods, who make them honours
Of men's impossibilities, have preserved thee.

GLOUCESTER

I do remember now. Henceforth I'll bear
Affliction till it do cry out itself
'Enough, enough', and die. That thing you speak of,
I took it for a man; often 'twould say
'The fiend, the fiend'; he led me to that place.

EDGAR

Bear free and patient thoughts.
          Enter Lear fantastically dressed with wild flowers

80   But who comes here?

The safer sense will ne'er accommodate
His master thus.

LEAR No, they cannot touch me for coining. I am the
King himself.

EDGAR O thou side-piercing sight!

LEAR Nature's above art in that respect. There's your
press-money. – That fellow handles his bow like a crow-
keeper. – Draw me a clothier's yard. – Look, look, a
mouse! – Peace, peace! this piece of toasted cheese will
90 do't. – There's my gauntlet; I'll prove it on a giant. –
Bring up the brown bills. – O, well flown, bird! I'the
clout, i'the clout! Hewgh! – Give the word.

EDGAR Sweet marjoram.

LEAR Pass.

GLOUCESTER I know that voice.

He falls to his knees

LEAR Ha! Gonerill with a white beard! They flattered me
like a dog and told me I had the white hairs in my beard
ere the black ones were there. To say 'ay' and 'no' to
everything that I said! 'Ay' and 'no' too was no good
100 divinity. When the rain came to wet me once and the
wind to make me chatter; when the thunder would not
peace at my bidding; there I found 'em, there I smelt
'em out. Go to, they are not men o'their words. They
told me I was everything. 'Tis a lie: I am not ague-
proof.

GLOUCESTER
The trick of that voice I do well remember.
Is't not the King?

LEAR   Ay, every inch a king.
When I do stare see how the subject quakes.
I pardon that man's life. What was thy cause?
110 Adultery?

Thou shalt not die. Die for adultery? No.
The wren goes to't, and the small gilded fly
Does lecher in my sight.
Let copulation thrive; for Gloucester's bastard son
Was kinder to his father than my daughters
Got 'tween the lawful sheets.
To't, luxury, pell-mell, for I lack soldiers.
Behold yon simpering dame
Whose face between her forks presages snow,
That minces virtue and does shake the head   120
To hear of pleasure's name –
The fitchew nor the soilèd horse goes to't
With a more riotous appetite.
Down from the waist they are centaurs,
Though women all above;
But to the girdle do the gods inherit,
Beneath is all the fiends' –
There's hell, there's darkness, there is the sulphurous
pit – burning, scalding, stench, consumption! Fie, fie,
fie! Pah, pah! Give me an ounce of civet; good apothe- 130
cary, sweeten my imagination. There's money for
thee.

He gives flowers

GLOUCESTER O, let me kiss that hand!

LEAR Let me wipe it first; it smells of mortality.

GLOUCESTER

O ruined piece of nature! This great world
Shall so wear out to naught. Dost thou know me?

LEAR I remember thine eyes well enough. Dost thou
squiny at me? No, do thy worst, blind Cupid; I'll not
love. Read thou this challenge; mark but the penning
of it.   140

GLOUCESTER

Were all thy letters suns, I could not see.

EDGAR (*aside*)
    I would not take this from report. It is;
    And my heart breaks at it.

LEAR Read.

GLOUCESTER What, with the case of eyes?

LEAR O, ho, are you there with me? No eyes in your head,
nor no money in your purse? Your eyes are in a heavy
case, your purse in a light; yet you see how this world
goes.

150 GLOUCESTER I see it feelingly.

LEAR What, art mad? A man may see how this world goes
with no eyes. Look with thine ears. See how yon justice
rails upon yon simple thief. Hark in thine ear – change
places and, handy-dandy, which is the justice, which is
the thief? Thou hast seen a farmer's dog bark at a
beggar?

GLOUCESTER Ay, sir.

LEAR And the creature run from the cur? There thou
mightst behold the great image of authority: a dog's
160 obeyed in office.
    Thou rascal beadle, hold thy bloody hand.
    Why dost thou lash that whore? Strip thy own back.
    Thou hotly lusts to use her in that kind
    For which thou whipp'st her. The usurer hangs the
        cozener.
    Thorough tattered clothes great vices do appear;
    Robes and furred gowns hide all. Plate sins with gold,
    And the strong lance of justice hurtless breaks;
    Arm it in rags, a pygmy's straw does pierce it.
    None does offend, none, I say none; I'll able 'em.
170   Take that of me, my friend, (*giving flowers*) who have
        the power
    To seal th'accusers' lips. Get thee glass eyes,
    And like a scurvy politician seem

To see the things thou dost not. Now, now, now, now!
Pull off my boots. Harder, harder – so.

EDGAR

O matter and impertinency mixed,
Reason in madness!

LEAR

If thou wilt weep my fortunes, take my eyes.
I know thee well enough; thy name is Gloucester.
Thou must be patient; we came crying hither.
Thou knowest the first time that we smell the air   180
We wawl and cry. I will preach to thee – Mark!

He takes off his coronet of flowers

GLOUCESTER Alack, alack the day!

LEAR

When we are born we cry that we are come
To this great stage of fools. – This's a good block.
It were a delicate stratagem to shoe
A troop of horse with felt. I'll put't in proof;
And when I have stolen upon these son-in-laws,
Then kill, kill, kill, kill, kill, kill!

He throws down his flowers and stamps on them
Enter a Gentleman and two attendants. Gloucester
and Edgar draw back

GENTLEMAN

O, here he is. Lay hand upon him. – Sir,
Your most dear daughter –   190

LEAR

No rescue? What, a prisoner? I am even
The natural fool of fortune. Use me well;
You shall have ransom. Let me have surgeons;
I am cut to the brains.

GENTLEMAN   You shall have anything.

LEAR

No seconds? All myself?

Why, this would make a man a man of salt,
To use his eyes for garden water-pots,
Ay, and laying autumn's dust. I will die bravely,
Like a smug bridegroom. What! I will be jovial.

200   Come, come, I am a king; masters, know you that?

GENTLEMAN

You are a royal one, and we obey you.

LEAR Then there's life in't. Come, and you get it you shall
get it by running. Sa, sa, sa, sa.

Exit running, followed by attendants

GENTLEMAN

A sight most pitiful in the meanest wretch,
Past speaking of in a king. – Thou hast one daughter
Who redeems nature from the general curse
Which twain have brought her to.

EDGAR (*coming forward*)

Hail, gentle sir.

GENTLEMAN   Sir, speed you; what's your will?

EDGAR

Do you hear aught, sir, of a battle toward?

GENTLEMAN

210   Most sure and vulgar. Everyone hears that
Which can distinguish sound.

EDGAR   But, by your favour,
How near's the other army?

GENTLEMAN

Near, and on speedy foot. The main descry
Stands on the hourly thought.

EDGAR   I thank you, sir; that's all.

GENTLEMAN

Though that the Queen on special cause is here,
Her army is moved on.

EDGAR   I thank you, sir.

Exit Gentleman

GLOUCESTER (*coming forward*)

    You ever-gentle gods, take my breath from me.

    Let not my worser spirit tempt me again

    To die before you please.

EDGAR   Well pray you, father.

GLOUCESTER Now, good sir, what are you?   **220**

EDGAR

    A most poor man made tame to fortune's blows,

    Who, by the art of known and feeling sorrows,

    Am pregnant to good pity. Give me your hand,

    I'll lead you to some biding.

GLOUCESTER   Hearty thanks;

    The bounty and the benison of heaven

    To boot, and boot!

    Enter Oswald

OSWALD   A proclaimed prize! Most happy!

    That eyeless head of thine was first framed flesh

    To raise my fortunes. Thou old unhappy traitor,

    Briefly thyself remember; the sword is out

    That must destroy thee.

GLOUCESTER   Now let thy friendly hand   **230**

    Put strength enough to't.

    Edgar intervenes

OSWALD   Wherefore, bold peasant,

    Darest thou support a published traitor? Hence,

    Lest that th'infection of his fortune take

    Like hold on thee. Let go his arm!

EDGAR

    'Chill not let go, zir, without vurther 'cagion.

OSWALD Let go, slave, or thou diest!

EDGAR Good gentleman, go your gate and let poor volk

    pass. And 'choud ha' bin zwaggered out of my life,

    'twould not ha' bin zo long as 'tis by a vortnight. Nay,

    come not near th'old man; keep out, che vor' ye, or I'ce **240**

try whether your costard or my ballow be the harder.
'Chill be plain with you.

OSWALD Out, dunghill!

EDGAR 'Chill pick your teeth, zir. Come; no matter vor
your foins.

They fight

OSWALD

Slave, thou hast slain me. Villain, take my purse.
If ever thou wilt thrive, bury my body
And give the letters which thou find'st about me
To Edmund, Earl of Gloucester. Seek him out
250 Upon the English party. O, untimely
Death! – Death –   *He dies*

EDGAR

I know thee well: a serviceable villain,
As duteous to the vices of thy mistress
As badness would desire.

GLOUCESTER   What, is he dead?

EDGAR

Sit you down, father; rest you. –
Let's see these pockets. The letters that he speaks of
May be my friends. He's dead. I am only sorry
He had no other deathsman. Let us see.
Leave, gentle wax; and manners blame us not;
260 To know our enemies' minds we rip their hearts;
Their papers is more lawful.

(*He reads the letter*)

*Let our reciprocal vows be remembered. You have many
opportunities to cut him off; if your will want not, time and
place will be fruitfully offered. There is nothing done if he
return the conqueror. Then am I the prisoner, and his bed
my gaol; from the loathed warmth whereof deliver me and
supply the place for your labour.*

Your – wife, so I would say – affectionate servant,
                                        Gonerill.

O indistinguished space of woman's will!   270
A plot upon her virtuous husband's life,
And the exchange, my brother! Here in the sands
Thee I'll rake up, the post unsanctified
Of murderous lechers; and in the mature time
With this ungracious paper strike the sight
Of the death-practised Duke. For him 'tis well
That of thy death and business I can tell.

GLOUCESTER

The King is mad; how stiff is my vile sense,
That I stand up and have ingenious feeling
Of my huge sorrows! Better I were distract;   280
So should my thoughts be severed from my griefs,
And woes by wrong imaginations lose
The knowledge of themselves.
        Drum afar off

EDGAR   Give me your hand.
Far off methinks I hear the beaten drum.
Come, father, I'll bestow you with a friend.   *Exeunt*

Enter Cordelia, Kent, and Doctor   IV.7

CORDELIA

O thou good Kent, how shall I live and work
To match thy goodness? My life will be too short
And every measure fail me.

KENT

To be acknowledged, madam, is o'er-paid.
All my reports go with the modest truth,
Nor more, nor clipped, but so.

CORDELIA   Be better suited.
These weeds are memories of those worser hours.

I prithee put them off.

KENT   Pardon, dear madam,
Yet to be known shortens my made intent.
My boon I make it that you know me not
Till time and I think meet.

CORDELIA
Then be't so, my good lord.
(*To Doctor*)   How does the King?

DOCTOR Madam, sleeps still.

CORDELIA
O you kind gods,
Cure this great breach in his abusèd nature!
Th'untuned and jarring senses O wind up
Of this child-changèd father.

DOCTOR   So please your majesty,
That we may wake the King. He hath slept long.

CORDELIA
Be governed by your knowledge and proceed
I'the sway of your own will. Is he arrayed?

DOCTOR
Ay, madam; in the heaviness of sleep
We put fresh garments on him.

> *Enter Gentleman ushering Lear in a chair carried by*
> *servants. All fall to their knees*

GENTLEMAN
Be by, good madam, when we do awake him;
I doubt not of his temperance.

CORDELIA   Very well.

> *Music sounds off stage*

DOCTOR
Please you draw near. – Louder the music there!

CORDELIA (*kneeling by the chair and kissing his hand*)
O my dear father! Restoration hang
Thy medicine on my lips; and let this kiss

Repair those violent harms that my two sisters
Have in thy reverence made.

KENT   Kind and dear princess!

CORDELIA

Had you not been their father, these white flakes   30
Did challenge pity of them. Was this a face
To be opposed against the jarring winds?
To stand against the deep dread-bolted thunder,
In the most terrible and nimble stroke
Of quick cross lightning? To watch, poor perdu,
With this thin helm? Mine enemy's dog,
Though he had bit me, should have stood that night
Against my fire; and wast thou fain, poor father,
To hovel thee with swine and rogues forlorn
In short and musty straw? Alack, alack!   40
'Tis wonder that thy life and wits at once
Had not concluded all. – He wakes! Speak to him.

DOCTOR Madam, do you; 'tis fittest.

CORDELIA

How does my royal lord? How fares your majesty?

LEAR

You do me wrong to take me out o'the grave.
Thou art a soul in bliss; but I am bound
Upon a wheel of fire, that mine own tears
Do scald like molten lead.

CORDELIA   Sir, do you know me?

LEAR

You are a spirit, I know. Where did you die?

CORDELIA Still, still far wide!   50

DOCTOR

He's scarce awake. Let him alone awhile.

LEAR

Where have I been? Where am I? Fair daylight?
I am mightily abused. I should even die with pity

163

To see another thus. I know not what to say.
I will not swear these are my hands. Let's see.
I feel this pin-prick. Would I were assured
Of my condition.

CORDELIA   O look upon me, sir,
And hold your hand in benediction o'er me.
        Lear falls to his knees
No, sir, you must not kneel.

LEAR   Pray do not mock me.
60 I am a very foolish fond old man,
Four score and upward, not an hour more nor less,
And, to deal plainly,
I fear I am not in my perfect mind.
Methinks I should know you, and know this man;
Yet I am doubtful; for I am mainly ignorant
What place this is; and all the skill I have
Remembers not these garments; nor I know not
Where I did lodge last night. Do not laugh at me,
For, as I am a man, I think this lady
70 To be my child Cordelia.

CORDELIA (*weeping*)   And so I am, I am.

LEAR
Be your tears wet? Yes, faith! I pray, weep not.
If you have poison for me I will drink it.
I know you do not love me, for your sisters
Have, as I do remember, done me wrong.
You have some cause; they have not.

CORDELIA   No cause, no cause.

LEAR
Am I in France?

KENT   In your own kingdom, sir.

LEAR Do not abuse me.

DOCTOR
Be comforted, good madam. The great rage,

You see, is killed in him; and yet it is danger
To make him even o'er the time he has lost.   80
Desire him to go in; trouble him no more
Till further settling.

CORDELIA   Will't please your highness walk?

LEAR You must bear with me. Pray you now, forget and
forgive. I am old and foolish.

Exeunt all but Kent and Gentleman

GENTLEMAN Holds it true, sir, that the Duke of Cornwall
was so slain?

KENT Most certain, sir.

GENTLEMAN Who is conductor of his people?

KENT As 'tis said, the bastard son of Gloucester.

GENTLEMAN They say Edgar, his banished son, is with   90
the Earl of Kent in Germany.

KENT Report is changeable. 'Tis time to look about. The
powers of the kingdom approach apace.

GENTLEMAN The arbitrament is like to be bloody. Fare
you well, sir.   *Exit*

KENT
My point and period will be throughly wrought,
Or well or ill, as this day's battle's fought.   *Exit*

*

Enter, with drum and colours, Edmund, Regan, V.1
gentlemen, and soldiers

EDMUND (*to a gentleman*)
Know of the Duke if his last purpose hold
Or whether since he is advised by aught
To change the course. (*To Regan*) He's full of alteration
And self-reproving. (*To gentleman*) Bring his constant
        pleasure.   *Exit gentleman*

REGAN

Our sister's man is certainly miscarried.

EDMUND

'Tis to be doubted, madam.

REGAN   Now, sweet lord,

You know the goodness I intend upon you.

Tell me but truly – but then speak the truth –

Do you not love my sister?

EDMUND   In honoured love.

REGAN

10   But have you never found my brother's way

To the forfended place?

EDMUND   That thought abuses you.

REGAN

I am doubtful that you have been conjunct

And bosomed with her, as far as we call hers.

EDMUND No, by mine honour, madam.

REGAN

I never shall endure her; dear my lord,

Be not familiar with her.

EDMUND   Fear not.

She and the Duke her husband!

> *Enter, with drum and colours, Albany, Gonerill, and*
> *soldiers*

GONERILL (*aside*)

I had rather lose the battle than that sister

Should loosen him and me.

ALBANY

20   Our very loving sister, well be-met.

Sir, this I heard; the King is come to his daughter,

With others whom the rigour of our state

Forced to cry out. Where I could not be honest,

I never yet was valiant. For this business,

It touches us as France invades our land,

Not bolds the King, with others – whom, I fear,
Most just and heavy causes make oppose.

EDMUND

Sir, you speak nobly.

REGAN   Why is this reasoned?

GONERILL

Combine together 'gainst the enemy.
For these domestic and particular broils   30
Are not the question here.

ALBANY   Let's then determine
With th'ancient of war on our proceeding.

EDMUND

I shall attend you presently at your tent.

REGAN Sister, you'll go with us?

GONERILL No.

REGAN

'Tis most convenient. Pray go with us.

GONERILL (*aside*)

O, ho, I know the riddle. (*Aloud*) I will go.

Exeunt both the armies

As Albany is going out, enter Edgar

EDGAR

If e'er your grace had speech with man so poor,
Hear me one word.

ALBANY (*to his captains*) I'll overtake you.

(*To Edgar*) Speak.

EDGAR

Before you fight the battle, ope this letter.   40
If you have victory, let the trumpet sound
For him that brought it. Wretched though I seem,
I can produce a champion that will prove
What is avouchèd there. If you miscarry,
Your business of the world hath so an end,
And machination ceases. Fortune love you.

ALBANY
Stay till I have read the letter.

EDGAR   I was forbid it.
When time shall serve, let but the herald cry
And I'll appear again.   *Exit*

ALBANY
50 Why, fare thee well. I will o'erlook thy paper.
       Enter Edmund

EDMUND
The enemy's in view; draw up your powers.
Here is the guess of their true strength and forces
By diligent discovery; but your haste
Is now urged on you.

ALBANY   We will greet the time.   *Exit*

EDMUND
To both these sisters have I sworn my love;
Each jealous of the other as the stung
Are of the adder. Which of them shall I take?
Both? One? Or neither? Neither can be enjoyed
If both remain alive. To take the widow
60 Exasperates, makes mad, her sister Gonerill,
And hardly shall I carry out my side,
Her husband being alive. Now then, we'll use
His countenance for the battle, which being done,
Let her who would be rid of him devise
His speedy taking off. As for the mercy
Which he intends to Lear and to Cordelia,
The battle done and they within our power,
Shall never see his pardon; for my state
Stands on me to defend, not to debate.   *Exit*

Alarum within. Enter, with drum and colours, Lear, V.2
Cordelia holding his hand, and soldiers, over the
stage, and exeunt
Enter Edgar and Gloucester

EDGAR

Here, father, take the shadow of this tree
For your good host. Pray that the right may thrive.
If ever I return to you again
I'll bring you comfort.

GLOUCESTER   Grace go with you, sir!

Exit Edgar

Alarum and retreat within. Enter Edgar

EDGAR

Away, old man! Give me thy hand; away!
King Lear hath lost; he and his daughter ta'en.
Give me thy hand; come on.

GLOUCESTER

No further, sir; a man may rot even here.

EDGAR

What, in ill thoughts again? Men must endure
Their going hence even as their coming hither;   10
Ripeness is all. Come on.

GLOUCESTER   And that's true too.   *Exeunt*

Enter in conquest with drum and colours Edmund; V.3
Lear and Cordelia as prisoners; soldiers, Captain

EDMUND

Some officers take them away. Good guard,
Until their greater pleasures first be known
That are to censure them.

CORDELIA   We are not the first
Who with best meaning have incurred the worst.
For thee, oppressèd King, I am cast down;

Myself could else out-frown false Fortune's frown.
(*To Edmund*)
Shall we not see these daughters and these sisters?

LEAR

No, no, no, no! Come, let's away to prison.
We two alone will sing like birds i'the cage;
10 When thou dost ask me blessing I'll kneel down
And ask of thee forgiveness; so we'll live,
And pray, and sing, and tell old tales, and laugh
At gilded butterflies, and hear poor rogues
Talk of court news; and we'll talk with them too –
Who loses and who wins, who's in, who's out –
And take upon's the mystery of things
As if we were God's spies; and we'll wear out,
In a walled prison, packs and sects of great ones
That ebb and flow by the moon.

EDMUND   Take them away.

LEAR
20 Upon such sacrifices, my Cordelia,
The gods themselves throw incense. Have I caught
      thee?
      (*He embraces her*)
He that parts us shall bring a brand from heaven
And fire us hence like foxes. Wipe thine eyes;
The good-years shall devour them, flesh and fell,
Ere they shall make us weep. We'll see 'em starved first.
Come.   *Exeunt Lear and Cordelia, guarded*

EDMUND
Come hither, captain. Hark.
Take thou this note; go follow them to prison.
One step I have advanced thee; if thou dost
30 As this instructs thee, thou dost make thy way
To noble fortunes. Know thou this, that men
Are as the time is; to be tender-minded

Does not become a sword; thy great employment
Will not bear question; either say thou'lt do't
Or thrive by other means.

CAPTAIN   I'll do't, my lord.

EDMUND

About it; and write happy when th' hast done.
Mark, I say 'instantly'; and carry it so
As I have set it down.

CAPTAIN

I cannot draw a cart nor eat dried oats;
If it be man's work, I'll do't.   *Exit* 40

    Flourish. Enter Albany, Gonerill, Regan, and
    officers

ALBANY

Sir, you have showed today your valiant strain,
And Fortune led you well. You have the captives
Who were the opposites of this day's strife;
I do require them of you, so to use them
As we shall find their merits and our safety
May equally determine.

EDMUND   Sir, I thought it fit
To send the old and miserable King
To some retention and appointed guard;
Whose age had charms in it, whose title more,
To pluck the common bosom on his side   50
And turn our impressed lances in our eyes
Which do command them. With him I sent the Queen,
My reason all the same; and they are ready
Tomorrow or at further space t'appear
Where you shall hold your session. At this time
We sweat and bleed; the friend hath lost his friend,
And the best quarrels in the heat are cursed
By those that feel their sharpness.
The question of Cordelia and her father

Requires a fitter place.

60 ALBANY   Sir, by your patience,
I hold you but a subject of this war,
Not as a brother.

REGAN   That's as we list to grace him.
Methinks our pleasure might have been demanded
Ere you had spoke so far. He led our powers,
Bore the commission of my place and person,
The which immediacy may well stand up
And call itself your brother.

GONERILL   Not so hot!
In his own grace he doth exalt himself
More than in your addition.

REGAN   In my rights,
70 By me invested, he compeers the best.

ALBANY
That were the most if he should husband you.

REGAN
Jesters do oft prove prophets.

GONERILL   Holla, holla!
That eye that told you so looked but asquint.

REGAN
Lady, I am not well; else I should answer
From a full-flowing stomach. (*To Edmund*) General,
Take thou my soldiers, prisoners, patrimony,
Dispose of them, of me; the walls is thine.
Witness the world that I create thee here
My lord and master.

GONERILL   Mean you to enjoy him?

ALBANY
80 The let-alone lies not in your good will.

EDMUND
Nor in thine, lord.

ALBANY   Half-blooded fellow, yes.

REGAN (*to Edmund*)
  Let the drum strike and prove my title thine.
ALBANY
  Stay yet; hear reason. Edmund, I arrest thee
  On capital treason, and, in thy attaint,
      (*he points to Gonerill*)
  This gilded serpent. For your claim, fair sister,
  I bar it in the interest of my wife.
  'Tis she is sub-contracted to this lord,
  And I her husband contradict your banns.
  If you will marry, make your loves to me;
  My lady is bespoke.
GONERILL   An interlude!   90
ALBANY
  Thou art armed, Gloucester; let the trumpet sound.
  If none appear to prove upon thy person
  Thy heinous, manifest, and many treasons,
  There is my pledge.
      He throws down his glove
                      I'll make it on thy heart,
  Ere I taste bread, thou art in nothing less
  Than I have here proclaimed thee.
REGAN   Sick, O sick!
GONERILL (*aside*)
  If not, I'll ne'er trust medicine.
EDMUND (*throwing down his glove*)
  There's my exchange. What in the world he is
  That names me traitor, villain-like he lies.
  Call by the trumpet. He that dares approach,   100
  On him, on you – who not? – I will maintain
  My truth and honour firmly.
ALBANY   A herald, ho!
      Enter a Herald
  Trust to thy single virtue; for thy soldiers,

173

All levied in my name, have in my name
Took their discharge.

REGAN   My sickness grows upon me.

ALBANY

She is not well. Convey her to my tent.

Exit Regan, supported

Come hither, herald; let the trumpet sound,
And read out this.

A trumpet sounds

HERALD (*reading*) *If any man of quality or degree within the*
110 *lists of the army will maintain upon Edmund, supposed*
Earl of Gloucester, that he is a manifold traitor, let him
appear by the third sound of the trumpet. He is bold in his
defence.

(*First trumpet*)

Again!

(*Second trumpet*)

Again!

Third trumpet
Trumpet answers within. Enter Edgar armed, a
trumpet before him

ALBANY

Ask him his purposes, why he appears
Upon this call o'the trumpet.

HERALD   What are you?
Your name, your quality, and why you answer
This present summons?

EDGAR   Know, my name is lost,
120 By treason's tooth bare-gnawn and canker-bit;
Yet am I noble as the adversary
I come to cope.

ALBANY   Which is that adversary?

EDGAR

What's he that speaks for Edmund, Earl of Gloucester?

174

EDMUND
　Himself. What sayest thou to him?

EDGAR　　　　　　　　　　　　　Draw thy sword,
　That if my speech offend a noble heart
　Thy arm may do thee justice. Here is mine.
　　　He draws his sword
　Behold; it is the privilege of mine honours,
　My oath, and my profession. I protest,
　Maugre thy strength, place, youth, and eminence,
　Despite thy victor sword and fire-new fortune,　　　　　130
　Thy valour and thy heart, thou art a traitor,
　False to thy gods, thy brother, and thy father,
　Conspirant 'gainst this high illustrious prince,
　And, from th'extremest upward of thy head
　To the descent and dust below thy foot,
　A most toad-spotted traitor. Say thou 'no',
　This sword, this arm, and my best spirits are bent
　To prove upon thy heart, whereto I speak,
　Thou liest.

EDMUND　　In wisdom I should ask thy name;
　But since thy outside looks so fair and warlike　　　　140
　And that thy tongue some 'say of breeding breathes,
　What safe and nicely I might well delay
　By rule of knighthood, I disdain and spurn.
　Back do I toss these treasons to thy head,
　With the hell-hated lie o'erwhelm thy heart,
　Which, for they yet glance by and scarcely bruise,
　This sword of mine shall give them instant way
　Where they shall rest for ever. Trumpets, speak!
　　　Alarums. Fights. Edmund falls

ALBANY (*to Edgar, about to kill Edmund*)
　Save him, save him!

GONERILL　　　This is practice, Gloucester.
　By the law of war thou wast not bound to answer　　　150

An unknown opposite. Thou art not vanquished,
But cozened and beguiled.

ALBANY   Shut your mouth, dame,
Or with this paper shall I stop it. – Hold, sir!
(*To Gonerill*)
Thou worse than any name, read thine own evil.
No tearing, lady! I perceive you know it.

GONERILL
Say if I do; the laws are mine, not thine.
Who can arraign me for't?

ALBANY   Most monstrous! O!
(*To Edmund*)
Knowest thou this paper?

EDMUND   Ask me not what I know.

Exit Gonerill

ALBANY
Go after her. She's desperate. Govern her.

Exit First Officer

EDMUND
160   What you have charged me with, that have I done,
And more, much more; the time will bring it out.
'Tis past; and so am I. But what art thou
That hast this fortune on me? If thou'rt noble,
I do forgive thee.

EDGAR   Let's exchange charity.
I am no less in blood than thou art, Edmund;
If more, the more th' hast wronged me.
My name is Edgar, and thy father's son.
The gods are just, and of our pleasant vices
Make instruments to plague us:
170   The dark and vicious place where thee he got
Cost him his eyes.

EDMUND   Th' hast spoken right. 'Tis true.
The wheel is come full circle; I am here.

ALBANY

  Methought thy very gait did prophesy
  A royal nobleness. I must embrace thee.
  Let sorrow split my heart if ever I
  Did hate thee or thy father.

EDGAR   Worthy prince,
  I know't.

ALBANY   Where have you hid yourself?
  How have you known the miseries of your father?

EDGAR

  By nursing them, my lord. List a brief tale;
  And when 'tis told, O that my heart would burst!   180
  The bloody proclamation to escape
  That followed me so near – O, our life's sweetness,
  That we the pain of death would hourly die
  Rather than die at once – taught me to shift
  Into a madman's rags, t'assume a semblance
  That very dogs disdained; and in this habit
  Met I my father with his bleeding rings,
  Their precious stones new lost; became his guide,
  Led him, begged for him, saved him from despair,
  Never – O fault! – revealed myself unto him   190
  Until some half hour past, when I was armed,
  Not sure, though hoping, of this good success,
  I asked his blessing, and from first to last
  Told him my pilgrimage; but his flawed heart –
  Alack, too weak the conflict to support –
  'Twixt two extremes of passion, joy and grief,
  Burst smilingly.

EDMUND   This speech of yours hath moved me,
  And shall perchance do good. But speak you on;
  You look as you had something more to say.

ALBANY

  If there be more, more woeful, hold it in;   200

    For I am almost ready to dissolve,
    Hearing of this.

EDGAR   This would have seemed a period
    To such as love not sorrow; but another
    To amplify too much would make much more
    And top extremity.
    Whilst I was big in clamour, came there in a man,
    Who, having seen me in my worst estate,
    Shunned my abhorred society; but then finding
    Who 'twas that so endured, with his strong arms
210   He fastened on my neck and bellowed out
    As he'd burst heaven, threw him on my father,
    Told the most piteous tale of Lear and him
    That ever ear received; which in recounting
    His grief grew puissant, and the strings of life
    Began to crack. Twice then the trumpets sounded,
    And there I left him tranced.

ALBANY   But who was this?

EDGAR

    Kent, sir, the banished Kent, who, in disguise,
    Followed his enemy king and did him service
    Improper for a slave.

       Enter a Gentleman with a bloody knife

GENTLEMAN

220   Help, help! O, help!

EDGAR   What kind of help?

ALBANY   Speak, man.

EDGAR

    What means this bloody knife?

GENTLEMAN   'Tis hot; it smokes!
    It came even from the heart of – O, she's dead!

ALBANY Who dead? Speak, man.

GENTLEMAN

    Your lady, sir; your lady! And her sister

By her is poisoned; she confesses it.

EDMUND

    I was contracted to them both. All three
    Now marry in an instant.

EDGAR   Here comes Kent.

    Enter Kent

ALBANY

    Produce the bodies, be they alive or dead.

                              Exit Gentleman

    This judgement of the heavens that makes us tremble
    Touches us not with pity. (*To Kent*) O, is this he?   230
    The time will not allow the compliment
    Which very manners urges.

KENT   I am come
    To bid my King and master aye good night.
    Is he not here?

ALBANY   Great thing of us forgot.
    Speak, Edmund, where's the King? and where's
           Cordelia?

      Gonerill's and Regan's bodies are brought out
    See'st thou this object, Kent?

KENT

    Alack, why thus?

EDMUND   Yet Edmund was beloved.
    The one the other poisoned for my sake
    And after slew herself.

ALBANY Even so. Cover their faces.   240

EDMUND

    I pant for life; some good I mean to do
    Despite of mine own nature. Quickly send –
    Be brief in it – to the castle, for my writ
    Is on the life of Lear and on Cordelia.
    Nay, send in time!

ALBANY   Run, run, O run!

EDGAR

To who, my lord? Who has the office? Send
Thy token of reprieve.

EDMUND

Well thought on. (*To Second Officer*) Take my sword,
Give it the captain.

EDGAR   Haste thee for thy life.

Exit Second Officer

EDMUND

250   He hath commission from thy wife and me
To hang Cordelia in the prison, and
To lay the blame upon her own despair,
That she fordid herself.

ALBANY

The gods defend her. Bear him hence awhile.

Edmund is borne off
Enter Lear with Cordelia in his arms, followed by
Second Officer and others -

LEAR

Howl, howl, howl! O, you are men of stones!
Had I your tongues and eyes I'd use them so
That heaven's vault should crack. She's gone for ever.
I know when one is dead and when one lives;
She's dead as earth. Lend me a looking-glass;
260   If that her breath will mist or stain the stone,
Why then she lives.

KENT   Is this the promised end?

EDGAR

Or image of that horror?

ALBANY   Fall and cease!

LEAR

This feather stirs - she lives! If it be so,
It is a chance which does redeem all sorrows
That ever I have felt.

KENT   O my good master!

LEAR

  Prithee away.

EDGAR   'Tis noble Kent, your friend.

LEAR

  A plague upon you, murderers, traitors all!
  I might have saved her; now she's gone for ever.
  Cordelia, Cordelia, stay a little. Ha!
  What is't thou sayest? Her voice was ever soft,   270
  Gentle and low – an excellent thing in woman.
  I killed the slave that was a-hanging thee.

SECOND OFFICER

  'Tis true, my lords; he did.

LEAR   Did I not, fellow?

  I have seen the day, with my good biting falchion
  I would have made him skip. I am old now
  And these same crosses spoil me. – Who are you?
  Mine eyes are not o'the best, I'll tell you straight.

KENT

  If Fortune brag of two she loved and hated
  One of them we behold.

LEAR

  This is a dull sight. Are you not Kent?

KENT   The same –   280

  Your servant Kent. Where is your servant Caius?

LEAR

  He's a good fellow, I can tell you that;
  He'll strike, and quickly too. He's dead and rotten.

KENT

  No, my good lord; I am the very man –

LEAR I'll see that straight.

KENT

  That from your first of difference and decay
  Have followed your sad steps –

LEAR   You are welcome hither.

KENT

Nor no man else. All's cheerless, dark, and deadly.
Your eldest daughters have fordone themselves,
290   And desperately are dead.

LEAR   Ay, so I think.

ALBANY

He knows not what he sees, and vain is it
That we present us to him.

EDGAR   Very bootless.

Enter a Messenger

MESSENGER

Edmund is dead, my lord.

ALBANY   That's but a trifle here.
You lords and noble friends, know our intent:
What comfort to this great decay may come
Shall be applied. For us, we will resign
During the life of this old majesty
To him our absolute power.

(To Edgar and Kent)   You to your rights
With boot, and such addition as your honours
300   Have more than merited. All friends shall taste
The wages of their virtue, and all foes
The cup of their deservings. – O, see, see!

LEAR

And my poor fool is hanged! No, no, no life!
Why should a dog, a horse, a rat have life,
And thou no breath at all? Thou'lt come no more;
Never, never, never, never, never.
Pray you undo this button. Thank you, sir.
Do you see this? Look on her! Look, her lips!
Look there! Look there!   *He dies*

EDGAR   He faints. My lord, my lord!

KENT

  Break, heart; I prithee break.

EDGAR   Look up, my lord.   310

KENT

  Vex not his ghost. O, let him pass. He hates him
  That would upon the rack of this tough world
  Stretch him out longer.

EDGAR   He is gone indeed.

KENT

  The wonder is he hath endured so long.
  He but usurped his life.

ALBANY

  Bear them from hence. Our present business
  Is general woe.
  (*To Kent and Edgar*)
                 Friends of my soul, you twain,
  Rule in this realm, and the gored state sustain.

KENT

  I have a journey, sir, shortly to go.
  My master calls me, I must not say no.   320

EDGAR

  The weight of this sad time we must obey;
  Speak what we feel, not what we ought to say.
  The oldest hath borne most; we that are young
  Shall never see so much nor live so long.

                      Exeunt with a dead march

COMMENTARY

In the Commentary and the Account of the Text the abbreviations 'Q' and 'F' refer to the Quarto text of *King Lear* (1608) and the text in the first Folio of Shakespeare's plays (1623). The terms 'Q corrected' and 'Q uncorrected' are explained at length in the Account of the Text (pages 316–18). Other Shakespeare works, where these are not yet published in the New Penguin Shakespeare, are referred to by the lineation in Peter Alexander's edition of the *Complete Works* (1951). Biblical quotations are taken from the Bishops' Bible (1568 etc.), the official English translation of Elizabeth's reign.

The Characters in the Play

GENTLEMEN. 'Gentleman' appears in several scenes of the play – II.4, III.1, IV.3, IV.6 (after line 188), IV.7, and V.3. There is no clear carry-over from one scene to another, and all these may be different characters. It is clear that the Folio text has a strong tendency to call all supporting actors 'Gentlemen'. Sometimes the Quarto is more discriminating, sometimes not. If he is a single person the 'Gentleman' (like the 'Knight' in I.5) attends Lear; he leaves Gloucester's castle with him (II.4), is sent by Kent to meet Cordelia (III.1), reports her reactions and is taken to meet Lear (IV.3), comes to find him (IV.6), and attends him in IV.7.

I.1   The scene which generates all the subsequent action. A short prelude introducing the names and natures of Gloucester and Edmund leads into a headlong ritual of

185

abdication and 'auction' of the country. Loyalty and sense are exiled from Britain in the persons of Cordelia and Kent, but taken up by the King of France. Hypocrisy and opportunism are left in charge of self-ignorant greatness.

(stage direction) *Edmund*. Normally the name used for this character in speech prefixes and stage directions throughout the play, in both Q and F, is '*Bastard*'.

1   *had ... affected* was fond of

3   *to us* to our people (perhaps an attempt to include Edmund in the conversation)

6   *curiosity in neither can make choice of either's moiety* not even the most scrupulous weighing of advantages can make either prefer the share given to the other *moiety* share

8   *His breeding ... hath been at my charge* I have been financially responsible for his upbringing (or 'I might be held responsible for his birth')

10   *brazed to it* brazen about it

11   *conceive* understand (with secondary reference to 'become pregnant')

15   *smell a fault. A fault* is both (1) a sin; (2) a loss of scent by the hounds.

17   *proper* handsome (but with, perhaps, an ironic undertone of *proper* meaning 'appropriate' (to the *fault*))

18   *by order of law* legitimate

19   *dearer in my account* (the first of the many financial puns in this scene, unless *charge* above, line 8, be so considered)

20   *knave* boy. The sense of 'villain' was available to Shakespeare and may be present by irony.
       something somewhat

29   *sue* beg

30   *I shall study deserving* I shall make every effort to deserve your esteem

31   *out* out of the country. This helps to explain the

ignorance of Edmund's nature shown both by his brother and by his father.

32 (stage direction) *a sennet* a trumpet call (announcing a movement of important characters)

a coronet. This seems to be designed to be part of a ritual of 'parting' the kingdom, expressed in a no doubt abbreviated form in line 139.

33 *Attend* usher into our presence

36 *darker* hitherto undivulged

37 *the map*. Marshall McLuhan says 'the map was also a novelty . . . and was key to the new vision of peripheries of power and wealth . . . the map brings forward at once a principal theme of *King Lear*, namely the isolation of the visual sense as a kind of blindness' (*The Gutenberg Galaxy* (1962), page 11).

37–8 *we have divided | . . . our kingdom*. The text 'Every kingdom divided against itself is brought to desolation' (Matthew 12.25) would occur to many Elizabethan minds. See Introduction, page 40.

38 *'tis our fast intent. Fast* means 'firm', and sorts oddly with *shake* in the following line. Notice the similar contradiction in line 41, where 'unburdening' leads to 'crawling'. The impression is given of the abdication as a charade rather than a necessity.

43 *constant will to publish* settled intention to promulgate

44 *several* separate

45 *prevented* forestalled

46 *Great* noble, powerful

49 *both*. Shakespeare sets 'both' before three (instead of the usual two) cognate nouns in several other places.

50 *Interest of territory* right or title to the territory

52 *largest* most generous

53 *Where nature doth with merit challenge* to the person in whom natural filial affection can be rewarded as if it were objective *merit* (since the merit and the filial love challenge one another as equals)

55 *I love you more than word can wield the matter* the

matter of my love is too weighty to be lifted or expressed by language

56   *space, and liberty* freedom from confinement, and the enjoyment of that freedom

59   *As much as . . . father found* as much as any father ever found himself to be loved

60   *breath* ('speech' rather than 'life' – repeating the idea of line 55)
      unable incompetent

61   *Beyond all manner of 'so much'* beyond all manner of ways of saying 'so much'

62   *Love, and be silent.* Gonerill has *spoken* of love. Cordelia therefore finds speech devalued; she cannot speak, but only love in fact, and so be silent.

63   *bounds* boundaries

64   *champains* flat open country

65   *wide-skirted meads* widely spread-out meadows

67   *Be this perpetual.* This is no temporary division of the kingdom. From now on, Britain will cease to exist as an entity.

69   *self* same
      mettle spirit. But the pun on 'metal' is given strength by *price* and *worth* in the following line (and by their opposition to *true heart*) – with the implication: 'My price can be measured in metal'.

70   *price me* evaluate myself. F reads 'prize', but the two words were not clearly differentiated, and *price* seems the more appropriate modern form.

71   *names my very deed* gives the very particulars of my deed
      deed (1) action; (2) legal instrument. Regan finds in her heart a document containing the very words that Gonerill has been using.

72   *that* in that

74   *Which the most precious square of sense possesses* which the senses, not 'out of square' (unbalanced) but in their proper constitution – the constitution that is so precious to us – possess

75   *felicitate* joyful

76   *poor* (because (1) she feels the lack of gifts within her;
      (2) she cannot join in the exchange of these high-flown
      'golden' sentiments, and must be *poor* as a result)

77–8 *my love's | More ponderous than my tongue.* Compare
      line 55 and lines 91–2, where we find the same sense
      of the glib tongue as the lever of the heart's weighty
      affections. This supports F's 'ponderous' against Q's
      'richer'.

79   *hereditary ever.* See the note on line 67.

81   *validity.* Shakespeare frequently uses the word in the
      sense of 'value'.

83   *least* littlest (or perhaps, as youngest, 'last in pre-
      cedence'). Cordelia's low stature may be implied
      elsewhere (for example, line 198 of this scene). The
      Q reading, 'last, not least', is easier, but the text may
      have been remembered in this form because of the very
      triteness of the phrase.

84   *milk of Burgundy.* Burgundy was notable for the fer-
      tility of its land, though not particularly devoted to
      milk production.

85   *interested* admitted (as to a privilege)

87   *Nothing* (I can say nothing designed *to draw | A third
      more opulent.* I refuse to enter this charade.)

93   *According to my bond* according to my bounden duty,
      the bond of natural affection and respect between child
      and parent

97   *those duties back as are right fit* the duties that are fitting
      to be returned, in answer to your kindnesses, and
      According to my bond

98   *Obey you, love you, and most honour you.* Shakespeare
      seems to be remembering the marriage service in the
      Prayer Book ('Wilt thou obey him, love, honour, and
      keep him . . .'), in preparation for the comparison with
      the duties owed to a husband.

100   *all* with the whole of themselves
      Haply perhaps

101   *take my plight* accept my troth-plight (vow of marriage)

106   *untender* inflexible, stiff in opinions

107   *true* growing straight; stiff, perhaps, but accurate and unerring

110   *mysteries.* F reads 'miseries', Q, 'mistresse'. This provides a good example of the way in which both texts can contribute to the true reading.

        Hecat and the night. Following the *radiance of the sun*, and preceding *the orbs*, this may refer to Hecat – more properly 'Hecatè' – as the moon; but *mysteries* suggests the Hecat who presides over witchcraft.

111–12   *the operation of the orbs | From whom we do exist, and cease to be* the influence of the stars on the lives of men, controlling life and death

116   *Scythian* (an inhabitant of the region now occupied by Russia, remarked by the Roman poets as savage and barbarous)

117–18   *he that makes his generation messes | To gorge his appetite* a barbarian, who chops up his parents (or his children) for food, just out of gluttony. The sense of *generation* as 'parents' gives a slightly better parallel with the actual parent-child situation that Lear sees.

118–19   *shall to my bosom | Be as well neighboured, pitied, and relieved* shall be as close to my bosom, and as within the kindnesses of intimate kinship. The forecast of his own situation in the heath scenes should be noticed.

120   *sometime* former

122   *dragon* (appropriate to the British (as against English) monarchy, imagined as carrying the Welsh red dragon emblem on their coats-of-arms)

123   *set my rest* (1) stake all I have on the bet (a term in the card game of primero); (2) repose in retirement

124   *nursery* nursing, loving care

        Hence and avoid my sight! (addressed, presumably, to Cordelia; but it appears that she does not obey, and that Lear accepts this, since he calls for France and Burgundy)

126 *Who stirs?* get moving, somebody! Don't stand staring!

128 *digest* assimilate, incorporate

129 *Let pride, which she calls plainness, marry her* instead of a dowry to win a husband, she will have to buy one with the pride which she thinks of as plain-speaking

131–2 *all the large effects | That troop with majesty* all the splendid panoply that accompanies the condition of being a king; and also all that *results* from being a king. Lear is to be a king outside the world of cause and effect.

132 *by monthly course* moving round, one month with Regan, one month with Gonerill, and so on

133 *With reservation* the privilege (of having the knights) being reserved or exempted from the agreement

135 *Only* as a sole exception

136 *th'addition* the external honours

137 *Revenue* (accented on the second syllable)

139 *This coronet part between you.* They are to divide royal authority (symbolized by the coronet) between them. Perhaps one should imagine an appropriate stage action in which Gonerill and Regan touch or grasp the coronet.

143 *The bow is bent and drawn; make from the shaft* you have wound up your speech in order to make some important point. Now let the point (barbed, no doubt) fly forward like an arrow. *Make from* is unknown to dictionaries, but must give some sense like 'let go'.

144–5 *Let it fall rather, though the fork invade | The region of my heart* I should prefer that my argumentative point should not hit you, even if the mis-shot arrow should kill me instead

145–6 *Be Kent unmannerly | When Lear is mad* my lack of manners could be justified only if you were mad

146 *thou.* The second-person singular, normally used to inferiors and intimates, is very extraordinary when applied to a king; Kent seems to be trying shock therapy in an attempt to bring Lear to his senses.

147-9   *duty . . . power . . . flattery . . . honour . . . majesty*. Kent presents an allegorical diagram of the relationships. *Duty* (Kent) must speak when *power* (Lear) bows to *flattery* (Gonerill and Regan); *honour* (Kent) must be plain-spoken when *majesty* (Lear) is foolish.

149   *stoops to folly*. The F reading, 'falls to folly', is easily explained by the conflation in the compositor's memory of the sound of *folly* and the idea of *stoops*.

       Reserve thy state. Both this (the F reading) and Q's 'Reuerse thy doome' make reasonable sense. Q is not only, however, the weaker text in general; here it gives a more obvious sense, more likely to be the product of a vulgarizing and simplifying memory than the F reading, which has the sense 'Don't give away your power' (repeated in *Revoke thy gift* below – line 164). There would be little point in linking 'Reverse thy doom' ('Cancel your sentence on Cordelia') to *best consideration*; but *Reserve thy state* links well: 'Do not give your power away; hold back your decision and consider it carefully'.

150-51   *in thy best consideration check | This hideous rashness* restrain this terrible speed of abdication by pausing and considering it well

151   *Answer my life my judgement* I will stake my life on my opinion

153-4   *whose low sounds | Reverb no hollowness*. 'Empty vessels sound most'; so, by inversion, those who make little noise may be thought to do so because they lack the hollow hearts of hypocrites. *Reverb* seems to be a Shakespearian coinage for 'reverberate'.

157   *motive* that which promotes (my action)

158-9   *let me still remain | The true blank of thine eye* instead of ordering me out of your sight, make me always the means of point-blank true aim from your eyes; looking through me you will see things accurately. *Blank* has usually been taken to mean 'the bull's-eye of a target'; but the evidence suggests rather that *true blank* means 'the direct line of sight', as of an arrow or gun directed 'truly', that is point-blank, at its target.

158   *still* always

160   *Apollo* (an appropriate god to invoke at this point, as he was both the archer-god (the god of straight aiming at targets) and the sun-god (the god of clear seeing))

161   *miscreant* unbeliever. Kent has denied the gods.

163–4   *thy fee bestow | Upon the foul disease* give the reward you should lavish on healthful advisers to those against whom they advise you, those who will be your death

168   *That* seeing that

169   *strained pride* pride that leads you to excess

170   *betwixt our sentence and our power* between my words and my deeds, my legal enactment and the fulfilment of it

171   *nor . . . nor* neither . . . nor

172   *Our potency made good* the potential of my power being fulfilled in execution. Lear says that since Kent has interposed himself between *sentence* and *power* he will find no gap between these two in his case: the sentence and power will appear together.

177   *trunk* body

179   *This shall not be revoked*. The emphasis is on *This*, with reference to line 164.

180–87   Kent's couplets, divided formally between the King, Cordelia, Gonerill and Regan, 'princes', mark the recession of the verse-level from immediate passion to sententious generality.

180–81   *sith thus thou wilt appear, | Freedom lives hence and banishment is here* since you are determined to act the tyrant, there can be no freedom in Britain

184   *approve* confirm

185   *effects* results, realizations. The antithesis in lines 184 and 185 is, once again, that between *words* and *deeds*.

187   *shape his old course* 'continue to act upon the same principles' (Dr Johnson) – of faithfulness, truth, and plain-speaking

187   (stage direction) *Flourish* a fanfare (used on stage to mark the ceremonial entry (or exit) of important persons)

191   *in the least* at the lowest

196   *so* dear, expensive, worth a large dowry

198   *little-seeming substance.* The phrase is difficult to disentangle (the hyphen is, of course, a modern addition). The charge can hardly be that Cordelia is *little*; but it is likely to involve *seeming* (hypocrisy) – a Shakespearian obsession. Perhaps the best interpretation is an ironic one, 'that girl so devoted to *substance* and fact, so *little* concerned with *seeming*'.

199   *pieced* augmented (here used ironically)

200   *fitly like* please by its fitness

202   *those infirmities she owes* the disabilities she possesses. He proceeds to enumerate them.
    owes owns

204   *strangered with our oath* made a stranger (to me) by my swearing to sever our relationship (above, lines 113 ff.)

206   *Election makes not up in such conditions* it is impossible to settle a choice (*Take her or leave her*) when the condition of the lady is of the kind you describe. This explains the *I know no answer* at line 201.

208   *tell* (1) report to; (2) count
    For you as for you

209   *make such a stray* stray so far

211   *T'avert your liking a more worthier way* to turn your love in the direction of some person more worth it

212–13   *Nature is ashamed | Almost t'acknowledge hers.* Lear seems to be denying Cordelia not only kinship to him, but kinship to the human species.

214   *your best object* the thing you best liked to gaze upon

215   *The argument of your praise* the theme you chose for praise

217   *to* as to

217–18   *dismantle | So many folds of favour* strip away the protective clothing of your favour (the first appearance of the idea of stripping clothes, later so important in the play)

219–20 *Must be of such unnatural degree | That monsters it* must be so far beyond ordinary human offences as to be monstrous

220–21 *or your fore-vouched affection | Fall into taint* if her offence is not monstrous then the alternative is for the affection for her you used to affirm to become suspect

221 *which to believe* to believe that her offence is so monstrous

221–3 *to believe ... Must be a faith that reason without miracle | Should never plant* to believe (in so impossible a thing) requires *faith*, and faith cannot be implanted by rational means, unaccompanied by the miraculous

224 *If for I want* if it is because I lack

225 *and purpose not* without intending to fulfil what I have spoken

227 *murder.* Critics have made the point that *murder* is a crime Cordelia need not clear herself of, for no one has accused her of it; but she is rehearsing here not her own real crimes, but the extremes that might be assumed of *a wretch whom Nature is ashamed | Almost t'acknowledge hers.*

228 *dishonoured* dishonourable

230 *for which* for want of which

231 *still-soliciting* always ogling for favours

235 *tardiness in nature* natural reticence

236–7 *leaves the history unspoke | That it intends to do* does not speak out the inner thoughts which, none the less, it purposes to enact

239 *regards that stands.* The coupling of a plural subject with a singular verb was not a clear breach of grammar in Elizabethan English.

239–40 *regards that stands | Aloof from th'entire point* considerations (of dowry etc.) that stand quite apart from the single unqualified issue (love)

242 *portion* dowry

248   *Since that* since. Elizabethan English adds 'that' to several conjunctions and relative adverbs ('if that', 'when that', etc.) without altering sense, but giving added emphasis.

      respect and fortunes are his love what he's in love with is worldly status and wealth

250–51   *art most rich, being poor, | Most choice, forsaken, and most loved, despised.* Some of the resonance of these lines no doubt comes from the reminiscence of 2 Corinthians 6.10, where Paul speaks of the ministry of Christ as 'poor, yet making many rich ... having nothing, and yet possessing all things'.

254–65   The couplets indicate (as usual) a formalization of the attitudes involved.

254–5   *from their cold'st neglect | My love should kindle.* He loves her because the gods seem to have abandoned her – the opposite process to that appearing in Burgundy.

258   *waterish Burgundy.* Burgundy is full of streams and rivers; but the principal implication of *water* here is of weakness, dilution (as against *wine*).

259   *unprized-precious* offered at no price at all by her father, but regarded as precious by me

260   *though unkind* though they have not acted like a family to you (yet you should preserve family decencies to them)

261   *Thou losest here, a better where to find. Here* and *where* are nouns: 'You are losing this place, in order to find a better place elsewhere'.

265   *benison* blessing

268   *washed* (1) washed with tears; (2) cleared, able to see you as you really are

271   *as they are named* by their true (unpleasant) names

272   *To your professèd bosoms* to the tender care you have alleged you felt

276   *study* effort, endeavour

278   *At Fortune's alms* as a charity give-away
      scanted stinted

279   *are worth the want that you have wanted* deserve the want of that (affection) which you have shown you lack (towards your father)

280   *plighted cunning* (the cunning that (1) is pleated, plaited, folded under, concealed; (2) involves 'plighting', or swearing as the truth, things that are false)

281   *Who covers faults, at last with shame derides* time begins by concealing faults, but at last reveals them, to the shame and derision of the malefactors

295   *look* expect

296   *imperfections of long-ingraffed condition* faults firmly implanted (grafted) in his character

297   *unruly waywardness* unpredictable petulance

299   *unconstant starts* sudden jerks (as of a frightened horse)

301   *compliment of leave-taking* ceremonious farewell

302   *hit together.* This probably means 'agree with one another', 'fit in with one another', but 'aim together' is also possible. In any case the sense of physical violence cannot be wholly discounted.

303-4   *If our father carry authority with such disposition as he bears, this last surrender of his will but offend us* if our father persists in acting over our heads, as he just has, this power that he has just surrendered to us will only do us harm

306   *We must do something.* The emphasis is on *do* as against *think* in the line before.

      and i'th'heat and strike while the iron is hot

I.2   Edmund reveals that he is as evilly calculating as Gonerill and Regan (though more self-analytical). Gloucester parallels Lear in folly, but on a lower level of energy. Superstition makes him a prey to ruthless intellectual exploitation – as does the relaxed guilelessness of Edgar.

1   *Nature* (a key-word in the play; see Introduction, pages 17–18. What seems to be meant here is a sanction that

precedes civilized law, the law of nations, and lays stress on those endowments that promote life in its most primitive conditions, nature red in tooth and claw.)

1   *goddess*. Edmund must be thinking of a mother-Nature goddess, a goddess of fertility, whose rights precede those of civilization.

      law (the 'law', that is, of the jungle)

2   *services are bound*. Edmund sees his relation to his 'goddess' as a parody of the feudal *service* owed to a liege lord.

3   *Stand in the plague of custom* be subject to the disabilities that customary law imposes on younger sons. Edmund might seem to be referring here to his bastardy – the audience already knows about this (I.1.12–15) – but it emerges in line 5 that he is talking about his status as a younger son.

4   *The curiosity of nations* the fine discriminations established by mere national laws

      deprive me (1) reduce my powers; (2) disinherit me (younger sons did not, bastards could not, inherit)

5   *For that* because

      moonshines months

6   *Lag of* lagging behind

      bastard . . . base. Edmund plays on *base*: (1) ('base-born') bastard; (2) low, vile, despicable. He proceeds to prove *bastard* untrue as a description, because he is not *base* in the second sense.

7   *my dimensions are as well-compact* I am as well formed

8   *generous* gentleman-like

      as true as truly stamped in my father's image

9   *honest madam* the legitimate's married mother

10–21   *base . . . legitimate*. 'Any word, if repeated over and over in a monotone, seems to lose its significance. Edmund plays this trick with *base* and *legitimate*, in order to prove that they are meaningless terms' (G. L. Kittredge).

11–12   *Who ... take | More composition and fierce quality* whose making requires more vigorous effort and energy

11   *lusty stealth of nature. Lusty* involves both vigour and lust: 'natural' love (or lust) has to be vigorously taken, or stolen.

14   *fops* fools

17–18   *Our father's love ... legitimate* (recalling Gloucester's words at I.1.19)

19   *speed* prosper

20   *invention* power of inventing (lies)

21   *top the.* This is an emendation from Q's 'tooth'' and F's 'to'th''. *Top* gives excellent and Edmund-like extension to the meanings of *base* in the preceding line: the *base* (low) will *top* (surpass, be higher than) the legitimate Edgar.

23   *France in choler parted.* We have not seen this; but the phrase serves as convenient and dramatic shorthand for the mode of relationship between Cordelia and the rest of her family.

24   *prescribed his power* instructed about what power he may possess. The Q reading, 'subscribd his power', is possible, but need not be preferred.

25   *Confined to exhibition* restricted to a small allowance

26   *Upon the gad* suddenly (as a horse is caused to bolt by a goad or *gad*)

28   *put up* pocket, conceal

33–4   *dispatch* (1) haste; (2) removal

34–5   *The quality of nothing hath not such need to hide itself* if there was nothing there, you wouldn't need to hide it; it is not the nature of nothing to require concealment

35–6   *If it be nothing I shall not need spectacles.* Note the anticipated irony: here Gloucester is confident of the power of his eyesight to distinguish *something* from *nothing*; later he learns, without eyes, the potentialities that stem from deprivation, or *nothing*.

38–9   *for so much as I have perused* as far as I have read it

39   *o'erlooking* perusal

42   *to blame* objectionable

45   *essay* (the same word as 'assay', a first trial or sip – used technically of the official 'tasting' of a great person's food)

46   *policy and reverence* (hendiadys for 'policy of reverence') politic trick of making us reverence

47   *to the best of our times* in the heyday of our life

48   *our oldness cannot relish them* we are too old to enjoy them

49–51 *an idle and fond bondage in the oppression of aged tyranny, who sways not as it hath power but as it is suffered* the tyrannical oppression of one's elders (in withholding patrimonies etc.) is a kind of slavery that it is needless and foolish to submit to, for it operates through our passivity, not because of its strength

51–2 *If our father would sleep till I waked him* if our father were put into my power to decide his sleeping or waking (that is, death or life)

53, 56 *revenue* (accented on the second syllable)

61   *closet* study

62   *character* handwriting

65   *in respect of that* considering what the subject-matter really is

70   *sounded you* taken soundings or measurements of your depths

73   *fit* appropriate
      at perfect age being fully mature and adult

74   *ward* a minor, under protection of a guardian who managed his affairs

77   *detested* detestable

83   *run a certain course* proceed through certainties
      where whereas

86   *pawn down* stake

87   *feel* test

88   *pretence of danger* dangerous intention

90   *meet* proper

91–2   *by an auricular assurance have your satisfaction* satisfy
        yourself with certainties based on what you yourself
        hear

98   *Wind me into him* screw yourself into his inmost
        thoughts. *Me* is the so-called 'ethic dative' and need
        not be construed in a modern paraphrase.
        Frame organize

98–9   *after your own wisdom* as you think best

99   *unstate myself* give up my rank and fortune

99–100 *a due resolution* a state where my doubts were duly
        resolved

101   *presently* at once
        convey manage

102   *withal* therewith

103   *late* recent (possibly remembering the eclipses of
        September and October 1605)

104–6   *Though the wisdom of nature can reason it thus and thus,*
        yet nature finds itself scourged by the sequent effects
        though science can explain natural events in rational
        terms, the results hurt us none the less for that

109, 114 *villain* (Edgar, who by the very breath of treachery has
        become ignoble, a *villain* (villein) in the sense of
        'peasant')

109–10 *the prediction* (1) the prediction implied by the eclipses;
        (2) the prediction of the end of the world in the New
        Testament, and especially the signs of this described in
        Mark 13, quoted in the Introduction, page 40.

111   *bias of nature* natural tendency (to love one's children,
        etc.)

112–13 *hollowness* lack of inner substance to support external
        appearance

115   *it shall lose thee nothing* ('a backhanded promise to
        reward his detective work' (G. L. Kittredge))

118   *excellent* (1) extreme; (2) splendid (from Edmund's
        anti-human point of view)
        foppery folly

119–20 *sick in fortune – often the surfeits of our own behaviour* reduced in fortune as a result of our excesses (as over-eating produces vomiting)

120   *guilty of* responsible for

123   *treachers* traitors

by spherical predominance because certain planets (in their spheres) were ascendant at the time of our birth

126–8   *An admirable evasion of whoremaster man, to lay his goatish disposition to the charge of a star* it is strange that lecherous man should evade responsibility for his lechery by saying that a star made him like that

126   *admirable* truly strange and wonder-worthy. Compare *excellent* (line 118).

129   *Dragon's tail* (a name given to the intersection of the orbit of the descending moon with the line of the sun's orbit. Chaucer (*A Treatise on the Astrolabe* II.4) names 'the Tail of the Dragon' among the 'wicked planets'.) *Ursa Major* the Great Bear. In astrological terms the horoscope is governed by Mars and Venus, producing a temperament not only daring and impetuous (*rough*) but also lascivious and adulterous (*lecherous*); but it may be that the Dragon and the Bear are mentioned only because of the associations with violence that these animals suggest.

130   *Fut!* (probably the same as "sfoot": by Christ's foot)

131   *that I am* what I am (that is, rough and lecherous)

132   *bastardizing* being conceived as a bastard

133   *pat* in the nick of time

like the catastrophe of the old comedy. Old-fashioned comedy, he implies, contrived the catastrophe (or ending) too mechanically, so that the required co-incidence always turned up just when convenient.

134   *cue* (a theatrical word, fitting to *comedy* and *catastrophe*. Edmund tells us he is about to play a new role.)

134–5   *a sigh like Tom o'Bedlam*. It is not clear why Tom o'Bedlam – the madman-beggar from the Bethlehem (*Bedlam*) or any other madhouse – should have a characteristic *sigh* – though he may well have *whined*.

136   *divisions* (1) conflicts – of father against son etc. as in
        lines 110–11; (2) musical 'divisions' – counterpoint
        against plainsong
        Fa, sol, la, mi. Edmund sings (I assume) the notes
        F, G, A, B natural (using the names given to these
        notes in the C and G hexachords of the musical system
        pertaining in Shakespeare's day). He thus moves
        across the interval of the augmented fourth, called
        diabolus in musica (the devil in music) in the current
        musical mnemonic: *Mi contra Fa est diabolus in musica.*
        The phrase reflects the enmity between the tritone and
        the normal system of harmony. Shakespeare seems to
        be creating something like a musical emblem or 'motto
        theme' for the character of his discordant Bastard.

142   *the effects . . . succeed* the results follow
146   *diffidences* mistrustings
147   *dissipation of cohorts* break-up of military companies
149   *sectary astronomical* devotee of astrology
158   *forbear his presence* avoid meeting him
159   *qualified* reduced
160–61 *with the mischief of your person it would scarcely allay*
        even if he did physical violence to you it would hardly
        diminish
163–4   *have a continent forbearance* contain your feelings (and
        keep away from him)
166   *fitly* at the appropriate time
171   *told . . . but faintly* given only a faint impression of
172   *the image and horror* the horrible picture that is true
173   *anon* soon
178   *practices* machinations
        I see the business I understand how my plot should
        advance
179   *if not by birth, have lands by wit* (because he is a bastard
        he cannot inherit lands by *birth*, but he may be clever
        enough to achieve them)
180   *All with me's meet that I can fashion fit* whatever I can
        turn to my purposes I will regard as justified

I.3   Time has elapsed since I.1, and Lear is now staying with Gonerill. This scene prepares us for what we see in I.4, and allows us to understand the calculation that lies behind the violences exposed there.

(stage direction) *Oswald.* Q and F directions and prefixes call him ' *Steward* '. The use of the personal name in the speech prefixes and stage directions of modern editions derives from its authentic use as a speech prefix in a passage of the Q text which gives two alternative perversions of I.4.332 (given to ' *Stew.* ' in F). The name *Oswald* also appears in the text, at I.4.310, 324, and 330. It is probable that Shakespeare used this name because he read that it was an Anglo-Saxon name for a steward. The Steward's costume should be an important facet of his character.

4   *By day and night.* This is sometimes taken to be an oath; but it is more likely, in the context of *every hour*, to mean 'at all times'.

5   *flashes* breaks out suddenly

7   *upbraids us.* Note the transfer of the royal plural from Lear to Gonerill.

10   *come slack of former services* are less attentive in serving him than previously

14   *come to question* be made an issue

15   *distaste it* find it offensive

21   *With checks, as flatteries, when they are seen abused.* This has been interpreted as 'with punishment instead of flattery when flattery becomes excessive' and as 'with punishments as well as flatteries when they (the old) are misled'.

25   *occasions* opportunities, excuses

26   *speak* rebuke him

     straight at once

I.4   The conflict implicit in I.1 and prepared for in I.3 breaks out in action. Bluntness in the disguised Kent and the nagging truth of the Fool lead up to Lear's violent repudiation of Gonerill and her calculated insults. Varieties of loyalty and respect for the past are opposed to icy and well-prepared control of the present situation.

1   *as well* (in addition to the disguise he is wearing)

2   *my speech* my normal way of speaking

    diffuse confuse, obscure

3   *carry through itself to that full issue* achieve my aim completely

3-4 *that full issue | For which I razed my likeness.* Kent is the first of several in this play (Edgar, Lear, Gloucester) who 'die into life', become effective morally by losing their old social personality.

4   *razed my likeness* altered my appearance. If he did this by shaving off his beard the word *raze* would be particularly appropriate.

    banished Kent. In case the audience have not recognized his voice, he announces his identity.

5   *where thou dost stand condemned* (in the presence of Lear)

6   *come* come to pass that

7   *full of labours* hard-working

    (stage direction) *Horns within* (to indicate the hunt that Lear returns from)

    Knights. F reads '*Enter Lear and Attendants*' (Q: '*Enter Lear*') but the speech prefixes below refer only to '*Knight*' (Q: '*Seruant*'). Some knights must be present if Gonerill's image of Lear's household is to make sense. The advice to the King in lines 63-5 suggests a rank above that of a common servant. On the other hand the imperiousness of Lear's commands would suggest that he is dealing with servants – though the orders given to the man who speaks in lines 63-5 are as imperious as any others in the scene. The usual modern stage direction gives 'Knights and Attendants', but I assume that knights are adequate to all the needs of the scene. Q keeps a '*Knight*' in II.4 (F: '*Gentleman*'); but thereafter neither text mentions Knights.

10   *A man* an ordinary human being (see lines 34–5; with a secondary sense of 'a servant')

11   *What dost thou profess?* Kent's point in *A man* – that he can offer only his basic humanity – is not understood by Lear. He asks 'What arts distinguish this man?', presuming that those who come to the King come because they have some special talent. Kent takes another sense of *profess*, and replies in his own terms: 'My art is to be myself – ordinary, decent, honest'.

13   *I do profess to be no less than I seem.* Kent's phrase has a second sense, aimed to remind the audience that he is, in fact, much *more* than he seems.

16   *judgement.* The most plausible sense is 'the Last Judgement', giving moral meaning to the rest of life.

16–17   *eat no fish.* It is not clear what this means; but certainly it is a joke of the brusque kind that comes to characterize Kent in his Caius persona.

25   *You.* Notice the distinction between *thou* and *you* in this passage.

30   *Authority.* This, like *Service* (line 23), suggests the tendency of this exchange to turn the characters into personifications of abstract qualities such as were characteristic of Morality plays. Compare I.1.147–9.

32   *curious* finely wrought. Kent implies that he is too blunt to be good at fine-spun rhetoric.

46   *clotpoll* one with a *clod* for his *poll* (head), a fool

53   *roundest* most downright and uncompromising

58   *ceremonious affection* (combination of the affection due to a father and the ceremony appropriate to a king)

60   *the general dependants* the mass of servants

     the Duke himself. If one were to examine dramatic evidence as if in a court of law this would be found unreliable. Albany later (line 270) is *ignorant* of the

situation, and the rest of his conduct in the play
confirms the truth of this ignorance. The speech of the
Knight here marks Shakespeare's anxiety to emphasize
the isolation of Lear.

66 *rememberest* remind

66–7 *mine own conception* what I have thought

67 *faint* (not 'imperceptible', but 'languid')

68–9 *jealous curiosity* tendency to suspect trifles as injuries
to my dignity

69 *a very pretence* an actual intention

73 *the Fool hath much pined away.* The first description of
the Fool characterizes him as delicate and sensitive.
Coleridge remarked that he 'is no comic buffoon. . . .
Accordingly, he is prepared for – brought into living
connexion with the pathos of the play, with the suffer-
ings' (*Coleridge on Shakespeare*, edited by Terence
Hawkes (1969), page 204).

83 *bandy.* The technical term for a stroke in tennis. The
dialogue following picks up the tennis metaphor; from
'bandying' looks, Lear turns to blows. Oswald objects
to being made a tennis-ball; Kent trips him and says
that football, a plebeian game, is more suitable for him
than tennis, a royal and noble game.

89 *differences* (the species or classes of men, dividing a
servant from a king, and, incidentally, football from
tennis)

90 *lubber* clumsy fellow

90–92 *Have you wisdom? So.* The Steward hesitates before
accepting the push through the door. Kent's phrase
means 'Surely you have more sense than to resist'. The
So marks the Steward's 'wise' acceptance of the
situation, and his exit.

94 *earnest.* Lear hires Kent as his servant with the usual
initial token-payment, a pledge of further payment to
come.

96 *pretty knave* dainty lad

97 *take my coxcomb* have my fool's cap (for your *earnest*,

for you show yourself apt to act as a fool if you bind
yourself to one who's out of favour)

100 *and if*

smile as the wind sits adapt your behaviour to the
currents of power

100–101 *thou'lt catch cold* (1) the *wind* of power will make you
suffer; (2) you'll be turned out of doors (ironic anticipation)

102–3 *banished two on's daughters, and did the third a blessing*
(a paradoxical inversion of the apparent situation. But
(the Fool implies) the values of I.1 *were* inverted.)

102 *on's* of his

104 *nuncle*. 'Mine uncle' in childish talk becomes transformed into 'my nuncle'. Hence *nuncle* becomes the
word of a fool for his guardian or superior.

107–8 *If I gave them . . . thy daughters* even if (like you) I had
given away all my possessions I should have something
left, good evidence of my folly (in giving things away).
I will give you one coxcomb as a first sign of folly; beg
from your daughters if you want a second sign

109 *the whip*. Domestic fools were (like madmen) whipped
into submission.

110 *must to kennel* must go out of doors to the dog-house

110–12 *he must be whipped out when the Lady Brach may stand
by the fire and stink* Truth is whipped out of doors like
a dog, but the falsely fawning bitch-hound (*Brach*) is
allowed to remain comfortably indoors, however unpleasant the result

113 *A pestilent gall to me!* This may refer to the Fool and
his speeches – 'How this fellow makes me wince!' –
but is more likely to pick up some inner train of
passion deriving from memory of Gonerill's household
– 'How intolerably bitter is the situation I'm in!' *Gall* is
both 'the bitter secretion of the liver' and 'a sore place'.

117–26 *Have more than thou showest . . . two tens to a score* if
you can be entirely prudent and self-concealing you
will accumulate possessions

208

119   *thou owest* you own

120   *Ride more than thou goest* (that is, use your horse's legs
       rather than your own)
       goest walk

121   *Learn more than thou trowest* listen to much and believe
       little

122   *Set less than thou throwest* (not clear; possibly 'gamble
       small stakes for large winnings')

125–6 *more | Than two tens to a score.* This has been thought
       to refer to usurious increase; but it is probably only a
       riddling way of saying 'more than you would expect'.

127   *nothing* nonsense

128   *like the breath of an unfee'd lawyer* (following up the
       proverb: 'A lawyer will not plead but for a fee' – no
       fee, no breath, nothing)

129   *use* usury. Lear's reply recurs to the arithmetical
       point that nothing cannot be multiplied into some-
       thing.

132–3 *so much the rent of his land comes to.* Dover Wilson
       suggests that the point being made is that all rent is
       'something for nothing', a return without work done
       to earn it. More simply, Lear has now no land.

138   *That lord* (an oblique way of pointing to Lear himself,
       as is implied by the following piece of play-acting)

141   *for him stand* impersonate him

143   *presently* immediately

145   *found out* discovered (in spite of his 'disguise' as a sane
       man)
       there. He points to where Lear is standing.

147–8 *that thou wast born with.* Probably Shakespeare does
       not intend the Fool to call Lear 'a born fool', but
       rather to make the point that we are all born with folly
       as a characteristic.

150   *No . . . will not let me.* Kent's *altogether fool* is taken by
       the Fool to mean 'having all the folly there is'.

151   *a monopoly out* a right to sole possession granted by the
       sovereign. This reference to a great abuse of the time

has been thought to account for the omission of the whole passage (lines 138–53) from the Folio.

151–2 *and ladies too.* Presumably these words should be illustrated by some indecency with the Fool's bauble.

157 *the meat* the edible part

159 *borest thine ass on thy back o'er the dirt* (like the old man in the fable who did not wish to overload his ass, and carried him to market (Poggio's *Facetiae* (1470), §24)

161–2 *If I speak like myself in this, let him be whipped that first finds it so* let the man who says that this is folly be whipped, for he is the real fool

163 *grace* favour

164 *foppish* foolish. The wise men now take the places of the fools, who in consequence lose their popularity.

165 *know not how their wits to wear.* The *wise men*, slavishly imitative of the manners of the time, don't know how to show their wisdom; in attempting to follow fashion they become fools.

166 *apish* foolishly imitative

168–9 *madest thy daughters thy mothers* gave your daughters the right to chastise you

173 *play bo-peep* (behave with childish folly)

177 *And if*

185 *What makes that frontlet on?* what are you doing, wearing that headband of frowns?

188–9 *an O without a figure* a zero with no other figure before it to give it value

193–4 *He that keeps nor crust nor crumb, | Weary of all, shall want some* he who (like Lear) in his weariness of the world gives away everything will come to want some of the things he has given away

195 *a shelled peascod.* Since a peascod is the *shell*, one that is *shelled* is nothing.

196–209 The rhetoric of Gonerill's speech seems designed to convey an impression of cold venom. Notice the length of sentence (lines 199–209 form one sentence), the elaboration of the subordinate clauses, the lack of concrete imagery, the sharpness of the alliteration (*found ... safe ... fearful*; *protect ... put*; *'scape censure ... redresses sleep*; etc.), the balance of abstractions, the deviousness of the rhythm.

196   *all-licensed* allowed to say and do what he pleases

197   *insolent* contemptuous of rightful authority

198   *carp* find fault, reprehend

199   *rank* gross

201   *safe redress* sure remedy

202   *too late* only too recently

203–4   *put it on | By your allowance* encourage it by your sanction

205   *nor the redresses sleep* and the remedies will not be slow

206–9   *Which in the tender of a wholesome weal ... call discreet proceeding* the process of remedy, resulting from care (*tender*) for the health of the state (*weal*), might well harm you in a way that under normal circumstances would be called shameful; but the necessities of the state will then allow that it is *discreet proceeding* to prefer your harm to the state's

211   *The hedge-sparrow fed the cuckoo.* The *cuckoo* is (like Gonerill) an admirable example of 'necessities of state'; laid in the hedge-sparrow's nest, it grows so big from the hedge-sparrow's (Lear's) nourishing that it becomes *discreet proceeding* for it to make room for itself by biting off its foster-parent's head.

212   *it's had* it has had. (Shakespeare is often careless of the sequence of tenses, as from the past (*fed*) above to the perfect tense here.)

        it head ... it young. The usual possessive of 'it' is 'his'; 'it' for 'its' seems especially common in 'baby talk'.

213   *So out went the candle.* Lear is presumably the candle of the state, whose extinction plunges the people into darkness.

216   *fraught* stored, loaded

217   *dispositions* states of mind

219–20   *May not an ass know when the cart draws the horse?* even a fool like me can see that things are the wrong way round here (a daughter giving instructions to the King her father)

221   *Whoop, Jug, I love thee!* (perhaps the refrain from a lost song. Obviously it repudiates the involvement with others which appears in the preceding line.) *Jug* Joan

224   *notion* power to understand

225   *Waking? 'Tis not so!* Lear assumes he must be dreaming (as later, with Cordelia, in IV.7).

228   *I would learn that* I seek an answer to the question 'Who am I?'

228–30   *for by the marks of sovereignty, knowledge, and reason, I should be false persuaded I had daughters.* An expanded paraphrase of this might read: 'When I look I see on myself the insignia of a king; and am not aware that in terms of knowledge and reason I have lost the right to rely on my assumptions; on these accounts I should suppose I was right in thinking I was King Lear, who had *daughters* (that is, children owing reverence and obedience). But no such *daughter* can be seen, so I cannot be King Lear.'

231   *Which.* This may (1) stand for 'whom', relating back to the *I* of Lear's speech, or (2) refer back to *Lear's shadow* in line 227. In the latter case we must suppose that the Fool is following his own uninterrupted train of thought, just as Lear is in lines 226 and 228.

233   *admiration* (perhaps 'astonishing behaviour'. G. L. Kittredge says 'Pretending to wonder who you are'.) *is much o' the savour* has the same taste or characteristics

234   *pranks* childish or malicious games

234–45   *beseech . . . desired . . . A little . . .* In this speech words of humility alternate with words of insolent censure, creating a rhetorical effect of calculated venom.

238   *disordered* disorderly

deboshed (a variant form of 'debauched')
bold impudent

240   *Shows* appears

240–41   *epicurism and lust | Makes it more like a tavern or a brothel.* The *epicurism* (gluttony) belongs to the *tavern*, the *lust* to the *brothel*.

242   *a graced palace* a palace which his grace, the King, graces

245   *disquantity your train* reduce the number of your followers

246   *the remainders that shall still depend* those who remain as your followers

247   *besort* be suitable for

248   *know . . . you.* Presumably she means 'know you to be a dangerous old man requiring restraint'.

254   *Woe that* woe to the person who

258   *the sea-monster.* The sea was traditionally a home of horrors, and perhaps *sea-monster* only means 'the kind of monster that the sea traditionally produces'. If any specific sea-monster is meant, that which destroyed Hippolytus probably fits best into the context: as described in the 1581 translation of Seneca's *Phaedra* it is a 'monster' with a 'marble neck'; it is sent as a punishment for filial ingratitude.

259   *Detested kite* vile carrion-bird

260   *of choice and rarest parts* of carefully selected, difficult-to-find qualities

262–3   *in the most exact regard support | The worships of their name* are punctilious, even in details, to live up to their honourable reputation

265   *engine* (usually said to be the rack, but the rack does not seem like the *small fault*, nor does it wrench the frame *From the fixed place*. Some device more like a lever or a crow-bar seems to be intended.)

266   *the fixed place* (1) the foundations of the *frame of nature*; (2) the natural affection which supports human existence

268   *this gate*. It is not clear which *gate* is intended – the ears, the eyes, or the mouth. It is very likely, however, that Lear beats his head as the general area of judgement and folly.

269   *dear* precious to me

275–8   *Into her womb . . . honour her*. Compare Deuteronomy 28.15, 18: '. . . if thou wilt not hearken unto the voice of the Lord thy God . . . cursed shall be the fruit of thy body.'

277   *derogate* degraded, dishonoured (in strong antithesis to *honour* below)

278   *teem* bear children

279   *Create her child of spleen* make her a child composed entirely of malice

280   *thwart disnatured* perverse and unnatural (that is, without filial affection)

282   *cadent* dropping
        fret wear away

283–4   *Turn all her mother's pains and benefits | To laughter and contempt* treat any cares and pains of motherhood that Gonerill may experience with scornful laughter, and treat her joys in motherhood with contempt

289   *disposition* mood

289–90   *that scope | As dotage gives it* (meaning, presumably, violent talk and little action)

291   *fifty of my followers*. Editors have usually sought to explain this by realistic means: fifty followers must have been removed, without comment, at some earlier stage. I think that we should rather praise the bold foreshortening that makes the loss of fifty followers seem the consequence of an absence during which only four lines are spoken. Certainly at line 320 there are *A hundred knights*, and at lines 322 and 330 the same number is repeated.
        at a clap at one stroke

292   *a fortnight* (the length of time he has been staying with Gonerill)

296   *Should make thee worth them* should value you as if you were worth the tears of a king

        Blasts and fogs blighting influences and disease-bearing fogs

297   *untented woundings* untentable wounds (too deep to be probed with a *tent* or roll of lint)

298   *fond* foolish

299   *Beweep this cause* if you shed tears over this matter

300   *loose.* The F word may be the common sixteenth-century spelling of 'lose' (the eyes lose water when they are plucked out), or it may be the modern 'loose' (the eyes release their water). It is probable that Shakespeare, given the overlap of spelling, did not distinguish clearly between the two words.

301   *To temper clay* to soften clay (a base use, like the 'treading of mortar', II.2.63–4)

301–2   *Yea, is't come to this? | Let it be so.* F omits Q's 'yea . . . this?', and prints instead 'Ha? let it be so'. Both versions are metrically defective, so it is likely that the 'F' correction should be added to the Q version, not simply substituted for it. But there is one word which the F corrector may have meant actually to remove from the text – the word 'yea', against which F has, throughout its length, a remarkable prejudice. If so, then 'Ha' should probably be regarded as a substitute rather than an addition; we cannot keep both exclamations, and I prefer to retain the earlier one.

303   *kind and comfortable* like a true daughter, affectionate and ready to give comfort

304–5   *with her nails | She'll flay thy wolvish visage.* Ironically, Lear is made to describe Regan attacking Gonerill in the manner of one wolf attacking another.

307   *Do you mark that?* Gonerill urges Albany to note the treason implied in Lear's statement – as if he had said 'I shall take steps to recover the throne and so depose you'.

308–9   *partial . . . | To* biased because of

312–13   *Take the Fool with thee*. 'The literal sense is obvious; but the phrase was a regular farewell gibe: Take the epithet "fool" with you as you go' (G. L. Kittredge).

314–18   *caught her ... daughter ... slaughter ... halter ... after*. The rhymes seem to have been perfect in Elizabethan English: ... 'hauter' ... 'auter'.

321   *At point* armed ready for action

322   *buzz* whisper of rumour

324   *in mercy* at his mercy

326   *still* always

327   *Not fear still to be taken* rather than live all the time in fear of being 'taken away' myself

334   *my particular fear*. What this particular (or 'personal') fear is does not appear.

336   *compact* confirm, strengthen

338   *milky gentleness and course* (hendiadys) effeminate and gentle course

340   *a-taxed for*. The various readings of the substantive texts are (1) Q uncorrected: 'alapt'; (2) Q corrected: 'attaskt for'; (3) F: 'at task for'. The uncorrected Q reading is almost certainly a misreading of 'ataxt' ('t' and 'x' were often misread as 'l' and 'p'). The Q correction is a variant spelling of this; and F is a 'regularization' of Q corrected. An editor's reading should be as close as it intelligibly can to the original form, and in this case an almost complete return is possible; 'a-taxed' is a variant form of 'taxed': 'complained of'.

341   *harmful mildness* gentleness that may harm the state

342   *eyes may pierce*. Albany means 'into hidden events'; but we are powerfully reminded of the description of Gonerill in II.4.167: *Her eyes are fierce*.

345   *Well, well – th'event!* Albany declines to continue the dispute, and puts the arbitration of their quarrel to the *event* – the outcome.

I.5   This scene follows straight after I.4. We are now outside Gonerill's castle. Lear makes his old-fashioned attempts to counter Gonerill's compact with Regan, while the Fool bodingly prepares us for disaster.

     (stage direction) *Knight.* F reads '*Gentleman*' – no doubt one of the Knights of the previous scene.

1   *before* ahead of me

     Gloucester (the town, presumably, rather than the Earl. But Shakespeare, no doubt, assumed that the Earl lived in or near the town. Dover Wilson prints 'Cornwall', on the grounds that Lear could not know that Regan, the recipient of the letter, is at Gloucester. But Shakespeare often makes these 'errors' of anticipation, not noticeable in the theatre.)

2–3   *Acquaint my daughter no further . . . the letter.* Lear already distrusts Regan, and wishes not to give her any ammunition for an attack on his interpretation of the recent past.

8   *in's* in his

     were't. The 'it' is his 'brain' or (alternatively) (the same sense) *brains.*

9   *kibes* chilblains

11–12   *Thy wit shall not go slipshod* there is no need for you to be shod in slippers (because of the chilblains in your wits), for your journey to Regan shows you lack wits, even in your heels. The train of thought is started by the *diligence* promised by Kent.

14   *use thee kindly.* As the next clause shows, he really means 'treat you according to her kind, or her nature', but he allows the possible meaning 'be kind to you' to point to Lear's expectation. Her 'kind' is as a sister to Gonerill rather than a daughter to Lear.

15   *she's as like this as a crab's like an apple* Regan is as like Gonerill as a sour apple is like an apple (that is, identical in *kind*)

18   *She will taste as like this as a crab does to a crab* the experience of Regan will be as sour and indigestible as the experience of Gonerill

19   *on's* of his

22   *of either side's nose* on either side of his nose

23   *what a man cannot smell out he may spy into.* The Fool is picking up his *I can tell what I can tell* (line 16). Man is given organs of perception that, used properly, may protect him from folly.

24   *I did her wrong.* Presumably Cordelia is meant. We recognize this immediately; but it is not clear *why* we do so.

29   *put's* put his

31   *forget my nature* (that is, cease to be a kind father)

37   *To take't again perforce!* 'He is meditating on his resumption of royalty' (Dr Johnson).
      perforce by violent means
      Monster ingratitude! Compare I.4.256–8.

43   *mad* (the first occasion when Lear leads our thoughts in this direction; no doubt he is picking up the *wise* of the preceding line, in its meaning 'sane'. As Coleridge remarks, 'The deepest tragic notes are often struck by a half sense of an impending blow' (*Coleridge on Shakespeare*, edited by Terence Hawkes (1969), page 205).)

48–9 *She that's a maid ... cut shorter.* This couplet with its indecent pun on *things* has been supposed to be not Shakespeare's; but indecency and authenticity are quite compatible.

48   *departure* (probably pronounced 'depart-er')

II.1   The parts of the plot begin to separate out into their constituent elements, evil with evil, good with good. Edmund completes his triumph over *A credulous father and a brother noble*; Cornwall and Regan move in to support him. Edgar, now associated with Lear's knights (lines 93–4), is exiled (like Kent and Cordelia).

218

(stage direction) Here, and at II.2.0 and III.1.0, I
have substituted a modern equivalent for the
stage direction in F ('*Enter ... seuerally*'). Entries
and exits 'severally' – at opposite stage doors
(compare III.1.55 and III.7.106) – are used by
Shakespeare to give visual effect to meetings from
far apart, or departures to undertake different
activities.

1   *Curan*. It is rare for Shakespeare to give a proper name
to a character as little individualized as Curan is here
(his only appearance). It is not clear why he does so at
this point.

6   *news* (here takes a plural agreement)

8   *ear-kissing*. Most editors prefer Q's 'eare-bussing'.
'Bussing' is certainly the more vivid word; but it is a
vulgar error to suppose that Shakespeare's vocabulary
is characterized principally by its use of quaint and
vivid elements.

arguments topics of conversation

10–11   *likely wars toward 'twixt the Dukes of Cornwall and
Albany* (the first of frequent references to wars likely
to occur (*toward*) between the Dukes)

14   *The better! best!* so much the better! In fact, nothing
better could happen

15   *perforce* of necessity, without my seeking it

17   *one thing of a queasy question* a matter that requires
delicate handling. He refers, presumably, to the dis-
posing of Edgar.

queasy (literally, 'liable to vomit')

18   *Briefness* speed of action

Briefness and fortune work! I hope that quick action
and good luck will help me

19   *Descend!* At I.2.174 Edgar retired to Edmund's lodging. Presumably it is from this hiding place that he
now *descends*.

23–6   *the Duke of Cornwall ... the Duke of Albany*. Edmund
was entirely ignorant of these matters only thirteen

219

lines before. This is a good example of his quick-thinking opportunism.

26　*Upon his party 'gainst the Duke of Albany.* First Edmund suggested Edgar's peril from Cornwall; now he reverses the case and suggests that Edgar may have spoken too boldly on the side of Cornwall against Albany and so excited the latter's wrath. The prime object is to create a world teeming with dangers.

27　*Advise yourself* consider the matter

29　*In cunning* as a clever device

30　*quit you* defend yourself in the fight (with also, perhaps, a sense of *quit* meaning 'depart')

34-5　*I have seen drunkards | Do more than this in sport.* 'Stabbing of arms', and mixing the blood with wine drunk to a mistress, was a practice of the gallants of Shakespeare's age.

37-9　*in the dark . . . auspicious mistress.* Note Edmund's gift for theatrical invention – these details are well designed to affect the credulous Gloucester.

38-9　*Mumbling of wicked charms . . . where is he?* Edmund appeals to Gloucester's tendency to superstition. Gloucester's reply is, however, severely practical. There is some comedy in the cross-purposes of Edmund trying to get Edgar out of the way, and divert attention to himself, and Gloucester bent on the capture of his son.

41　*Fled this way.* As the eighteenth-century editor Capell said, Edmund should point in the wrong direction.

45　*bend* aim (like a bow). Compare II.4.222.

48-9　*how loathly opposite I stood | To* with what loathing I opposed

49　*fell motion* with a fierce thrust

50　*preparèd sword.* At I.2.167 Edmund told Edgar to go armed. We may assume that Edgar has given substance to the story by entering (line 19) with his sword drawn (*preparèd*).

51　*unprovided* unprepared, unprotected

latched. The F reading is less easy than Q's 'lanch'd' (or 'lanced'); but the fact that the change was made gives it a claim to credence. To *latch* is to 'catch' or 'nick', and this may seem more appropriate to the minor wound that Edmund has inflicted on himself than the stronger 'lanced'.

52 *my best alarumed spirits* my best energies called up by the *alarum* of battle

54 *gasted* terrified

55 *Let him fly far* however far he flies

57 *And found – dispatch.* Presumably the pause is filled in by some gesture, such as drawing his hand across his throat.

58 *arch and patron* (hendiadys) arch-patron

61 *to the stake* (metaphorically: 'to the place of final inescapable reckoning')

64 *pight* (past participle of 'pitch') firmly fixed (like tent-pegs)
  curst speech angry words

65 *discover* reveal

66 *unpossessing bastard.* Bastards were in law deemed incapable of inheriting land.

67–9 *would the reposal | Of any trust, virtue, or worth in thee | Make thy words faithed?* would the fact that trust has been placed in you, or any virtue or worth that you possess in yourself, make people believe what you say?

71 *character* handwriting (in the letter Edmund showed in I.2)

71–2 *turn it all | To thy suggestion, plot, and damnèd practice* explain it as being due to your temptations, your plotting, and your wicked intriguing

73–6 *thou must make a dullard of the world . . . make thee seek it* you would have to make mankind very stupid to stop them thinking that you had full, ready, and powerful motives to seek my death, given the advantages that would come to you if I were dead

76 *strange and fastened* fixed firm in his unnaturalness

77   *deny his letter* (in lines 70–71)
       got begot
       (stage direction) *Tucket* personal trumpet call

79   *ports* (probably 'seaports'; but it may mean the gates
       of walled towns)

80–81 *his picture | I will send far and near* (an early version of
       the 'wanted' poster outside police-stations)

83   *natural boy.* Gloucester means one who has expressed
       'natural' loyalty to his father; but since a 'natural son'
       is a bastard, there is an ironic twist to the phrase.

84   *capable* (of inheriting land; that is, legitimized by
       process of law)

89   *my old heart is cracked; it's cracked.* The repetition
       suggests the sentimental self-pity that is a part of
       Gloucester's basic temperament. Compare *lady, lady*
       (line 92) and *too bad, too bad* (line 95).

90, 91 *my father's godson ... He whom my father named.* Regan
       immediately capitalizes on the new situation, to identify
       all wickedness with her father.

95–6   *I know not ... Yes, madam. ...* Gloucester's response
       to Regan's efforts to blame her father is not very satis-
       factory; he is too sunk in self-pity to catch her drift. It
       is Edmund, with his clear eye for the main chance, who
       gives her the reply she wants, thus establishing at first
       sight the natural rapport between them.

96   *consort* (accented on the second syllable). This is
       usually derogatory: 'gang, mob'.

97   *though* if
       ill affected ill disposed

98   *put him on* urged him to undertake

99   *expense* spending

102   *my house.* Notice the mannish and commanding air of
       Regan and the merely confirmatory role of Cornwall in
       this exchange.

105   *A child-like office* the duties that are appropriate to a
       true son. Coming from Cornwall the words have an
       irony appropriate to Edmund.

106   *He did bewray his practice* Edmund revealed Edgar's plot

110   *Be feared of doing harm* give rise to the fear of his harmful deeds

110–11   *Make your own purpose | How in my strength you please* fulfil your purpose (of capturing Edgar) by whatever means you like, drawing on my resources as it suits you

113   *ours* one of my followers. Note the royal plural.

114   *we shall much need* (with the implication: 'in the troubled times ahead of us' – whether in wars with Lear or wars with Albany is not certain)

116   *Truly, however else* even if my imperfections prevent me from being as efficient as I am true

118   *Thus out of season, threading dark-eyed night.* Notice how imperiously Regan takes over Cornwall's narrative and makes it her own. *Out of season* may imply that it is winter, a bad time for travelling, or may only be repeating the point that, in their haste to avoid Lear, they have travelled all night. The idea of threading the eye of a needle in the dark, implicit in the imagery used, conveys the sense of effort and difficulty.

119   *Occasions . . . of some price* there are reasons (or 'personal requirements') of some importance. *Price* rather than 'prize' seems the most suitable modernization; see the note on I.1.70.

122–3   *which I best thought it fit | To answer from our home* which letters I thought it best and most appropriate to reply to away from home. Regan wishes to delay receiving Lear till she has consulted with Gonerill.

123–4   *The several messengers | From hence attend dispatch* the men carrying the respective letters are waiting here for their dismissal

127   *Which craves the instant use* which requires to be dispatched at once. It is not clear whether *Which* refers to *counsel* or *businesses*. In Elizabethan English the singular form *craves* would be equally correct with either.

II.2   The physical conflict between the two servants, Kent and Oswald the Steward, foreshadows in a semi-comic and pathetic vein the grander conflict to come. Gloucester and Cornwall move into sharper definition.

2   *Ay.* It is not clear why Kent says he is of Gloucester's household, unless it is to give occasion for further attacks on Oswald.

3   *we . . . our.* Presumably the plural refers to the attendants who accompany Oswald.

5   *if thou lovest me* (a conventional and rather affected phrase for 'please', which Kent chooses to take literally)

7, 9   *care . . . care.* Oswald says he does not *care for* ('like') Kent. Kent says he could make him *care* ('worry').

8   *Lipsbury pinfold.* No place called *Lipsbury* is known; so it is usually supposed to be an equivalent to 'lip-town', the space between the lips. A *pinfold* is a pound for stray animals. The two words may well imply 'the strongly fenced area between the teeth', the whole phrase meaning 'If I had you between my teeth I would make you care'.

11   *I know thee* I can see through you. Notice the pejorative second-person singular throughout this dialogue.

13   *eater of broken meats.* After meals the scraps were collected into a basket, and these were the food of the lowest menials. Kent's general picture of Oswald is of a jumped-up menial pretending to be a gentleman – he is both *base* and *proud*.

14   *shallow* incapable of thought

    three-suited (servant-like. Servants were allowed three suits a year. Compare III.4.129.)

    hundred-pound (a great sum if the point is simply that Oswald is a menial. But about this time James I was making knights for a hundred pounds; so that the phrase carries the idea of 'beggarly pretender to gentility'.)

15   *filthy-worsted-stocking knave.* Real gentlemen wore silk
      stockings.

      lily-livered bloodless, cowardly

15–16 *action-taking* going to law (instead of fighting)

16   *super-serviceable.* This seems to be the only appearance
      of the word, so it is not clear exactly what it means –
      perhaps 'anxious to be of service in any way, however
      dishonourable'.

      finical fussing about details

17   *one-trunk-inheriting* who inherited only as much as
      would go into one trunk

17–18 *wouldst be a bawd in way of good service* would do any
      service, however improper or disgusting, if that was
      required of you

19   *composition* compound

22   *addition* (something added to a man's name to denote
      his rank – here the names that Kent has 'added' to
      Oswald)

28–9 *make a sop o'the moonshine of you* make a mash of you,
      soak you in blood, while the moon shines (or 'while
      you talk "moonshine"' – nonsense)

29–30 *cullionly barbermonger* base fop, never out of the
      barber's shop

33   *Vanity the puppet* (Gonerill, seen as a Morality-play
      figure of Self-Regard, performed in a puppet play.
      There is also the sense of Gonerill as a puppet who
      should not speak except with her father's voice – the
      sense of the unnatural revolt of the puppet against the
      puppeteer.)

      puppet. We should be aware of not only the modern
      sense of 'marionette', but also the earlier sense of
      'doll' (poppet).

35   *carbonado your shanks* slash your legs as if they were
      meat for broiling

35–6 *Come your ways* come on

39   *neat slave* elegant rascal

42   *With you* I'll fight with you

42   *goodman boy* master child, you who have set yourself up with more authority than your years authorize

       and you please if you like. For *and* F prints 'if', which is probably a modernization. See the Account of the Text, page 320.

43   *flesh ye* introduce you to bloodshed

48   *difference* dispute

51   *disclaims in thee* denies any part in making you

51–2   *a tailor made thee.* The proverb is that 'The tailor makes the man' – with the sense that social status is derived from clothes. Kent pushes this one stage further: Oswald is made, not simply socially but in every sense, by his clothes.

55–6   *A tailor . . . A stone-cutter or a painter could not have made him so ill. . . .* The tailor was one of the more despised of Elizabethan tradesmen, often thought of as cringing and effeminate.

62   *thou unnecessary letter.* Zed was thought *unnecessary* because most of its functions in English are taken over by 's', and because Latin manages without it. Similarly Oswald is a superfluous element in society.

63   *unbolted* unsifted, unkneaded; requiring to be trodden down (like lumpy mortar) before he can be useful

64   *jakes* lavatory

65   *wagtail.* G. L. Kittredge suggests that Oswald is too scared to stand still, and therefore reminds Kent of the uneasy tail-jerking of the wagtail. The word was often used in this period to mean 'wanton'.

67   *beastly* beast-like (not knowing the *reverence* etc. proper to human society)

68   *privilege* (to break the bounds of normal social decorum)

70–71   *should wear a sword | Who wears no honesty* carries the symbol of manhood, but lacks an honourable character

72   *the holy cords* the bonds of natural affection that bind the individual to society

73   *t' intrinse t'unloose* too inward, secret, hidden (in their

mode of tying) to be untied. Thus the bonds of matrimony or of filial obedience (or of royal duty) cannot be 'untied' (returned to their separate condition), but can be 'bitten' apart so that *love cools, friendship falls off*, etc. Oswald's nature is thus turned towards one of the central problems of the play.

smooth promote by flattery

74   *rebel*. In the typical image of man, passion can only emerge when it *rebels* against its overseer, reason.

75   *Being*. F's 'Being' and Q's 'Bring' seem equally good; and therefore, in the absence of other evidence, we must prefer the F reading.

76   *Renege* deny. Compare IV.6.98–100.

       turn their halcyon beaks. The kingfisher (or *halcyon*) was supposed, if hung up, to vary direction with the wind. So flattering servants only possess opinions to point in whatever direction the passions of their masters require.

79   *epileptic visage*. Oswald is presumably trying to smile and at the same time twitching with terror.

80   *Smile*. F follows Q's unusual spelling 'Smoile'. Editors have sometimes thought that this reflected Kent's dialect disguise as Caius; but such an isolated expression of it would be pointless.

81–2 *Goose, if I had you ... Camelot* (an obscure passage, which must have the general sense: 'If I had you at command I would make you add flight to your cackling laughter, like a goose being driven')

81   *Goose* foolish person

       Sarum Plain Salisbury Plain

82   *Camelot* (the legendary capital of Arthur's kingdom; it is not known where it was situated; some Elizabethans believed it was at Winchester)

88   *likes me not* does not please me

94–6 *doth affect ... from his nature* pretends to a blunt rudeness of manner, and twists the habit (*garb*) of

227

plain-speaking away from its (*his*) true nature (truth), turning it towards deception

98   *And they will take it, so ; if not, he's plain* if people will swallow his rudeness, then that's all right; if they object, then he defends himself by the claim that this is just plain-speaking

100   *more corrupter.* The double comparative is a common Elizabethan usage.

101   *silly-ducking observants* obsequious attendants making themselves foolish with their low bows

102   *stretch their duties nicely* strain themselves to carry out their duties with the greatest finesse

104,   *aspect . . . influence* (astrological terms. Kent's parody
105   of the *observants'* courtly dialect leads him to describe Cornwall as a planet.)

104   *aspect* (accented on the second syllable)

106   *flickering Phoebus' front* the fiery forehead of the sun

107   *my dialect* (that of a plain-spoken man)

110–11   *though I should win your displeasure to entreat me to't.* It is difficult to paraphrase this; perhaps the easiest interpretation is: 'though I should manage to overcome your displeasure to the extent that you would entreat me to be a knave'.

115   *upon his misconstruction* as a result of his (the King's) misunderstanding of me

116   *he, compact* Kent, being in league with the King
    flattering his displeasure to gratify his mood of anger

117   *being down, insulted* when I was down, he abused me

118–19   *put upon him such a deal of man | That worthied him* made himself out to be such a hero that others thought him worth something

120   *For him attempting who was self-subdued* for attacking a man who gave in without a struggle

121   *fleshment* excitement of accomplishing. To *flesh* was to inflict injury in warfare, especially for the first time.
    dread exploit (ironical)

122–3   *None of these rogues and cowards | But Ajax is their fool.*

Either (1) 'To hear people of his kind speak you would think the great hero Ajax was a fool beside them' or (2) 'Rogues and cowards can deceive great men like Cornwall (or Ajax)'.

124   *ancient knave . . . reverend braggart.* The same idea is repeated: Kent is old and therefore should be revered; but he is a knave and a braggart.

129   *grace and person* (both his mystical body as King and his *person* as man)

132   *till noon.* The moon is still shining; the sun begins to rise some thirty lines later (line 161).

135   *being* since you are

136   *colour* character

137   *bring away* bring along

140   *check* rebuke

141   *contemned'st* most despised

152   *Will not be rubbed* cannot bear to be hindered. A *rub* in bowls is anything that impedes the bowl.

153   *watched . . . hard* made myself stay awake

158   *approve the common saw* prove the truth of the well-known saying. The particular *saw* is no doubt suggested by the rising of the sun.

159–60   *out of Heaven's benediction comest | To the warm sun* come from good to bad

161   *beacon to this under globe* (the sun)

162   *comfortable* comforting

163–4   *Nothing almost sees miracles | But misery* miracles (like this letter from Cordelia) are especially likely to occur to those in the lowest and most depressed condition. Maynard Mack thinks there is a reference to Acts 16, where Paul and Silas, placed in the stocks in Philippi, 'sang praises unto God' and were released by an earthquake (*King Lear in Our Time* (1966), page 56).

166   *my obscurèd course* my disguised way of life

166–8   *and 'shall find time . . . their remedies'* (obscurely worded and perhaps corrupt. Some of the dislocation of sense may be due to Kent's reading out phrases from the letter. The general meaning must be that Cordelia will intervene and try to put things right.)

167 *this enormous state* this abnormal and wicked state of affairs

168–9 *o'erwatched ... eyes* eyes made weary by being kept from sleep

171 (stage direction) *He sleeps.* I give no exit here. I believe that Kent remains on stage throughout the next scene and is discovered by Lear in II.4 still on stage. We may prefer to imagine that the stocks are set in a recess and are concealed by the drawing of a curtain.

I.3 This one-speech scene serves to give a short breathing-space in the effectively continuous action in the court-yard of Gloucester's castle which occupies II.2 and II.4. It also allows us to be aware of the transformation of Edgar into Poor Tom so that when we hear his name (III.4.37 and 41) and see him (III.4.43) we know with whom we are dealing.

1 *proclaimed* (as an outlaw. See II.1.59.)

2 *by the happy hollow of a tree* by the fortunate accident that there was a hollow tree in which I could hide

3 *No port is free.* See II.1.79.

6 *am bethought* have a mind

7 *most poorest.* The double superlative, like the double comparative (see II.2.100), is a means of giving emphasis.

8 *in contempt of man* despising the pretensions of humanity (to be superior to the beasts)

10 *Blanket my loins* (a useful indication of the stage appearance of the 'naked' Tom – he wore a piece of blanket as a loin-cloth)

elf tangle into elf-locks. (Matted hair was thought to be the result of elvish malice.)

11 *with presented nakedness outface.* By persecuting him-

self, by *presenting* his nakedness to the storm, Edgar 'stares down' the hostile world.

14   *Bedlam beggars* beggars who claim they have been in-
      mates of the Bethlehem (*Bedlam*) madhouse, and have
      licences to go about begging for their keep. 'This
      fellow . . . that sat half-naked . . . from the girdle up-
      ward . . . he swears he hath been in Bedlam and will
      talk franticly of purpose; you see pins stuck in sundry
      places of his native flesh, especially in his arms, which
      pain he gladly puts himself to . . . only to make you
      believe he is out of his wits; he calls himself by the
      name of *Poor Tom* and, coming near anybody, cries
      out, *Poor Tom is a-cold*' (Thomas Dekker, *The Bellman
      of London*, 1608).

15   *mortified* dead to feeling (like *numbed*)

17   *object* spectacle
      low lowly, humble

18   *pelting* paltry

19   *bans* cursings

20   '*Poor Turlygod! Poor Tom!*'. Edgar enacts the role he
      must now fulfil. *Turlygod* is a word no one has ex-
      plained.

21   *That's something yet; Edgar I nothing am* as Poor Tom
      there is some kind of existence for me; as Edgar I
      cannot exist

II.4   The climactic scene at the end of the protasis or exposi-
        tion of the play. Beginning at the level of the affront to
        Kent, the tension mounts through Lear's dispute with
        Regan and Cornwall – conducted via Gloucester and so
        avoiding full-scale confrontation – and reaches its first
        climax when Gonerill arrives and we have the full
        orchestration of I.1 repeated, answering the 'I give
        you' of the opening with a conclusive 'We take'. This
        dispute only dies into another kind of climax as Lear's
        speeches expand to prophetic frenzy, as the storm

thunders closer, and as Lear rushes to join the cosmic furies, and the wicked withdraw to safety.

3–4　　*purpose ... Of this remove* intention to move from one house to another

6　　*Makest thou this shame thy pastime?* do you sit in the stocks for fun?

7　　*cruel garters* (1) the stocks; (2) crewel (worsted) cross-garters

10　　*wooden nether-stocks* stocks as stockings

11　　*place* (1) rank (as King's messenger); (2) the place (where you sit) due to you

13　　*son* son-in-law

19　　*Yes.* Given the regular symmetry of this exchange one might expect 'Yes, yes' here; but one can hardly change the text for such a reason, even though the unreliable Quarto is the only authority for lines 18–19.

23　　*upon respect* (either (1) 'against a man whose role required respect' or (2) 'deliberately')

24　　*Resolve me with all modest haste* tell me with speed, but be temperate

26　　*Coming from us* given that you came as a royal messenger

28–9　　*from the place that showed | My duty kneeling* from the kneeling posture that showed my duty

29–30　　*a reeking post, | Stewed in his haste* a sweating messenger, soaked in the sweat his haste had produced

32　　*spite of intermission* in spite of the gasps and pauses that his breathless condition required

33　　*presently* immediately
　　　　on whose contents when they had read them

34　　*meiny* household menials

40　　*Displayed so saucily* acted in so obviously insolent a way

41　　*man than wit* courage than discretion

45　　*wild geese.* They fly south in the autumn. The events that Kent has described convey the same message as do wild geese seen flying south – the winter of displeasure and unkindness is to get worse.

47   *blind* (to the needs of their parents)

48   *bear bags* keep their money-bags

51   *turns the key* opens the door

52-3   *dolours for thy daughters* (1) griefs because of your daughters; (2) dollars in exchange for your daughters

53   *tell* (1) speak of; (2) count

54, 55   *mother ... Hysterica passio* (a feeling of suffocation and giddiness thought to begin in the womb ('mother', *hystera* in Greek) and to affect the patient by climbing to the heart and then to the throat. One of the demoniacs in Harsnet's *A Declaration of Egregious Popish Impostures* (1603) suffered from the mother.)

56   *Thy element's below* your appropriate place is below. The 'mother' is not simply a medical condition appropriate to Lear; it is a visceral symbol of the breakdown in hierarchy, when the lower elements climb up to threaten or destroy the superior ones.

62   *And* if

62-3   *set i'the stocks for that question.* The question is subversive, for the answer must be that kings who lose their power also lose their followers.

65-6   *an ant ... no labouring i'the winter.* Aesop's provident ant laboured when labour was profitable (in the summer); so Lear's followers stopped following when the winter of their master's fortune made following unprofitable.

66-9   *All that follow their noses ... him that's stinking* those who go straight still follow what they see, and they ca˙ see Lear's downfall. Even the blind man who canno˙ *see* his downfall can smell the stink of failure

69   *a great wheel* (a great man)

73   *ha' ... use.* This emendation assumes that the F reading, 'I would hause none but knaues follow it' (where 'hause' replaces the Q 'haue'), derives from a correction 'ha use' written in the margin of Q. It is assumed that this was intended to replace Q's 'haue' by 'ha' and Q's 'follow' by 'use'. The F compositor,

however, attributed both the corrections to 'haue' and left 'follow' intact.

74-7 *That sir . . . in the storm.* The servant's progress described here is very close to that which Iago praises in *Othello*, I.1.49–54.

74 *sir* man (here specifically a servant)

75 *for form* out of habit or convention

76 *pack* depart

80-81 *The knave turns fool that runs away ; | The fool no knave, perdy.* If this is textually correct it implies a sudden switch from worldly wisdom to spiritual truth: 'The knave (servant) who deserts his master must eventually be seen as a fool; but this fool will stay, and so, in God's name, is no knave'.

83 *Not i'the stocks, fool.* In the context this is equivalent to saying that Kent is no knave.

85 *fetches* tricks

86 *images of revolt and flying-off* (representative of disobedience and desertion and the rejection of natural ties)

88 *quality* character

91 *What 'quality'?* Lear is still in the world where individuality is far less important than status and relationship. When king and father command, character is no excuse.

97 *commands, tends, service.* This is F's reading. The text here is difficult if not impossible to sort out. The Q corrector's 'commands her seruice' is probably mere tidying up without authority. The original (uncorrected) Quarto's 'come and tends seruice', because it is nonsense, probably represents an honest attempt to read the manuscript. If the Folio was printed from the uncorrected form of the Quarto page we could base little on its preservation of the Q reading; on the other hand, if F was printed from the corrected page, its readings would imply a fresh look at the manuscript, and the coincidence with the uncorrected Q reading

would prove authenticity. I think we must print either 'commands, tends' or something that looks like 'come and tends' in Elizabethan handwriting. The usual reading of modern editors, 'commands, tends', makes sense, but not good sense. Lear is making plain forceful demands, not complex or ironic ones like 'commands her service and tends his own'. 'True service' is a possible reading, and one easily misread in Elizabethan handwriting as 'tends service'.

101   *still* always

101–2   *neglect all office | Whereto our health is bound* fail to fulfil the duties which are required of us when we are in health

105   *am fallen out with my more headier will* am no longer friendly to my more reckless impulse

107   *Death on my state!* (an oath – 'May my kingly power come to an end' – which is already fulfilled)

109   *remotion* (either (1) 'removal from one house to the other' or (2) 'holding themselves remote from me')

110   *practice* stratagem

111   *and's wife* (not 'my daughter')

112   *presently* at once

113   *chamber* bedroom

114   *cry sleep to death* kills off sleep by the noise it makes

116   *rising heart* (a further stage in the hysterica passio)

117–20   *as the cockney did . . . down!'. Cockney* probably means here 'a pampered and foolish person'. She had little experience of making eel-pies, put the eels in without killing them, and, when they tried to wriggle out of the pastry, rapped them on the heads, crying 'Down, you roguish creatures'. So Lear's heart tries to *rise* out of the situation his folly has created and must be *knapped* ('struck').

120–21   *'Twas her brother . . . buttered his hay.* Cheating ostlers were said to butter hay to stop the horses eating it. The cockney's *brother* (that is, one of the same breed of

tender-hearted fools) tries to be kind and succeeds in
being destructive (like Lear).

126–7   *divorce me from thy mother's tomb, | Sepulchring an
adult'ress* posthumously divorce your mother, proved
unfaithful to me (by your unfilial conduct)

127   It has been suggested that Kent should exit here.

129   *naught* wicked

130   *like a vulture.* Shakespeare may be remembering the
torment of Prometheus, whose liver (believed to be the
seat of the passions) was endlessly devoured by a
vulture.

133–5   *I have hope . . . she to scant her duty.* The sense is clear:
'I trust that she does not know how to scant her duty
as well as you know how to undervalue her'; but it is
not easy to make the words mean this. The most
probable explanation of the fact that the literal sense
seems opposite to the required sense is that *scant* adds
a second negative idea to that in *less know*; Shakespeare is anxious to stress the negative, but fails to
notice that he has one too many, and that 'she to do
her duty' would be more accurate.

138   *riots.* Regan and Gonerill use the same vocabulary for
the knights. See I.3.7, I.4.199 and 240, and II.1.93.

144   *state* physical and mental condition (but with an ironic
echo of *state* meaning 'power, royalty')

148   *becomes the house* is appropriate to the household
(where the father is 'the head of the house')

150   *Age is unnecessary.* In a survival-of-the-fittest world
(which Gonerill and Regan are setting up) the aged
cannot be justified; no one needs them. If they are to
be given *raiment, bed, and food* it must be out of
charity.

154   *abated* deprived

158–9   *Strike her young bones . . . with lameness* deform the
bones of her unborn child

159   *taking airs* infectious vapours

161–3   *Infect her beauty . . . blister* you noxious vapours that

236

rise from bogs when the sun shines on them, fall down
on her, blister her face and mar her beauty

166   *tender-hefted* (literally, 'set into a delicate handle')
endowed with a tender sensibility

170   *sizes* allowances

171–2 *oppose the bolt | Against my coming in.* The climax of
these deprivations is, ironically enough, the one which
Regan is shortly to put into practice.

173   *The offices of nature, bond of childhood* the duties that
are natural to our state, such as the bond of affection
between child and parent

174   *Effects of courtesy* manifestations of a courtly disposition

174–5 *gratitude. | Thy half o'the kingdom. . . .* It is worth
noticing that Lear, even at this point, climaxes his
arguments, not with the claims of nature or courtesy,
but with the economic argument.

178   *approves* confirms

180   *easy-borrowed pride.* 'Pride' often means 'ostentatious
adornment'. Oswald's splendid livery and his steward's
chain (compare Malvolio) are easy to put on and take
off. What is more, they depend on the whim of 'her
grace'.

186   *Allow* approve

188   *beard* (an emblem of age, and therefore of authority
and deserving)

191   *that indiscretion finds* that want of judgement (like
yours) discovers to be so

192   *sides* (the sides of the chest, strained by the swellings
and passions of the heart)

193   *hold* hold out, remain intact

195   *Deserved much less advancement.* The stocks are a low
seat, and a disgraceful punishment; but they are higher
than he deserves.

196   *being weak, seem so* don't act as if you had strength
you do not possess. Shakespeare quickly transfers
the contest from Cornwall to the daughters. The

central conflict must not be obscured by subsidiary issues.

201   *entertainment* proper reception

204   *wage against the enmity o'th'air* struggle against the hostile environment of the open air

205   *the wolf and owl* (solitary and rapacious animals, hunting by night)

206   *Necessity's sharp pinch!* The phrase is governed by *choose*, in apposition to *To be . . . owl*. *Necessity* is both 'poverty' and 'fate'.

207   *hot-blooded* passionate (supposed to be a French characteristic) and therefore likely to be violent

209   *knee* kneel before
      squire-like like a body-servant

211   *sumpter* pack-horse, drudge

212   *groom* servant

219   *embossed* swollen (to a knob or *boss*)

220   *corrupted* (by the *disease . . . Which I must needs call mine*)

221   *come when it will*. Notice the confidence that shame is bound to be visited upon her, sooner or later.

222   *the thunder-bearer shoot* Jupiter aim his thunder-bolts (at you)

223   *high-judging* who judges from on high

229   *mingle reason with your passion* view your passionate outbursts with the cold eye of reason

230   *Must be content to think you old, and so* – have no choice but to see you as senile, with the result that. . . . Regan's contempt for his failure to accept his own senility chokes her utterance: the whole thing is so obvious that there is no point in speaking further.

234   *sith that* since. On *that*, see the note on I.1.248.
      charge expense

240   *slack ye* be negligent to you (as Oswald was commanded in I.3.10)

241   *control them* call them to account

244   *place or notice* lodging or official recognition

246   *Made you my guardians, my depositaries* put you in charge of my estate, made you my trustees

251   *well-favoured* fair of face

257   *To follow* to be your followers

259   *reason not the need!* don't try to apply rational calculation to *need* (as in line 256)

259–60   *Our basest beggars | Are in the poorest thing superfluous* even the most deprived of men have among their few possessions something that is beyond (*superfluous* to) their basic *needs*

261–2   *Allow not nature more than nature needs – | Man's life is cheap as beast's.* The usual punctuation of this involves a comma after *needs*, with the sense: 'If you do not allow nature more than is necessary, then man's life will have to be reckoned as cheap as a beast's'. This seems to me too rational and hypothetical an argument for Lear at this point. He is (I take it) angrily mimicking the computational arguments of his daughters: 'In your terms even the beggar's rags are superfluous. Don't bother to believe that human nature has needs greater than those of animal nature, for it is as easy (or *cheap*) to buy a human life as an animal life.'

263–5   *If only to go warm . . . keeps thee warm* let us define 'the gorgeous' in dress as 'able to keep you warm'; yet nature does not need even that kind of gorgeousness in spite of the little warmth your gorgeous dresses do provide

265   *for* as for

268   *wretched in both.* This is the first time that Lear has described the wretchedness as against the dignity of age.

270   *fool me not so much* don't let me be such a fool. Realizing the wretched passivity of age, Lear prays to be given the *nobility* of manly anger, even of revenge.

276–7   *they shall be | The terrors of the earth.* Shakespeare does not hesitate to show Lear's alternative to weeping, his *noble anger*, as absurd boasting. Lear's nobility depends not on his power to terrorize the earth, but on his ability to assimilate into his passions those terrors of the earth which begin to make their sounds heard almost immediately.

280–81 *break into . . . flaws | Or ere I'll weep. O Fool, I shall go mad!* The alternative to melting into tears (the woman's way) is to explode into fragments (*flaws*). And immediately Lear indicates the nature of this explosion, the fragmentation of sanity that is to ensue.

283 *and's* and his

284 *bestowed* accommodated

285 *from rest* from his bed

287 *For his particular* as far as he himself is concerned

293 *He leads himself* he is under no guidance but that of his own will

296 *ruffle* rage, brawl

298–9 *The injuries that they themselves procure | Must be their schoolmasters* they have to learn their lesson in being punished by the consequences of their own wilful actions

300 *a desperate train* (the *riotous knights* once again)

301–2 *apt | To have his ear abused.* This is an example of a standard shift to which Regan and Gonerill resort: that their unkindness to their father is provoked by others, such as *riotous knights*, who mislead him ('abuse his ear'), and must therefore bear the responsibility for his suffering.

III.1 A bridge-passage between two scenes of higher dramatic tension. The narrative account of Lear's behaviour describes some of the meanings that we should attach to the *action* of III.2. Shakespeare gives here, at the very moment when evil has established its undisputed ascendancy, a glimpse of the countermovement gathering momentum at Dover.

(stage direction) *still* (perhaps 'as before' (at II.4.279), but more probably 'continuously')

2   *One minded like the weather* (the first statement of the equation between the inner world and the stormy weather which is so important in the next few scenes)

4   *Contending* (both (1) 'physically struggling against' and (2) 'competing in violence and anger')

     the fretful elements the angry weather

5–6   *Bids the wind ... 'bove the main.* Lear commands the earth to return to the state before creation separated water and earth.

6   *main* mainland

8   *eyeless rage* blind, indiscriminate wrath

9   *make nothing of* treat as worthless

10   *his little world of man* (Lear as a microcosm or model of the external world)

     out-storm. The Q reading, 'outscorne', is possible and therefore tempting (there is no F text at this point). But Elizabethan printers and transcribers frequently confused 'c' and 't', as well as 'm' and 'n'. *Out-storm* picks up and develops the important and central idea of the microcosm in a way which would be typically Shakespearian.

11   *to-and-fro conflicting* blowing now one way, now another

12   *the cub-drawn bear would couch* the bear, drained of her milk by her cubs and therefore ravenous, would lie in shelter

14   *unbonneted* not wearing a hat (a stronger idea then than now: totally abandoning self-respect as well as self-protection)

15   *bids what will take all* offers the world to any power which cares to have it. *Take all* is usually associated with the gambler's cry when he stakes everything on the last throw.

16   *out-jest* overcome by the force of his jokes

17   *heart-struck injuries* injuries that are like blows on the heart

18   *upon the warrant of my note* justified by my knowledge (of you)

19   *Commend . . . to you* recommend to your care
        dear important

22   *their great stars* their fortune of being great

23   *who seem no less* who seem indeed to be real servants

24   *France* (the King of France)

24–5   *speculations | Intelligent of our state* observers collecting political intelligence

26–9   *Either in snuffs . . . but furnishings.* Three things that the King of France may have learned, and that may be encouraging him to invade, are: (1) the division between Albany and Cornwall; (2) the harsh treatment of King Lear, as if he were a horse pulled back on a tight rein (a pun on 'reign'), given no freedom of movement; (3) *something deeper*, which explains both (1) and (2), making these mere *furnishings* or accidentals. It seems pointless to speculate on the nature of this *something deeper*; it is part of the deep shadow that belongs to the picture.

26   *snuffs and packings* huffiness and secret plots to secure revenge

29–30   *furnishings – | But true it is.* The dash expresses a refusal by Kent to speculate further; he returns to what is known as a fact – the French invasion.

30   *power* army

31   *scattered* (presumably refers to the dispersal of the royal power shown in the first scene of the play)

32   *Wise in our negligence* taking advantage of our neglect (of national security)
        feet footholds

33–4   *are at point | To show their open banner* are prepared to unfurl their flag, and declare themselves

34   *Now to you* now I am going to suggest what you can do

35   *my credit* your belief in me

35–6   *so far | To* so far as to

37   *making just report* for making an exact report

38   *unnatural and bemadding sorrow* sorrow caused (unnaturally) by his own flesh and blood, so as to drive him mad

39   *plain* complain

42   *office* duty, function

45   *out-wall* outside appearance. Kent is still dressed as Caius the servant.

46   *What it contains* (the *ring* mentioned in the next line)

48   *fellow* (sometimes glossed 'companion'; but more likely to mean 'lower-class person, servant')

52   *to effect* in their consequences

53–4   *in which your pain | That way* in which matter I beg you to take pains by searching in that direction

III.2   Lear and the Fool stumble across a stage now representing 'the heath' where man is fully exposed to the hostile physical world. Shakespeare uses the extension of this hostility in the storm to talk about the storm of passions in Lear's mind. Kent remains an emblem of loyal endurance; but Lear is more and more detached from any sense of an individual self to which one may be usefully loyal.

1   *your cheeks.* The image is derived from the personifications of the winds shown puffing their cheeks at the corners of old maps.

2   *cataracts and hurricanoes* water from the heavens and from the seas. Here, as in *Troilus and Cressida*, V.2.170 – the only other occurrence of the word in Shakespeare – *hurricano* is used to mean 'waterspout'. Lear is asking for a second deluge, or for a return to the state before the creation of man.

3   *cocks* weathercocks (on the top of the *steeples*)

4   *thought-executing* acting as fast as thought

5   *Vaunt-curriers of oak-cleaving thunderbolts.* The *fires* of the lightning are the advance guard of the thunder's *bolts* or missiles, which are so powerful that they split

the oak-tree. *Vaunt-curriers* are those who run in the 'van' of the main body. I have avoided the usual modernization 'Vaunt-couriers' (F has 'Vaunt-curriors', Q, 'vaunt-currers') because it brings distracting associations into the line.

7   *Strike flat the thick rotundity o'the world* hit so hard that the roundness of the world will be smashed flat. The suggestion of round-bellied fertility being frustrated may also be present; this would lead directly to the imagery of the following lines.

8   *Crack Nature's moulds* break the patterns by which all things are created in their kinds

     all germens spill destroy all the seeds out of which all matter is formed

10   *court holy-water* the flattery a man must sprinkle to belong to the court

16   *I tax not you . . . with* I do not accuse you of

18   *subscription* obedience, allegiance

21–2   *yet I call you servile ministers,* | *That will* I call you servile agents, in that you are willing to

23   *high-engendered battles* battalions coming from the heavens

25–6   *a good head-piece* (1) a good head covering; (2) good sense

27–9   *The cod-piece that will . . . shall louse* the man who finds a home for his penis before he has a roof over his head is destined for lice-infested beggary

27   *cod-piece* (a case for the male genitalia ('cods') attached to the breeches, often, as Alexander Dyce says, 'ostentatiously indelicate' in this period. Here (by metonymy of the covering for the thing covered) the penis.)

30   *So beggars marry many* (obscure; does *many* refer to the lice or the women?)

31–3   *The man that makes . . . cry woe* (another inversion of order; based on the proverb 'Set not at thy heart what should be at thy heel'. If you lay your delight in what you should spurn, you will be liable to suffer for it, just as, if you valued your toe as highly as you should value your heart, its ailments would loom as large.)

35–6 *For there was never yet fair woman but she made mouths in a glass.* To 'make mouths' carries, as well as the obvious meaning, the sense of 'treat with contempt'. Apparently a foolish *non sequitur*, the sentence may be a return to the theme of the daughters: 'Women are by nature likely to despise what they see'.

40 *grace and a cod-piece* the spiritual and the physical, the King (his grace) and the fool. The idea of *a wise man* is introduced to make the choice of roles uncertain. The professional fool often wore a particularly prominent cod-piece; but Lear, like the cod-piece above (line 27), had children before he had wisdom.

44 *Gallow* (more properly 'gally') frighten
wanderers of the dark nocturnal animals

48–9 *carry | Th'affliction nor the fear* endure the physical affliction or the terror it inspires

49–60 *Let the great gods . . . than sinning.* Lear's speech should be contrasted with the preceding one by Kent. Kent speaks of the physical effect of the storm. Lear, careless of this, concentrates on its moral meaning.

50 *pudder* (a variant form of 'pother') hubbub

51 *Find out their enemies now.* The *enemies* (criminals), terrified by the storm, will confess their crimes.

53 *bloody hand* (murderer. Compare III.4.89.)

54 *simular of virtue* false claimant to chastity

55 *Caitiff* base wretch

56 *under covert and convenient seeming* behind a surface appearance that was effective to conceal the truth and fitting for the nefarious purposes planned

57 *practised on* plotted against

58 *Rive* break out
continents hiding-places, bounds that hold you in

58–9   *cry* | *These dreadful summoners grace* cry for mercy to
         the elements that are sounding a summons to God's
         court (as the *summoners* call offenders before the
         ecclesiastical courts)

59–60   *I am a man* | *More sinned against than sinning.* *I* should
         be emphasized, in contrast to the *Close pent-up guilts* of
         other people.

60   *bare-headed.* See the note on III.1.14.

63, 64   *hard* unpitying

67   *scanted* limited

69   *my fellow* (Kent)

70–71   *The art of our necessities is strange* | *And can make vile
         things precious* necessity has a strange art (like that of
         the alchemist who turns base metal into gold) which
         makes things that we despised when we were pros-
         perous seem precious when we are in need

71   *vile.* Here and at III.4.138, III.7.82, IV.2.38 and 47,
         and IV.6.278, Q and F read 'vild' (or 'vilde'), com-
         mon alternative forms of the word in Elizabethan
         English.

72–3   *I have one part in my heart* | *That's sorry yet for thee.*
         This may seem to imply a radical limitation on Lear's
         sympathy for a *fool and knave.* Perhaps we should read
         '... sorry yet – for thee' ('I have a part of me still
         capable of feeling sorrow, and that part is concerned
         with you').

74–7   *He that has . . . every day.* This is a stanza derived from
         the popular song that Feste sings at the end of *Twelfth
         Night.* Lear's mention of his *wits* (line 67) reminds the
         Fool of the song, with its obviously appropriate refrain-
         line, and he uses it to enshrine the lesson that our wits
         must be adapted to our fortunes.

79   *a brave night to cool a courtesan.* It is not clear why the
         comment on the weather takes this form. Perhaps a
         pun is intended on 'night'/'knight'. If so, this would
         explain the sudden switch to medieval parody in the
         lines following.

81–94   *When priests . . . used with feet.* The *prophecy* begins as
a parody of a passage attributed in the Elizabethan
period to Chaucer:

> When faith faileth in priestès saws,
> And lordès hests are holden for laws,
> And robbery is holden purchase,
> And lechery is holden solace,
> Then shall the land of Albion
> Be brought to great confusion.

Shakespeare turns this into a satiric statement of things
that really do happen in his own day. The next 'stanza'
involves a list of things not satirical and real, but
utopian and ideal. In F this is followed by four lines of
generalization (lines 85–6, 93–4), but as the passage is
made up of two separate couplets saying different
things, and as the first couplet completes the pseudo-
Chaucerian matter of the first stanza, it seems best to
follow the practice of those editors who have placed
the couplets one at the end of each stanza.

81   *more in word than matter* better at talking about virtue
than practising it

83   *nobles are their tailors' tutors* fashion-mad noblemen
tell their tailors how to cut their elaborate clothes (as in
Shakespeare's time)

84   *No heretics burned but wenches' suitors* when love is
more important than religion. *Burned* may be a reference to the flames of love or to the physical effects of
the pox.

86   *confusion* (four syllables: con-fu-si-on)

90   *Nor . . . not.* In Elizabethan English two negatives do
not necessarily make a positive.

cutpurses come not to throngs. The cutpurse, like his
modern equivalent, the pickpocket, pushed in among
large crowds, where he could cut and steal purses –
commonly worn hanging from the belt – with greater
ease.

91   *When usurers tell their gold i' the field.* Usurers were a

part of city life, opposed to the traditional agricultural sources of wealth. Perhaps *gold i'the field* refers to grain, so that the phrase means 'when usurers turn farmers', or perhaps 'are willing to lend to farmers'.

91   *tell* count

92   *do churches build* (use their wealth for religious purposes)

94   *going shall be used with feet* feet will be used for walking on ('an intentionally absurd truism', says G. L. Kittredge)

95-6   *Merlin . . . I live before his time.* According to Geoffrey of Monmouth, Lear lived during the eighth century B.C., and Arthur during the sixth century A.D.

III.3   In this prose scene, Gloucester's fate marches forward to the same betrayal as has already overtaken Lear. His pity for Lear keeps before us what is happening on the heath, but interrupts the lyrical passions of approaching madness with reminders of ordinary life.

1-2   *unnatural* (because it is their father that Gonerill and Regan have mistreated)

3   *pity* be merciful to (a use of the verb not elsewhere recorded, but cognate with 'have pity on' in the same sense)

7   *Go to* no more of that

8   *a worse matter.* Perhaps this refers to the French invasion, which is what the letter in fact describes (III.5.9-10). But in lines 9-10 the invasion seems a separate matter. Perhaps the *worse matter* is yet another piece of the 'shadow' in which Shakespeare chooses to place the conflict of Albany and Cornwall; compare *something deeper* (III.1.28, and the note on III.1.26-9).

10   *closet* cabinet for private papers

11   *home* all the way, thoroughly

12   *footed* landed, got a foothold. The same unusual word

is used at III.7.45 of the French invasion (compare III.1.32).

13   *look* seek

18   *toward* about to happen

19   *This courtesy forbid thee* (helping Lear, which he was forbidden to do)

21   *a fair deserving* deserving of a fair reward

III.4   A direct continuation of III.2. Kent's concern for the physical well-being of the King is frustrated finally by the appearance of naked Tom, an apparition that releases Lear's last hold on his own identity and submerges his sanity in his sense of all the oppressed and dispossessed of the world. Fool, King, and Bedlam begin to forge a new dialect, a rapt recitation of inner visions, compared to which the common-sense solicitudes of Kent and Gloucester seem external and superficial.

3   *nature* human nature

11-12   *When the mind's free | The body's delicate* when the mind is free of worry, it can afford to attend to the body's petty complaints of discomfort

15   *as this mouth should tear this hand* as if one part should harm another part of the same body (all of whose functions are for the united good of the whole). Lear sees himself and his daughters as part of such a body.

20   *frank heart* generous love

25   *things would hurt me more* (the internal *tempest* of his thoughts of filial ingratitude)

26   *houseless poverty* (*Poor naked wretches* who have no covering from the storm)

27   *I'll pray.* The 'prayer' that Lear says before he goes to sleep is a highly unorthodox one, not for his own safety during the night, but for that of *wretches*; and not to the gods, but to the objects of their power.

31   *Your looped and windowed raggedness* your ragged
      clothes, full of 'windows' (which were normally un-
      glazed in Shakespeare's time) and loop-holes

32   *seasons* times, weather conditions

33   *Take physic, pomp* let the pompous man of authority
      learn how to be (morally) healthy

35   *shake the superflux* shake off superfluous possessions

37   *Fathom and half.* Edgar takes up the cry of the sailor
      singing out the depth of water his ship is passing
      through. The hovel is presumably half-submerged by
      the rainstorm.
      Poor Tom. See the note on II.3.14.

44   *Away!* keep away from me
      The foul fiend follows me. The mad were often supposed
      to be possessed or followed by devils.

45   *Through the sharp hawthorn blow the cold winds.* This
      has the air of a quotation from a song. Bishop Percy
      (1729–1811) has, in his *Reliques of Ancient English
      Poetry* (1765), a ballad ('The Friar of Orders Grey')
      with the line 'See through the hawthorn blows the
      cold wind, and drizzly rain doth fall'; but this ballad
      appears to be Percy's invention, patched together from
      scraps of Shakespeare. The Q reading, 'cold wind',
      is supported by the same song-fragment below (line
      95).

46   *Humh!* Edgar shivers with cold.
      Go to thy bed and warm thee. The beggar Christopher
      Sly says something very similar in *The Taming of the
      Shrew*, Induction 1.7–8 – so it may well be another
      catch-phrase, possibly in reply to Jeronimo's famous
      'What outcries pluck me from my naked bed' (*The
      Spanish Tragedy*, II.5.1).

47   *Didst thou give all to thy daughters?* (the first words that
      can be used to prove that Lear has finally lost his hold
      on external reality, is 'mad'. The appearance of 'Poor
      Tom' is undoubtedly intended to be the catalyst that
      releases the inner forces that have been beating in

Lear's mind. Immediately after the *Poor naked wretches* speech he finds a figure with whom he can wholly identify himself and whose role (of madman) he can take over.)

52, 53 *knives . . . halters . . . ratsbane*. These are the traditional gifts (the poison is usually less specific) given by the Devil to the man who is in a state of despair, in the hope that he may kill himself and bring his soul into a state of perpetual damnation.

53 *porridge* soup

55 *course* hunt

thy five wits. These were defined as 'common wit, imagination, fantasy, estimation, memory'; or perhaps this is another way of saying 'your five senses' (taste, smell, sight, hearing, touch).

56 *O do, de, do, de, do, de*. This set of sounds is probably meant to represent Tom's teeth chattering with cold.

57 *star-blasting* being struck down by disease (disease was often supposed to be the result of the 'influence' of the stars)

taking being 'taken' with an infection

58–9 *There could I have him now*. Tom searches for lice and devils at the same time.

64–5 *plagues that in the pendulous air | Hang fated*. Like *star-blasting* (line 57), this alludes to the idea that disease is poured down by planetary influence as a punishment on the wicked. Stored up in the stars, it hangs (*pendulous*) like fate over the future of wrong-doers.

65 *light* alight

67, 68 *subdued . . . unkind*. The accent in both cases falls on the first syllable.

67 *subdued nature* brought down the human state

70 *little mercy on their flesh* (referring to Edgar's nakedness, and to the thorns and sprigs (or splinters) stuck in his arms. When Edwin Booth was playing Lear he 'drew a thorn or wooden spike from Edgar's arm and

thrust it into his own': A. C. Sprague, *Shakespeare and the Actors* (1944), page 291.)

71   *Judicious* appropriate, fitting

72   *pelican daughters.* The pelican's young (according to the medieval bestiaries) smite their father and kill him. The mother pelican first hits back, and then revives the dead children by shedding her own blood over them – thus becoming the symbol of Christ-like loving self-sacrifice. Lear sees Gonerill and Regan as assaulting him and also demanding that he sacrifice himself for them.

73   *Pillicock* (suggested by *pelican*. It seems both to have meant a darling, a beloved, and to have been a playful word for penis (picking up the idea from *flesh begot* in line 71).)

74   *Alow, alow, loo, loo!* Some sort of cry of sporting encouragement seems to be intended.

75   *This cold night will turn us all to fools.* Note that as Edgar takes over the role of the broken, rhapsodic, song-singing madman, the Fool is reduced to the role of the balanced observer.

77–9   *Take heed ... proud array* (a crazy parody of the ten commandments)

78–9   *commit not with man's sworn spouse* do not commit adultery with one who is sworn wife to another

79   *proud array* fine clothes. The idea of clothes leads Tom naturally to his next remark about the cold.

82   *servingman.* It is not clear whether this refers to a servant in the ordinary sense (with a *mistress* whose first role is to command the household) or to a 'servant' (that is, lover) with a 'mistress' (that is, a beloved).

83   *wore gloves in my cap.* Gallants wore their mistress's gloves in their cap.

88   *the Turk* (the Grand Turk, the Sultan, famous for his seraglio)

89   *light of ear* 'credulous of evil' (Dr Johnson)

89–90 *hog in sloth . . . lion in prey.* The seven deadly sins were often represented in art and literature by animals, illustrating the predominant passion or the particular 'beast in man' that was intended.

90 *stealth* (both 'stealing' and 'stealthiness')

dog in madness. The dog represents madness because the transmission of rabies to man makes the mad dog particularly notable.

prey the act of preying, pillage, violence

93 *plackets* slits in the front of petticoats

95 *Still . . . cold wind* (the same song-fragment as in line 45)

96 *Says suum, mun, nonny.* Some kind of refrain seems to be intended, and the Q version, 'hay no on ny', is an approximation to the traditional 'hey, nonny, nonny'. The F reading, given here, is likely to be nearer to the original, because more difficult. Perhaps it represents an imitation of the *cold wind* whistling through the hawthorn.

97 *Dolphin, my boy, boy, sesey! Let him trot by.* Perhaps these are more song-fragments – but, if so, the songs have perished. *Dolphin* may be a horse, *sesey* may be the French '*cessez*' – but all this is merest conjecture.

98 *answer* encounter

99 *body . . . skies* (the microcosm/macrocosm analogy once again)

99–100 *Is man no more than this? Consider him well.* Shakespeare may have been remembering Hebrews 2.6, 'What is man, that thou shouldst be mindful of him? Or the son of man, that thou wouldst consider him?', or Florio's Montaigne: '. . . miserable man; whom if you consider well, what is he?' ('An Apology of Raymond Sebond', 'Tudor Translations' (1893), Volume II, page 172).

100–101 *Thou owest . . . no* you are not indebted to . . . for

101 *beast* (specifically 'cattle')

102 *cat* civet cat (the source of some perfumes)

102   *sophisticated* adulterated by the addition of clothes etc. away from the pure (naked) state of man (*the thing itself*)

103   *Unaccommodated* unfurnished (with clothes etc.), unsupported by a well-fitting environment

104   *forked* having two legs

105   *lendings* (the clothes *lent* to man by the *beast*, the *worm*, the *sheep*, etc. Lear aims, by tearing off his clothes, to identify himself with *the thing itself*, with Poor Tom.)
unbutton. As a king he commands his *valet de chambre* to undress him; as a demented moralist he tears off his clothes with his own hands.
(stage direction) *He tears off his clothes*. Capell added '*Kent and the Fool strive to hinder him*'.

106   *naughty* bad. The word was quite without the childish connotations it has since acquired.

107   *swim* (suggested both by the rain and by Lear's stripping off his clothes)
a wild field a waste heath, a wilderness

107–8   *an old lecher's heart*. This undoubtedly refers to Gloucester with his torch, the lechery which begot Edmund, and the evidence of *heart* shown by his succouring of the King. To secure a naturalistic explanation, we must suppose that the Fool spies Gloucester after *swim in*, though it is not clear how an actor could convey this.

110   *Flibberdigibbet* (the name of one of the devils who danced with a supposed demoniac in Harsnet's *Declaration*. See IV.1.60.)

111   *curfew ... till the first cock* (said to be from 9 p.m. till midnight; but may have the more general sense of 'from dusk till dawn' – when evil spirits were most free)

111–12   *the web and the pin* cataract of the eye

112   *squenies* causes to squint

113   *white* almost ripe

115–18   *S'Withold ... aroint thee*. F's '*Swithold*' presumably refers to Saint Withold, elsewhere in Elizabethan

literature a defender against harms. Here he is a
defender against the *nightmare* – the demon that
descends on people when they are asleep. The saint
paces the wold (*'old*) three times (the magic number)
and when he meets the nightmare and her nine (three
times three) offspring he commands her to *alight* (get
off the sleeper's chest) and *plight her troth* (swear – that
she will do no harm). And so he (Edgar) can bid all
witches *aroint* (begone!).

115   *'old* wold (rolling upland)

124   *todpole* (an alternative form of 'tadpole')

      the wall-newt and the water the lizard and the water-
newt

124–5 *in the fury of his heart, when the foul fiend rages* (when
the fit of madness is on him)

126   *sallets* salads, tasty morsels

      the ditch-dog the dead dog thrown into a ditch

127   *the green mantle of the standing pool* the scum of the
stagnant pond

128   *whipped from tithing to tithing.* Elizabethan law required
vagabonds to be whipped publicly and sent into another
parish (*tithing*), where presumably the same thing happened again.

      stock-punished set in the stocks

129–30 *three suits . . . six shirts* (the allowance of a servingman,
such as Edgar alleges he has been (line 82))

132–3 *But mice . . . seven long year.* This is a version of a
couplet from the popular medieval romance, *Bevis of
Hampton.* In the old-fashioned language of *Bevis*, *deer*
means 'animals'.

134   *Beware my follower! Peace, Smulkin!* Edgar warns
them of the dangers of his familiar spirit or devil,
called Smulkin after one of the devils in Harsnet's
Declaration. The name must have been suggested by
mice, since in Harsnet Smulkin went out of the
possessed man's right ear 'in the form of a mouse'.

136–7 *The prince of darkness is a gentleman; Modo he's called and Mahu.* To Gloucester's complaint about the company, Edgar replies that the devils he has about him are noblemen. In Harsnet, Modo and Mahu are grand commanders of legions of devils.

138–9   *Our flesh and blood ... doth hate what gets it* our children hate their parents

138   *vile.* See the note on III.2.71.

139   *gets* begets

140   *Poor Tom's a-cold.* Edgar fends off the relevance of Gloucester's complaint about his son by retreating into the role of the Bedlam beggar.

147   *philosopher* (expert in 'natural philosophy' or science. Perhaps it is Edgar's 'philosophical approach' (that is, acceptance of his hardships) that gives Lear the idea that he is a philosopher.)

148   *the cause of thunder* (one of the 'secrets of nature' which a 'philosopher' or professional wise man would be expected to explain. It is apposite both to the immediate weather and to the larger questions of God's justice.)

150   *learnèd Theban* Greek sage

151   *What is your study?* in which branch of learning do you specialize? Edgar picks up *study* in the other sense: 'zealous endeavour'.

152   *prevent* forestall

154   *Importune* (accented on the second syllable)

160   *outlawed from my blood* (1) legally made an outlaw (as in II.1.59–62 and 109–10); (2) disowned as my son and heir (II.1.82–4)

164   *I do beseech your grace –.* Some action is clearly intended. The New Cambridge edition suggests: 'Gloucester takes his arm, trying to separate him from his "philosopher"; Lear refuses'.

       cry you mercy I beg your pardon (I didn't notice you)

169   *With him!* Both words are heavily emphasized. Lear is impatient of the efforts to divert him from the conference with his 'philosopher'.

170   *still* continuously

171   *soothe him* humour him

172   *Take him you on.* Kent should take ahead the 'philosopher' Edgar so that Lear can be persuaded to follow to the farmhouse.

175   *No words. . . . Hush!* (presumably an indication (to the audience) that they are approaching the castle)

176   *Child Roland to the dark tower came* (perhaps another line from a romance. *Child* is '*Infante*' ('Prince'); Roland or Orlando is the most famous of Charlemagne's paladins. The *dark tower* is certainly Gloucester's castle in the immediate reference, sinister enough in the *King Lear* story, whatever it may have been in the lost Roland story referred to here.)

177–8   '*Fie, foh, and fum, | I smell the blood of a British man.*' Here the Roland fragment seems to modulate into 'Jack, the Giant-killer'. It may be no accident that Edgar, returning to his home, remembers the story of another son's triumphant return. The *tower* may have suggested the beanstalk.

III.5   The final fruits of Edmund's 'nature' are shown in the planned destruction of his natural father, his adoption into the love of Cornwall, and his acquisition of the 'legitimate' title of Earl of Gloucester.

2   *censured* judged

2, 3   *nature . . . loyalty* family affection . . . loyalty to the state

3   *something fears me* somewhat concerns me

6–7   *a provoking merit set a-work by a reprovable badness in himself.* This is puzzling, because it is not clear whether the reference is to Edgar or Gloucester. Most probably the meaning is: 'The fact that death was only Gloucester's due reward (*merit*) must also have provoked Edgar to act; but a man must be bad before he will allow himself to be provoked to parricide for such a reason'.

9   *to be* that I am
       just loyal to the state

9–10   *approves him an intelligent party to the advantages of*
       France proves that he is a spy, seeking to give advantage
       to the French side

17–18 *that he may be ready for our apprehension* so that we may
       arrest him without any trouble

19   *comforting* giving aid to

20   *stuff his suspicion more fully* augment Cornwall's
       suspicion of Gloucester as a spy
       persever (equivalent to the modern 'persevere', but
       with the accent on the second syllable)

22   *my blood* my natural loyalty to my father

III.6   The scene takes us inside the farmhouse towards which
         Gloucester was conducting his companions at the end
         of III.4. The antiphonally placed voices of the three
         madmen – lunatic King, court fool, feigned Bedlam –
         weave the obsessive themes of betrayal, demoniac
         possession, and injustice into the most complex lyric
         structure in modern drama.

2   *piece out* augment

6   *Fraterretto* (one of the demonic names in Harsnet)

7   *Pray, innocent* (often thought to be addressed to the
         Fool (the *innocent*))

10   *yeoman* (a man who owns property but is not a gentle-
         man, that is, does not have a coat-of-arms)

15–16   *To have a thousand . . . upon 'em.* While Edgar
         and the Fool follow their separate trains of
         thought, Lear's mind is fixed on Gonerill and Regan;
         here he imagines them suffering the torments of
         Hell.

17   *bites* (the foul fiend in the form of a louse or flea; com-
         pare III.4.152)

18   *the tameness of a wolf.* The implication is that the wolf
         can never be tamed.

18–19   *a horse's health*. 'A horse is above all other animals subject to diseases' (Dr Johnson).

20   *arraign them*. Lear abandons the idea of the torments of Hell, and turns to the image of a trial for Gonerill and Regan.

21   *justicer* judge

23   *he* (possibly Lear, but probably 'the Fiend', with whom Edgar's speeches are continuously concerned)

23–4   *Want'st thou eyes at trial, madam?* The *madam at trial* must be Gonerill or Regan; but it is not clear what *Want'st thou eyes* means. It must connect with the glaring of the fiend in the previous sentence. Perhaps it means 'Can't you see who's looking at you?'

25–6   *Come o'er the burn . . . hath a leak*. Edgar sings a snatch of popular song, which the Fool completes, providing a reason (doubtless obscene) why Bessy should avoid having to do with her lover. See page 344.

29–30   *in the voice of a nightingale* (no doubt suggested by the Fool's singing)

30   *Hoppedance* (derived from Harsnet's 'Hoberdidance')

31   *white herring* unsmoked herring

     Croak. The Elizabethans spoke of 'croaking guts' where we speak of 'rumbling tummies'. The noise is supposed to indicate hunger, which explains the next sentence. In Harsnet some 'croaking' was said to be the voice of a demon.

     black angel. Black being the devil's colour, a *black angel* would be a demon.

33   *amazed* (stronger than the modern sense) in a maze dumbfounded

34   *cushings* (an earlier form of 'cushions')

35   *their evidence* the witnesses against them

36   *robed*. This no doubt refers to Tom's *Blanket* (II.3.10).

     thy place (on the judges' bench)

37   *yokefellow* fellow

     yokefellow of equity. The Courts of Justice and of Equity were the two main branches of the English legal system. In this trial, exceptionally, the two are combined (as at the trial of Mary, Queen of Scots).

38   *Bench by his side* join him on the judges' bench
      commission (a body to whom power (in this case, judicial power) is delegated from the crown, specifically 'the commission of the peace', the body of justices of the peace)

41-4 *Sleepest or wakest . . . no harm.* Dr Johnson remarked: 'This seems to be a stanza of some pastoral song. A shepherd is desired to pipe, and the request is enforced by a promise that though his sheep be in the corn, i.e. committing trespass by his negligence, yet a single tune upon his pipe shall secure them from the pound'. The nursery rhyme of 'Little Boy Blue' is an obvious analogy.

43   *for one blast* as a result of even a single blast
      minikin (either (1) shrill or (2) pretty, neat, fine)

45   *Pur, the cat is grey.* The cat may be another demon or familiar, as often in witchcraft. *Pur* may be the noise it makes, or its name ('Purre' is the name of a devil in Harsnet).

51   *I took you for a joint-stool* (a proverbial insulting 'excuse' for not noticing someone. A *joint-stool* is a stool made by jointing together pieces of wood.)

52   *another* (Regan)
      warped looks twisted, distorted features

53   *What store her heart is made on* what kind of material her heart is made of. Compare lines 75–6.

54   *Arms, arms, sword, fire!* It is not clear what *fire* is doing in this list, which is concerned with means of stopping Regan's escape. If 'fire' could mean 'fire your muskets', this would be acceptable; but there is no evidence that the word could be so used in 1605.
      Corruption in the place! Even the court of law is corrupt; the judge has connived at the prisoner's escape.

56   *Bless thy five wits!* Edgar lapses into his jargon (compare III.4.55), unable, as his next utterance shows, to sustain his part in the charade.

61–2   *The little dogs and all . . . they bark at me* I am now so despicable that even the little lap-dogs (perhaps bitches, by their names) know they can bark at me

65   *or . . . or* either . . . or

66   *Tooth that poisons.* The only sense in which a dog's tooth *poisons* is through rabies.

68   *brach or lym* bitch-hound or bloodhound

69   *bobtail tike* cur with its tail 'bobbed' (cut short)
       trundle-tail dog with a long drooping tail trundling (trailing) behind it

72   *leapt the hatch* jumped over the closed lower half of a divided door

73   *Do, de, de, de.* At III.4.56 a similar collection of syllables was supposed to represent Tom's teeth chattering.
       Sese. Most editors change to 'Sessa', but one unexplained sound seems as good as another. Compare III.4.97.

73–4   *Come, march . . . market-towns.* Tom addresses himself, to take his attention away from the painful scene before him. He resolves to set out for the places of resort most likely to yield good begging.

74   *thy horn is dry* (a formula used by the Bedlamites in begging for drink. It appears that they wore an ox-horn round their necks into which they poured the drink that was given them. In the present context it must also mean 'I have no more words for this situation'; in this scene Edgar says no more in his Tom persona.)

75   *anatomize* dissect

75–6   *what breeds about her heart* (as if some hard deposit was forming on it. Lear's mind may have moved in this direction because of Edgar's *dry* (line 74) and his reference to *horn*, which is formed by the process to which Lear alludes in reference to Regan's heart.)

76-7   *Is there any cause in nature that makes these hard hearts?*
        Hard hearts were well-known theological phenomena,
        caused by falling from grace. Despairing of super-
        natural causes, Lear asks for a natural, anatomical,
        reason.

77   *entertain* take into my service

78-9   *fashion of your garments ... Persian.* Tom's blanket
        now reminds Lear of the traditionally pompous gar-
        ments of the Persians.

81-2   *draw the curtains. So, so.* Lear imagines himself on a
        luxurious bed, with his servant drawing the bed-
        curtains.

82   *We'll go to supper i'the morning.* Lear presumably re-
        members he has not had his supper. 'Never mind,' he
        says to himself, 'we can eat it at breakfast time.'

83   *I'll go to bed at noon.* These are the last words that the
        Fool speaks in the play and they have been thought
        (rather sentimentally) to refer to his going to his grave
        in the prime of life. But they are more likely to draw on
        the proverbial sense of *going to bed at noon*: that is,
        'playing the fool'.

89   *drive.* The *litter* is presumably horse-drawn.

94-5   *to some provision | Give thee ... conduct* take you where
        you can get supplies

96   *balmed thy broken sinews* healed your shattered nerves.
        Shakespeare gives to Lear the physical condition that
        followed torture on the rack; but the rack he has been
        on is a mental one.

98   *Stand in hard cure* will be hard to cure

100-101 *When we our betters see bearing our woes, | We scarcely
        think our miseries our foes* it is so disturbing to see our
        superiors oppressed by the same miseries as beset us
        that we almost cease to notice our own pains; we begin
        to think of these pains as not ours at all, but only
        levelled against the superior people

102-3 *Who alone suffers, suffers most i'the mind, | Leaving free
        things and happy shows behind* the principal suffering of

the man who suffers on his own is the sense of having left behind him the whole world of carefree lives and joyful sights

104–5 *But then the mind much sufferance doth o'erskip | When grief hath mates, and bearing fellowship* we avoid much suffering when we know other people in the same plight who have to bear the same woes (a proverbial idea)

106 *portable* bearable

108 *He childed as I fathered* he with children who seek his life, as I have a father who seeks my life

109 *Mark the high noises* watch what's going on in the world of important people
thyself bewray reveal yourself (as Edgar)

110–11 *When false opinion, whose wrong thoughts defile thee, | In thy just proof repeals and reconciles thee* when the false story about you, which has made you seem morally corrupt, is proved wrong and you are shown to be just, so that you can be recalled to your true station and reconciled (with your father)

112 *What will hap more* whatever else happens

113 *Lurk* keep in hiding

I.7 The violent assaults on the mind and dignity of Lear are now paralleled by a physical assault on the eyes of Gloucester. No counter-movement is strong enough to stop this barbarism; but the intervention of the servants marks the beginning of an upswing of the pendulum. A first defeat for wickedness appears in the death of Cornwall.

1 *Post speedily* hasten
my lord (of Albany)

2 *this letter* (the letter about Cordelia's landing that Gloucester told Edmund about (III.3.9) and that Edmund conveyed to Cornwall (III.5.9))

7 *sister* sister-in-law (Gonerill, on her way to Albany)

9–10   *Advise the Duke where you are going to a most festinate preparation* advise the Duke of Albany, to whom you are going, to make speedy preparations (for war)

10–11   *Our posts shall be swift and intelligent* our couriers will move rapidly and convey full information

12   *my lord of Gloucester*. Edmund has already been promoted though his father is still alive. Compare line 14.

16   *Hot questrists after him* eagerly searching for him. 'Questrist' seems to be Shakespeare's invention (from 'quest').

17   *the lord's* (Gloucester's)

24   *pass upon his life* pass a death sentence on him

25–6   *our power | Shall do a curtsy to our wrath* we will use our power (as co-sovereigns) in a way that gives precedence to our wrath

26   *curtsy*. I have modernized to the form that gives the better rhythm, and (marginally) the better sense, but we should notice that 'courtesy' and 'curtsy' were not distinguished by the Elizabethans.

27   *control* curb, restrain

28   *Ingrateful fox*. He has shown ingratitude by failing in loyalty to his *arch and patron* Cornwall; he has been foxy in his sly and secretive dealing with Lear and his friends.

29   *corky* dry, withered

33   *none* no traitor

37   *Naughty* wicked

39   *quicken and accuse thee* come to life (as people) and speak against your actions

40   *hospitable favours*. This is usually said to mean 'the features (*favours*) of your host'; but perhaps 'the indulgences of my hospitality' is simpler.

41   *ruffle thus* treat with this outrage

42   *late* lately

43   *Be simple-answered* give us a straight answer

45   *footed* landed

46   *To whose hands you have sent the lunatic King?* This

completes the question begun in line 44. *Lunatic King* is a good example of Shakespearian foreshortening: Regan has had no opportunity to learn about Lear's lunacy.

51　　*at peril* under the threat of punishment

53　　*I am tied to the stake, and I must stand the course* like a bear in bear-baiting, I am tied to the stake, the dogs are attacking me, and I must endure it till the bout is ended

57　　*anointed flesh*. The holy oil with which he was anointed at his coronation sanctified his person, and made physical assault on him a sacrilege.

　　　　rash boarish fangs. Rash, the Q reading for F's 'sticke', is not only more picturesque but also more accurate, since it is the hunting term for the slashing sideways movement of the boar's tusks. The three 'sh' sounds in the line imply a slow deliberate delivery.

59–60　*would have buoyed up | And quenched the stellèd fires* would have risen up, like a buoy on the swell, high enough to extinguish the stars (with the implication of formlessness overcoming the pattern of order)

60　　*stellèd fires*. The context shows that these must be the stars. 'Stelled' is not known elsewhere as an adjective. Shakespeare uses it as a participle, meaning 'delineated'; but it is easier to suppose that here he is making up a new word, meaning 'starry', from the Latin *stella*.

61　　*holp* (old form of the past tense of 'help')

62　　*dern* dread, dark

64　　*All cruels else subscribe*. This is a famous crux, for which any interpretation must be tentative. One problem is whether the clause belongs with what precedes or what follows. Supposing the former, I suggest 'Assent to any other cruel thing you like (but open the door to these poor creatures)'; the usual interpretation is: 'All other cruel creatures yield to pity (so you should do so too, and turn the key)'.

65　　*wingèd Vengeance*. Perhaps this means only 'swift

vengeance'; but it is more likely to imply vengeance as an angel of divine wrath.

75–6   *If you did wear a beard upon your chin* | *I'd shake it* if you were a man I would attack you

77   *My villain!* my serf (daring to argue with me! – the same point as in line 79)

78   *the chance of anger* the risk of what may happen when angry men fight

82   *Lest it see more, prevent it* so that your remaining eye shall not see any more mischief done to Cornwall, I will anticipate the mischief, on that very eye

    vile. See the note on III.2.71.

85   *enkindle all the sparks of nature* let your family loyalty blaze into anger

86   *quit* repay

88   *overture* (accented on the second syllable) revelation

90–91   *Edgar was abused.* | *Kind gods, forgive me that.* Gloucester's insight into moral and factual truth comes with great suddenness: 'So Edgar was slandered – forgive me for my part in that'. Note the absence of recrimination and the assumption that normal goodness still exists.

93   *How look you?* how do you look on yourself, how are you?

97   *Untimely.* Cornwall's one feeling seems to be regret that the wound will interfere with his schedule for leading the army against Cordelia.

100   *meet the old course of death* die in the normal way

101   *Women will all turn monsters* (a repetition of the point made about men in lines 98–9: 'In that case women too will lose their moral sense, and behave monstrously')

103   *roguish madness.* This is the reading of Q uncorrected; Q corrected omits *roguish.* The epithet seems, however, too Shakespearian to be accidental and we must suppose that the corrector made a slip.

104   *Allows itself to anything* lends itself to any task that may be imposed on him

V.1   A scene showing the struggle to recover meaning and value in the world. Edgar's determination to endure and Gloucester's determination to die counterpoint one another in a tone moving between the grotesque and the affectionate.

1–2   *better thus, and known to be contemned,* | *Than still contemned and flattered* it is better to be a beggar and know what people think about you (contempt) than to be despised (as at a court) though flattered. The punctuation in F and that in Q both allow the following phrase, *To be worst*, to be included in the sentence; but it seems better to attach it to the following lines, and F's punctuation can be read in this way.

3   *most dejected thing of fortune* thing most dejected (or cast down) by fortune

4   *Stands still in esperance* remains always in possession of hope
    fear (of something worse about to happen)

6   *The worst returns to laughter* any change, when you are at the worst, is bound to be change for the better

7   *Thou unsubstantial air that I embrace* (with my nakedness I embrace the air, and I approve of it, even though it is lacking in substance, in wealth, in gifts, in comforts)

9   *Owes nothing to thy blasts.* Because the wind's help led only to the worst, Edgar is free of obligation, and therefore can embrace his 'creditor' without fear.

10   *parti-eyed.* The uncorrected Q reading, 'poorlie, leed', was no doubt responsible for the F reading, 'poorely led'; but since this gives a modicum of sense it has been generally accepted. The Q correction, 'parti, eyd', on the other hand, must be the result of a second attempt to read the manuscript, and is the nearest to Shakespeare we can come. It is usually supposed to be unintelligible as it stands; but in F a comma is often a substitute for a hyphen, and may be so here. If we make this substitution we then have *parti-eyed*, a

phrase like 'parti-coloured' or 'parti-coated' (*Love's Labour's Lost*, V.2.754), 'party-bow' (the rainbow), 'party-flowers', or 'parti-membered' (having different members). *Parti-eyed* would mean 'having his eyes looking like a fool's coat in the red of blood and the white of eggs'. This provides a grotesque image, but there is no shortage of these in *King Lear*. Gloucester's eyes are the striking point about him, and Edgar would be expected to mention them. It may be better that he should refer to them as grotesque than dilute his response (and ours) by noticing only the social quality of his guide.

11–12   *But that thy strange mutations make us hate thee | Life would not yield to age* if it were not for these strange switches in fortune from good to bad, and the hatred of life that this generates, we would not be willing to accept old age and death (or perhaps 'we would not age at all')

18   *I have no way* I have lost my path through life

19   *I stumbled when I saw* when I had my eyes I missed my moral footing, and tripped over false judgements

20–21   *Our means secure us, and our mere defects | Prove our commodities* our possessions (such as eyes) make us secure or over-confident, and total (*mere*) deprivation may prove an advantage

22   *The food of thy abusèd father's wrath* I used you to feed my anger on, when I was deceived (*abusèd*)

23   *in my touch* by touching you

25   *Who is't can say 'I am at the worst'?* The scene up to this point may be taken as an illustration of the folly of Edgar's initial confidence in *To be worst.*

27–8   *The worst is not, | So long as we can say 'This is the worst'* the kind of consolation in which you say to yourself (as Edgar did in lines 1–6) 'I am now at the lowest point' is a sure indication of a buoyancy of hope that separates you from the real *worst*

33   *think a man a worm* (perhaps a reminiscence of Job

25.6: 'man a worm, even the son of man, which is but a worm')

36–7   *As flies to wanton boys are we to the gods; | They kill us for their sport* as playful and irresponsible boys make games out of the lives of flies, not really caring whether they live or die, so the gods (on this evidence) seem to be having fun with mankind's misery and death

37   *How should this be?* how can the mental even more than the physical condition of Gloucester have changed so radically?

38   *Bad is the trade that must play fool to sorrow* it is a bad business to have to spend your time uttering folly to a man (like my father) distressed by sorrow

39   *Angering itself and others* creating general anger, because of its inappropriateness

43   *I'the way toward Dover* along the Dover road

46   *'Tis the time's plague* it is the kind of horror appropriate to our times

47   *or rather do thy pleasure.* Gloucester withdraws the command, remembering that it is quite inappropriate to his condition; 'Do what you wish' is the most he is entitled to say.

49   *'parel* apparel

50   *Come on't what will* whatever may happen (to me) as a result

51   *I cannot daub it further* that's the best I can do (in pretending to be Poor Tom)

55   *stile and gate, horse-way and footpath.* Each kind of path has its appropriate obstacle – the stile for the footpath, the gate for the horse-way (bridle-path).

56   *Tom hath been scared.* The landscape is for Tom a series of places to be scared in, where the foul fiend has appeared.

58–60   *Obidicut; Hobbididence ... Mahu ... Modo ... Fliberdigibbet.* Harsnet's forms are 'Hoberdicut', 'Hoberdidance', 'Maho', 'Modu', 'Fliberdigibbet', and,

allowing for the probability that the Q reporters would
have difficulty in remembering these outlandish names
correctly, perhaps we should prefer Harsnet's spellings.
Q's 'Stiberdigebit' is a clear compositor's misreading
of a manuscript form like Harsnet's (F is defective at
this point). Compare the Q form at III.4.110: '*fliber-
degibek*'. Above (III.6.30) Shakespeare represents
Harsnet's 'Hoberdidance' as *Hoppedance*.

60–62 *Flibberdigibbet, of mopping and mowing, who since
possesses chambermaids and waiting-women.* 'Fliberdigibbet' is a dancing devil in Harsnet, and a 'flibber-
tigibbet' is a flighty chattering woman (hence,
presumably, Harsnet's devil's name). The vices he
represents here are in an appropriate key: *mopping and
mowing* – grimacing and twisting the face, like chambermaids in their mistress's looking-glass. There are three
'possessed' chambermaids in Harsnet.

61 *since* (since they left Tom)

64 *Have humbled to all strokes* have brought to the acceptance of every kind of misery

64–5 *That I am wretched | Makes thee the happier* (since (as
in III.6.104–5) misery loves company)

65 *Heavens deal so* (so that one man's misery should be
comforted by another's)
still always

66 *the superfluous and lust-dieted man* the man who has too
much (compare *superflux*, III.4.35) and who sates himself on his pleasures

67 *slaves your ordinance* does what he likes with (makes a
slave out of) the divine rule (that one man should help
another)

67–8 *will not see | Because he does not feel. See* means 'under-
stand' and *feel* 'have fellow-feeling with'; but
Gloucester is also thinking of his own condition,
brought to 'see' how things are when he can only
know them by touch. Compare lines 23–4.

69 *So distribution should undo excess* (the gods' powers

would deprive the superfluous man of his excess and *shake the superflux* to those in need)

72 *bending* bending over, overhanging

73 *fearfully* frighteningly

confinèd shut in (by the land on both sides of the English Channel)

IV.2   The upswing towards good is advanced by an extraordinary and unprepared volte-face. Albany has now become a man of clear moral commitment (though less clear in his commitment to action), opposed to the faction of his wife Gonerill and her intended paramour, Edmund.

1-2   *Welcome ... way.* She welcomes him to her castle, where they have now arrived. She is surprised that her house-keeping husband has not come out of the castle to greet them.

8   *sot* fool

9   *turned the wrong side out* (that is, reversed the moral judgements – called Gloucester's loyal service *treachery* and Edmund's treachery *loyal service*)

11   *What like* what he should like

12   *cowish* cowardly, effeminate

13   *undertake* take responsibility for any enterprise

13-14   *He'll not feel wrongs | Which tie him to an answer* he will ignore insults which require him to 'answer' them by challenging the wrong-doer to fight. It is for this reason he is ignoring the French invasion.

14-15   *Our wishes on the way | May prove effects* what we talked of and wished for as we came here together may well come to pass. Presumably the idea of Albany's cowardice gives Gonerill the further idea of getting rid of him, so making effective their wish for union.

15   *my brother* my brother-in-law (Cornwall)

16   *Hasten his musters* speed up his enlistment of soldiers

powers troops

17   *I must change arms* . . . (1) I must change into military
      accoutrements; (2) my husband and I must exchange
      the work we do with our arms: he must take the dis-
      taff, and I will get the sword

20   *in your own behalf* thinking of yourself (and not of
      your loyalty to the cause)

21   *mistress* (with a *double-entendre*)

21-8 *mistress's command* . . . *bed*. The passage is full of
      sexual innuendoes stronger than anything said expli-
      citly, as in *stretch thy spirits, Conceive, ranks of death,
      services, usurps my bed*.

24   *Conceive* think what this implies

25   *Yours in the ranks of death.* Edmund slightly over-acts
      the role of swashbuckling lover that has been foisted
      on him, though Gonerill does not seem to notice any-
      thing amiss.
      death (often used as a metaphor for 'orgasm')

27   *a woman's services* (the service that a woman naturally
      gives to a real *man*)

28   *A fool usurps my bed* I am possessed by a fool (Albany)
      who does not know how to command. The uncorrected
      Q reading, 'My foote usurps my body', is the source
      of F's 'My Foole usurpes my body'; Q corrected
      reads 'A foole usurps my bed', which implies a
      second look at the manuscript, whereas the F reading
      need imply no more than an obvious correction of the
      copy-text (Q uncorrected). *Bed* seems better in mean-
      ing also, since it is the connubial possession of her she
      objects to rather than sexual possession. Compare
      IV.6.265-6, where in her letter of *mistress's command*
      she speaks of *his bed my gaol ; from the loathed warmth
      whereof deliver me.*

29   *I have been worth the whistling.* This is based on the
      proverb 'It is a poor dog that is not worth the whist-
      ling'. The meaning is: 'So you have decided at last to
      come looking for me, since even "a poor dog is worth
      whistling for" '.

30–31 *not worth the dust . . . your face.* Albany picks up *worth the whistling* and twists it round so that the sarcasm rebounds: 'Even the wind that cares nothing for you whistles as it throws dust at you and that's too good for you; that's how much whistling you are worth'.

31 *I fear your disposition.* That Gonerill was worthless and neutral (like the *dust*) would not cause *fear*; but her *disposition*, the tendency of her character, is not neutral, but frighteningly destructive.

32 *contemns its origin* disdains the source from which it springs (Lear in this case)

 its. Q uncorrected reads 'it', which could sometimes be used for 'its', but usually appears in Shakespeare in contexts of childish talk. The fact that the Q corrector changed 'it' to 'ith' implies either that he did not find the reading plausible or that it did not correspond to what he thought he saw in his copy. 'Ith' (that is, 'in the') does not make sense; but it would be easy to mistake 's' for 'h' in the manuscript.

33 *Cannot be bordered certain in itself* cannot be contained, or trusted to act in one way rather than another (and therefore must be *feared*)

34–5 *herself will sliver and disbranch | From her material sap* will tear herself from the stock on which she grew, as one tears a branch from a tree. *Material* means 'which gave her her (moral and physical) substance'.

36 *to deadly use* (a use proper to dead wood – to be burned. Compare Hebrews 6.8: 'But that which beareth thorns and briars is rejected and is nigh unto cursing; whose end is to be burned'. It may be that this is referred to below in *text*.)

37 *No more ; the text is foolish* stop preaching at me on a subject that makes no sense

38, 47 *vile.* See the note on III.2.71.

39 *Filths savour but themselves* filthy minds can only smell (and relish) their own odour

42   *head-lugged bear* bear pulled along by the ring in its nose (and therefore in no good temper)

44   *brother* brother-in-law (Cornwall)

45   *A man, a prince, by him so benefited* (a cumulative list of three reasons why Cornwall should not have acted thus: (1) he was a human being; (2) what is more, he was a prince, one with moral standards higher than those of mere humanity; (3) most of all, he was greatly in Lear's debt)

46   *their visible spirits* (not their invisible spirits (who are, presumably, all around us all the time) but manifest interventions, like those which will precede the Last Judgement)

49–50   *prey on itself | Like monsters of the deep.* The life of the sea creatures, where the big fishes eat up the little ones, was a common image of final moral disorder or chaos.

50   *Milk-livered man!* Gonerill can only see Albany's feverish moral vision as a result of lack of courage to seize the real situation, lack of blood in his liver, a substitution of female *Milk* for male blood. In this she resembles Lady Macbeth before the murder of Duncan.

51   *bear'st ... a head for wrongs* your head is only an object for other people to rain their wrongful blows on

52–3   *an eye discerning | Thine honour from thy suffering* a capacity to see how far endurance is proper and how far suffering ought to be resented and revenged. Compare lines 13–14.

54–5   *Fools do those villains ... their mischief* it is foolish to object to punishment which *precedes* crimes. Lear has not yet collaborated with the French, but he will; Gloucester's case must also be in the mind of Gonerill and of the audience, though Albany has not yet heard of his punishment.

56   *noiseless land.* Noise is made equivalent to warlike preparation or resistance: Albany should beat his drum and march against the enemy.

57   *thy state begins to threat.* The Q corrector's change
from 'slayer' to 'state' seems quite acceptable. A new
grammatical subject in line 57 could only weaken the
antithesis between *France* and *thou*. But the other
change – 'begin threats' to 'begins thereat' – cannot
be accepted as it stands, since it makes no sense. What
would be ideal would be a relevant word easily mistaken for 'thereat', but none has been found; *to
threat* makes good sense but it is not very like 'thereat'.

58   *a moral fool* foolish enough to sit and argue to moral
pros and cons (instead of taking up arms)

59   *See thyself* contemplate your own condition (not
mine)

60–61 *Proper deformity shows not in the fiend* | *So horrid as
in woman* devilish grimaces are uglier in a woman than
they would be on the devil's face, for they are appropriate (*Proper*) to him

62   *changèd and self-covered thing* one who has *changèd*
her appearance so that it no longer corresponds to her
reality, who has *covered* or concealed the fiend within
her behind the female graces of her external self

63   *Be-monster not thy feature* don't show in your external
appearance the monster that lives within you
Were't my fitness if it were appropriate for me

65–6 *dislocate and tear* | *Thy flesh and bones* dislocate the
bones and tear the flesh

66   *Howe'er thou art a fiend* however great a fiend you are,
in reality

68   *Marry, your manhood! Mew!* good heavens, you and
your talk of your 'manhood' (in shielding my *woman's
shape*)! I'll show you what I think of it. (*Mew* is a
derisive cat-call.)

73   *that he bred* that he kept or supported in his household
thrilled with remorse pierced through with feelings of
compassion

76   *amongst them* (presumably 'amongst the other servants')

78   *Hath plucked him after* has made him follow his servant into death

79   *justicers* (heavenly) judges
        nether crimes crimes committed down here on earth

83,   *One way I like this well. . . . Another way | The news*
86-7   *is not so tart.* These both refer to the same thought: Cornwall's death brings one step nearer the possibility of undivided rule over Britain.

85   *the building in my fancy* the dream of marrying Edmund that my amorous inclinations (*fancy*) have built up

86   *hateful* (because she will be left as Albany's wife, and will have to watch her sister enjoying Edmund)

90   *back* on his way back

.V.3   A series of short scenes (in or near Dover) marks, as often at this point in a Shakespearian tragedy, the alternate postures of the competing armies. But the battle in *King Lear* is less important than the moral attitudes of those involved. In IV.3 Kent and a Gentleman narrate the facts of the coming reunion between Lear and Cordelia, and (more important) the values that attach to Lear's shame and to Cordelia's radiant and healing beauty.

3   *imperfect* incomplete

9   *letters.* If the mission which the Gentleman undertakes to Cordelia in III.1 is the same one referred to here, the verbal message has been transformed into *letters.* This is understandable, as the inconsistency would allow Shakespeare to make better dramatic effects at both points.

12   *trilled.* The *Oxford English Dictionary* says that 'trill' implies 'a more continuous motion than is expressed by trickle'.

14   *her passion who* . . . her emotion which . . .

16–17   *patience and sorrow strove | Who should express her goodliest* her passions and her power of control appeared like competitors in her face and her temper, each seeming to make her more lovely than the other

19   *Were like a better way.* This is difficult to construe, and so to punctuate: *like* may refer back to *Sunshine and rain* (the smiles and tears were like simultaneous sunshine and rain), or it may mean 'were like one another' (each resembled the other and in this relationship revealed *a better way*), or perhaps 'were like a vision of the way to Heaven'. In any case the meaning aimed at must be that she expressed a new mode of connexion, not found in nature and better than what is found there.

20   *seem* (historic present. Since the eighteenth century this has been regularized to the past 'seemed'; but Shakespeare's usage elsewhere justifies the original reading.)

23   *a rarity most beloved* (as much sought-after and precious as *pearls* and *diamonds* – or the beauty of Cordelia in her patience)

24   *become* adorn
       verbal in words (beyond what was conveyed by her looks)

25–6   *heaved the name of father . . . as if it pressed her heart.* The use of *heave* and *heart* should remind us of *I cannot heave | My heart into my mouth* in I.1.91–2. Cordelia is throughout the play characterized by a lack of fluent rhetoric.

29   *Let pity not be believed* let me believe (on this evidence) that pity does not exist

31   *clamour moistened* sprinkled with this *holy water* the outcry of her grief

34   *one self mate and make* one and the same husband and wife. ('Make' like 'mate' can apply to either spouse.)

37   *the King* (of France)

42   *A sovereign shame so elbows him* a dominating sense of shame so crowds and jostles him

44   *foreign casualties* the chances of existence in a foreign land

51   *Some dear cause* an important reason. The real reason is Shakespeare's desire to keep the revelation of Kent's identity till the last scene.

IV.4   Cordelia enacts the part the preceding scene described. The fertile English landscape is used to evoke both the ungoverned wildness of the King (in preparation for IV.6) and the natural powers of restoration that Cordelia can call up.

       (stage direction) *with drum and colours* with drums beating and flags waving (indicative of battle order)

1   *he* (the one you have just been describing to me)

2   *mad as the vexed sea* tossed and turned by his passions, as unpredictable as the movement of a stormy sea

3-5   *rank fumiter . . . Darnel.* These flowers seem, so far as they are identifiable, to be of bitter, pungent, or poisonous kinds and therefore an appropriate 'crown of thorns' for the mad King; but they also reflect the state of natural growth to which he has allied himself.

3   *furrow-weeds* weeds that spring up in the furrows of ploughed land

4   *hardokes* (F; Q: 'hor-docks'; not accurately identifiable; sometimes equated with burdocks, hoar-docks, harlocks (= charlocks), and other possibilities)

5-6   *idle weeds that grow | In our sustaining corn.* Lear is associated with the rank and random uselessness of the weeds, set in contrast to the planned and useful grain which sustains life. The *century* of soldiers, the organized life of Cordelia's army, is, on the other hand, like the *sustaining corn*.

6   *century.* Is it an accident that Cordelia sends forth a hundred men to restore the King who lost his 'hundred knights'?

7   *the high-grown field.* It is now, for symbolic purposes,

high summer at Dover. The height of Lear's escape into 'natural' chaos is supported by a natural riot of vegetation.

8   *What can man's wisdom* what can human science do

10   *outward worth* wealth. We should recognize the same Cordelia as in I.1, despising the outward shows that others prize.

12   *foster-nurse* she who cherishes and supports

13   *provoke* induce

14   *simples* herbs
       operative effective

15–17 *blest secrets ... unpublished virtues of the earth,* | *Spring with my tears.* The hidden or unknown recuperative powers of herbs are to spring out of the earth as the herbs themselves do after a spring shower.

17   *aidant and remediate* (rare words, with the sense of 'aiding and remedying', used here to fit into the remote and incantatory atmosphere of Cordelia's prayer)

19   *ungoverned rage* violent and unchecked temper

20   *means* (that is, his reason)

24   *It is thy business that I go about.* Cordelia forswears personal political ambition and proclaims Lear's restoration as her only war-aim. But the echo of Christ's answer when found by his parents in the temple, 'I must go about my father's business' (Luke 2.49), is presumably not accidental.

26   *importuned* importunate, beseeching. The Q reading, 'important', has the same meaning.

27–8 *No blown ambition ... But love.* 1 Corinthians 13.4–5 seems to have been in Shakespeare's mind: 'Charity ... is not puffed up, is not ambitious, seeketh not her own' (Rheims version). In the Bishops' Bible it reads: 'Love ... swelleth not, dealeth not dishonestly, seeketh not her own'.

IV.5   The self-seeking wickedness of Gonerill and Regan has found out its own punishment in the desire that both feel for the person of Edmund. General destructive hate here is in strong contrast to the love and protectiveness that was the keynote of the preceding scene.

(stage direction) *Oswald*. Oswald has delivered to Regan the letter that Gonerill promised to send at IV.2.87; and he has mentioned, it appears, that he is carrying another letter, from Gonerill to Edmund.

2   *with much ado* making a great fuss about it. This reflects Gonerill's view of Albany's moral scruples.

4   *Lord Edmund spake not with your lord at home?* Regan asks Oswald to confirm what he has already told her.

8   *Faith.* Regan's uncharacteristic oath is presumably designed to make palatable what may seem to Oswald to be a mere evasion.

9   *ignorance* lack of (political) understanding

13   *nighted* (1) benighted; (2) on which (since he is blind) night has fallen

13–14   *moreover to descry | The strength o'th'enemy.* The quick shift from moral pretension – which she does not properly understand – to practical political realities is typical of Regan.

20–21   *Belike – | Some things – I know not what.* . . . Regan's incoherence betokens her attempt to think how she can overcome her sister's advantage with Edmund and Oswald's unco-operativeness.

22   *I had rather –.* Presumably Oswald wished to state (once again) his loyalty to his mistress, in something like 'I had rather die than disobey my lady'.

25   *œillades.* This French word (defined in Cotgrave's French dictionary of 1611 as 'an amorous look, affectionate wink ... passionate cast of the eye, a sheep's eye') was almost naturalized in the Elizabethan age (in the pronunciation indicated by the F spelling, 'Eliads'), but has now reverted to foreignness.

26   *of her bosom* in her confidence

29   *I do advise you take this note* I recommend that you take note of what I am about to say

30   *talked* (here almost a technical term for the coming to agreement which preceded marriage)

31   *more convenient is he for my hand* it is more fitting that he should marry me. In normal parlance the lady's hand is *given* in marriage. Here, as elsewhere, Regan and Gonerill take the masculine role; their hands are not there to be given, but to seize on what they desire.

32   *You may gather more* I have left things unsaid, which you can well guess at

33   *give him this.* Some commentators assume that she gives a love-token rather than a letter. Certainly only one letter is clearly mentioned when Oswald dies – that from Gonerill; but it may be implied that he was carrying more than one (see the note on IV.6.248); one given by Regan at this point is not ruled out.

40   *What party I do follow.* Like a good politician Oswald seizes on the opportunity to conclude by expressing the solidarity of Gonerill and Regan.

IV.6   The expected reconciliation of Lear and Cordelia is postponed to allow the stories of the blind Gloucester and the mad Lear to cross and reach a common climax. This stupendous scene covers three different actions: (1) Gloucester in despair is brought to accept his lot by the strange exercise of falling over an imaginary Dover Cliff. This grotesque and emblematic episode prepares us for (2) the entry of Lear crowned with flowers, now the master of a torrential vein of mad moral eloquence. The broken reverence of Gloucester, never far from despair, and the free-wheeling phantasmagoric energy of Lear point up two opposite ways of reacting to oppression and impotence. But both are now in the care of loving children. The 'capture' and

cure of Lear belong to the next scene; in the third part
of this scene we see Gloucester saved from the courtly
wickedness of Oswald by the cudgel of Edgar (now
A most poor man). The denouement of the Gloucester
plot is prepared for by the time-honoured device of an
intercepted letter.

(stage direction) *in peasant's clothes*. This is added to
show that the Old Man has kept the promise given at
IV.1.49; Oswald below (line 231) calls Edgar a *peasant*.

1   *that same hill* the hill we talked about (Dover Cliff as
described in IV.1.72–3)

7–8   *thou speak'st | In better phrase*. (Edgar now speaks in
verse.)

11–24   *How fearful . . . headlong*. Marshall McLuhan calls the
Dover Cliff speech a 'Unique piece of three-dimen-
sional verbal art. . . . What Shakespeare does here is to
place five flat panels of two dimensions one behind the
other. By giving these flat panels a diagonal twist they
succeed each other, as it were, in a perspective from
the "stand-still" point' (*The Gutenberg Galaxy* (1962),
pages 16, 17). The set-piece description built up, layer
by layer, by accumulation of small details is designed
both to convey to the blind Gloucester the standards of
measurement he should apply to the precipice and to
convey to the audience the powerful and coherent
nature of poetic illusion, by which Gloucester's 'cure'
is to be effected.

13   *choughs* (pronounced 'chuffs'; members of the crow
family)

15   *sampire* samphire (or 'Saint Pierre'; a maritime rock-
herb, used in pickling, and gathered on cliffs for this
purpose)

18   *yon*. Here and at lines 118 and 152, F changed Q's
'yon' to 'yond'. This is a recurrent Folio mannerism,
spread across several plays, and seems to reflect its
modernizing tendencies (see the Account of the Text,
page 320) rather than its concern for accuracy.

yon tall anchoring bark that sailing vessel there at anchor

19 *Diminishea to her cock* looking as small as her cock-boat or dinghy

  her cock, a buoy her cock-boat looks as small as a buoy

21 *th'unnumbered idle pebble* the innumerable loosely shifting pebbles. *Pebble* is the old collective plural.

23–4 *Lest my brain turn, and the deficient sight | Topple down* lest I lose my mental (and physical) balance, so that the eyes which have failed me fall down with the rest of me

27 *Would I not leap upright* if I were as close to the edge as you are I would not dare even to jerk myself into an upright position (or 'dare to jump up vertically, so as to land on the same spot')

28 *another purse* (in addition to the one given at IV.1.63)

30 *Prosper it with thee* make it multiply when in your possession

32 *With all my heart* I endorse heartily what you have said; I am going to fare well where I am going (to my death)

36 *Shake patiently my great affliction off* end my painful life, but not in passionate despair

38 *opposeless* that permit no opposition

39 *My snuff and loathèd part of nature* the mere blackened wick of my senility, with its offensive smell – all that is left of the candle of my natural life

41 *Gone* I have gone (as he was instructed in line 30)

42–4 *I know not . . to the theft* I think that imagination may cause death when life gives itself up willingly

44 *where he thought* (at the foot of the cliff)

47 *pass indeed* pass away, die, in reality

49 *gossamer.* The Q and F spellings – 'gosmore', 'Goze-more' – indicate the expected two-syllable pronunciation.

52 *Hast heavy substance* are made of flesh, are not a ghost

53 *at each* one on top of the other

57   *chalky bourn* chalk boundary (of England: Dover Cliff)

58   *The shrill-gorged lark* even the lark with its shrill, penetrating voice

63   *beguile* trick

        beguile the tyrant's rage. Gloucester is thinking not of his own particular case, but of the traditional defence of suicide as it appeared among the Romans, and especially the Roman Stoics under the tyranny of such emperors as Nero or Domitian.

65   *Feel you your legs?* have you any feeling in your legs?

71   *welked and waved like the enridgèd sea* twisted and ridged like the waves of the sea. F's 'enraged' is an obvious vulgarization.

72   *happy father* fortunate old man. Here, as in lines 255 and 285, the true relationship is expressed by Edgar in a context which muffles its specific meaning.

73   *the clearest gods* the spotless and most pure gods

73–4   *make them honours | Of men's impossibilities* do things that are impossible for men to do, and so make themselves to be honoured by men

75   *remember.* Perhaps he remembers the fiend-like behaviour of the Bedlamite; perhaps he remembers the morality of endurance proper to a religious man.

76–7   *till it do cry out itself | 'Enough, enough', and die* till affliction itself tire of afflicting me and give up (as I have been tempted to do)

80   *free* unburdened by guilt or self-reproach. Typically, the moral poise that Edgar achieves here is immediately subverted by the entry of Lear.

81–2   *The safer sense will ne'er accommodate | His master thus.* This is usually said to refer to Lear's mad clothes ('Nobody sane would go around like that'). I take Edgar to be saying: 'Sights like this cannot be accommodated inside a sane view of the world', *His master* referring not to Lear, but to the possessor of such a *safer sense* ('saner view').

83–92   *they cannot touch ... Give the word*. Lear's madness
expresses itself in a string of commands and observa-
tions, entirely disjointed in content, but linked by
modulations of imagery. Thus *touch* – (1) arrest; (2)
test gold – leads to *coining*, which leads to *press-money*;
the idea of recruiting soldiers with *press-money* leads
to images of archery, of challenges, of *brown bills* (hal-
berdiers) and passwords – a tissue of ideas interrupted
only by the *mouse* and the *toasted cheese*.

83   *they cannot touch me for coining*. Coining lay within the
royal prerogative.

85   *side-piercing* heart-rending (but with a reminiscence of
Christ on the Cross (John 19.34))

86   *Nature's above art in that respect* (perhaps 'It is better
to be the king who creates the coinage than the image
of the king that the coin bears', for only the latter can
be counterfeited)

87   *press-money* (the sum paid to a recruit when he was
'impressed', seized for the army)

87–8   *a crow-keeper* (a farmer's boy, not a military expert)

88   *Draw ... a clothier's yard* extend the bow for the full
length of an arrow (a cloth-yard long)

90   *do't* (catch the mouse)
There's my gauntlet; I'll prove it on a giant. Lear throws
down his 'gauntlet' and challenges anyone (be he a
giant) to dispute his verdict.

91–2   *O, well flown, bird! I'the clout*. The *bird* may be a falcon,
or may refer to the arrow which hits the *clout* (the
target).

92   *Hewgh!* (the noise made by the arrow)
Give the word. For the first time in the scene, Lear
shows an awareness of other people beside him; and
his immediate impulse is to challenge them, demand
the password that distinguishes friend from foe.

93   *Sweet marjoram* (an appropriate password, since the
herb was used for diseases of the brain)

96   *Gonerill with a white beard*. It seems as if something in

Gloucester's action or tone of voice suggests flattery. I have suggested that Gloucester, when he recognizes the King's voice, falls to his knees like a loyal servant. Lear's mind immediately harks back to Gonerill as archetype of flatterers – and *this* Gonerill has a white beard.

96–7   *They flattered me like a dog.* As always, Shakespeare sees the dog species as characterized by false fawning on its master.

97–8   *told me I had the white hairs in my beard ere the black ones were there.* Since this refers to flattery, the *white hairs* must be those of wisdom rather than age. The *I* must be emphasized, for he is reminded of all this by the sight of Gloucester's beard.

98–9   *To say 'ay' and 'no' to everything that I said* agreeing (or pretending to agree) with everything I said

99–100   *'Ay' and 'no' too was no good divinity.* Several passages in the New Testament might seem to supply the *divinity* that the flatterers erred against. Matthew 5.37 – 'But your communication shall be yea, yea; nay, nay. For whatsoever is added more than these, it cometh of evil' – is possible as a source; the actual injunction is against the oaths that may be added to 'yea, yea' or 'nay, nay', but it is preceded by 'Neither shalt thou swear by thy head, because thou canst not make one hair white or black', which might seem to have suggested lines 96–8 here. In 2 Corinthians 1.17–20 Paul defends himself against a charge of lightness by asserting that 'our preaching to you was not yea and nay' (was not ambiguous).

102–3   *there I found 'em, there I smelt 'em out* in these matters I was able to see through their lies and discover them for the flatterers they were

106   *trick* individual peculiarity

107   *Is't not the King?* Nevill Coghill (*Shakespeare's Professional Skills* (1964), pages 25–6) says 'the act of homage that brings Gloucester to his knees, a loyal

subject, leaves him there a seeming culprit, for that is
how Lear interprets the ambiguity in kneeling; and
now Gloucester's guilt is to be thrust home'.

109   *thy cause* your case; the charge against you

110   *Adultery.* The key distinction here and throughout
the speech is between 'natural' or illegal sexuality,
which gradually moves from *Adultery, lecher, copulation*, to the more violent representation of *luxury,
pell-mell, riotous appetite*, and (on the other hand) the
legal proprieties embodied in the *King*, the *lawful
sheets*, the *women all above*. The process of the speech
mimics the collapse of these legal safeguards into the
horror of animal sexuality.

115   *kinder* (with the usual sense – 'more naturally child-
like')

117   *luxury* lechery
pell-mell (as if in headlong, indiscriminate, and con-
fused battle)
for I lack soldiers. Indiscriminate lechery is promoted
by the King, for surplus population swells his army.

118   *yon.* See the note on line 18.

119   *Whose face between her forks presages snow.* Her *forks*
are her legs. Her face *presages* or indicates that the
other face *between her forks* is frigid or chaste.

120   *minces virtue* affects virtue by a show of squeamishness

120–21   *does shake the head | To hear of pleasure's name* shakes
her head in disapproval at the very name of pleasure

122   *fitchew* polecat or weasel. 'Polecat' was a cant term for
a prostitute.
soilèd full-fed with fresh grass (and therefore bursting
with sexual enthusiasm)

124   *Down from the waist they are centaurs.* He means that,
like centaurs, they are bestial like horses (*soilèd horses*,
as above) below the waist. Centaurs were from early
times used as images of man's lustful animal im-
pulses.

126   *girdle* waist

126 *inherit* possess, hold power over

128-9 *hell ... darkness ... the sulphurous pit – burning, scalding, stench, consumption.* The obvious sexual references point to a climax of hysterical disgust at female sexuality. At the same time the fairly free verse form of the preceding lines breaks down into prose.

129 *consumption* destruction (especially by fire)

130-31 *Give me an ounce of civet; good apothecary, sweeten my imagination.* The imagination that has just conjured up *stench* and *consumption* needs a perfume to sweeten its atmosphere. For the purpose Lear will buy civet from Gloucester, now imagined to be an apothecary.

135 *piece of nature.* Probably *piece* has the sense of 'masterpiece'; but the following phrase suggests a contrast between this *ruined piece* (portion) and the *great world* or macrocosm also in the process of being ruined.

137 *I remember thine eyes.* In Lear's unsweetened imagination the horror of Gloucester's eyeless sockets provides an image of the world he recognizes, though he may not be able to recognize unmutilated forms.

138 *squiny* squint through half-shut eyes
  blind Cupid. Cupid's traditional blindness and romantic associations give a horrid appropriateness to the use of his name for Edmund's progenitor.

139 *challenge.* Lear seems to revert to the obsession of line 90.

142 *take this* accept this scene as real. (The speech is an oblique Shakespearian defence of the non-realism of what is before us.)

145 *the case of eyes* the sockets where the eyes used to be

146 *are you there with me?* is that the point you are making?

147-8 *in a heavy case* in a sad way (with a pun on *case* meaning 'socket')

150 *I see it feelingly* (1) I recognize it with keen feelings; (2) having no eyes, I can only 'see' it by the feel of it

151 *What, art mad?* Lear takes Gloucester's *see it feelingly*

in the sense of 'know it only imperfectly because I know it only by feel'; and says 'You must be mad to require eyes to know the way of the world; all the senses convey the same message, the same image of the world as a place of merely superficial social distinctions, with no moral basis'.

152   *yon*. See the note on line 18.

153   *simple* of humble condition

153–5   *Hark in thine ear – change places and, handy-dandy . . .* a whisper to the justice of the peace bribes him to reverse his decision. Then he is as like the thief as one hand is like another. Lear puts his hands behind his back and pretends to shift an object from one to the other. This is the guessing-game of *handy-dandy*: which hand holds the object? Here the object is social status, and it is mere luck to guess which thief is called to the dock and which to the bench.

William R. Elton, in *King Lear and the Gods* (1966), page 86, note 24, quotes Thomas Powell's *The Attorney's Academy* (1623), page 217: '. . . and play at handy-dandy, which is the guardian, or which is the fool'.

158   *creature* man in his lowest state and therefore nearest to the animal. 'Creature' was often used of the animal in contradistinction to the human state. An ironic awareness of this may be intended.

159–60 *a dog's obeyed in office* (obedience is given not to intrinsic worth but to the accident of status)

161   *beadle* parish constable (charged with the duty of whipping offenders)

       bloody (from the lashing)

164   *The usurer hangs the cozener* the big cheat is given the sanction of society and condemns the little cheat. In this period usurers or capitalists were acquiring respectability and were being appointed to offices such as that of magistrate, against the protests of preachers and poets.

165   *Thorough* (an alternative form of 'through')

    great vices do appear. The Q reading, 'smal vices do appeare', makes perfect, if fairly trite, sense. But F corrected it to 'great Vices do appeare', for no reason that is discernible, unless the corrector found it in his 'copy'. We must either accept *great* or explain it away. The F reading can be defended in terms of sense as well as of text: it is not the smallness of their vices that distinguishes the poor, but the exposure to which they are subject. It must be allowed, however, that the antithesis is somewhat muffled by *great*. If the corrector's 'great', written in the margin, was inserted by the compositor of F in the wrong place, we might suppose that 'do great appear' was the original reading; the rhythmical emphasis in the line would then, however, seem to be in the wrong place.

166   *Robes and furred gowns* (the robes of the judges, and perhaps also of the usurers, as in *Measure for Measure*, III.2.7)

    Plate arm in plate mail

167   *And the strong lance of justice hurtless breaks.* Notice the sense of effort conveyed by the sound of this line.

    hurtless without hurting

168   *a pygmy's straw* (a weak weapon, opposite to a strong *lance* (compare *Othello*, V.2.268–9: 'Man but a rush against Othello's breast, | And he retires'). The frogs in the pseudo-Homeric *Battle of the Frogs and Mice* carried rushes for spears. The parallel mock-battle of the cranes and pygmies was also well known in Shakespeare's age, but had not been described in so much detail.)

169   *able* fortify, give power and capacity to

170   *Take that of me.* What we think the exact sense of *that* is depends on whether we suppose that Lear is more obsessed with kingship or with corruption at this point. If he is concerned with his kingship, what he gives Gloucester to *able* him will be some document

of the royal prerogative. If corruption is uppermost
in his mind (as I suppose) what he gives is 'money',
and what *seals th'accusers' lips* is (as in lines 153–5)
a bribe. In either case his flowers would seem the only
things he can give.

171–3   *Get thee glass eyes ... thou dost not.* Lear returns, at
the end of his speech, to the subject with which he
started it – Gloucester's failure to 'see' without eyes.
You should be, he says, like a *politician*, one of those
vile persons concerned to control affairs through
'policy' or trickery, who have the art of seeming to
see what they cannot actually see (discovering, for
example, imaginary plots so as to justify repression).
You should be like them and conceal your blindness
behind glass eyes.

171   *glass eyes* spectacles

173–4   *Now, now, now, now! | Pull off my boots. Harder,*
harder – so. Exhausted by his speech, Lear sinks down
and gives the command that might accompany such a
feeling in ordinary life – on returning from hunting
or a journey, for example. The *so* implies satisfaction
when the job is done.

175   *matter and impertinency* relevant substance and ir-
relevancy

181   *wawl* cry out

184   *This's a good block.* It seems possible to detect a series
of actions here. In accordance with good Anglican
practice he takes off his 'hat' (his crown of flowers, I
suppose) when he begins to 'preach' (line 181). His
sermon has not, however, got beyond a line and a half
when his attention is diverted to the hat he notices he
is holding in his hand. *This's a good block*, he says:
'This is a well-made hat'.

185   *delicate stratagem* cunning trick

185–6   *to shoe | A troop of horse with felt.* The idea of the *felt*
no doubt comes from the hat-block mentioned before.
The horsemen so shod could steal up on Albany and

Cornwall (seen as responsible for their wives' crimes) and kill them.

186   *put't in proof* put it to the test

192   *The natural fool of fortune* born to be the plaything of fortune (just recently leading a charge against the sons-in-law, and now a prisoner)

194   *cut to the brains.* Notice how the expression combines both physical and mental wounding.

195   *seconds* supporters

196   *a man of salt* a man of tears

197–8   *To use . . . I will die.* The text is difficult to determine at this point. Q reads as here, except that after *dust* there is a new line and a new speech prefix: '*Lear.* I will . . .'. This suggests that something is missing, and the second Quarto (1619) supplies it: '*Gent.* Good Sir.' This is tempting, but there is no evidence that Q2's corrections of Q1 are the result of anything more than the compositor's ingenuity. F omits everything between *water-pots* and *I will die*, no doubt because the compositor's eye moved from 'I [Ay] and laying' to the 'I' in the same line.

198–9   *I will die bravely,* | *Like a smug bridegroom. Bravely* means not only 'with courage' but also 'in my fine attire' (flowers and all). It is this latter sense that leads to the image of the *smug* (neat, spruce) bridegroom.

202   *there's life in't* there's still a chance; at least I can make you run for your captive. Hearing them say that they obey him, he realizes that the captivity is not as absolute as he had supposed.
       and if

203   *Sa, sa, sa, sa* (a cry of encouragement to the hounds in hunting)

206–7   *the general curse* | *Which twain have brought her to.* On the most factual level the *twain* are Gonerill and Regan, and the *general curse* brought about in nature is the current state of Britain, with brother against

brother etc. (I.2.106–11). Behind this is the larger idea
of the fallen condition of mankind caused by Adam
and Eve (*twain*). On this level Cordelia is a Christ-like
redeeming figure.

208   *gentle* honourable

       speed you God speed you, God prosper you

210   *sure and vulgar* it's certain and everybody knows about
       it

210–11 *Everyone . . . Which can distinguish sound* everyone who
       has ears to hear

213   *on speedy foot* on foot, and advancing rapidly

213–14 *The main descry | Stands on the hourly thought* a sighting
       of the main force of their army is expected from hour
       to hour

218   *my worser spirit* (usually taken to be 'my evil angel';
       but it may mean no more than 'my ill thoughts')

219   *Well pray you* that's a good thing to be praying for

221   *tame to* submissive, resigned to

222   *by the art of known and feeling sorrows* as the result of
       the workings of sorrows that I have both felt in myself
       and known in others

223   *pregnant to* disposed to feel

224   *biding* place to stay

226   *To boot, and boot!* (probably means 'in addition, and
       may you make *boot* (profit) out of it')

       proclaimed prize outlaw proclaimed as having a price
       on his head

       Most happy! how lucky I am! The self-centred insen-
       sitivity of Oswald makes an effective contrast, set
       against the mutual support of the other characters in
       the scene.

229   *Briefly thyself remember* say your last prayer, and make
       it short

230   *friendly* (friendly to him, since he desires death more
       than anything else)

231   *bold peasant.* Oswald's words here, as well as the
       general affectation of his language, give Edgar the

idea of the vocabulary and the identity he can assume to answer him.

232 *published* proclaimed

233-4 *th'infection of his fortune take | Like hold on thee* his outlawry attach itself to you as well (for helping him)

235-40 *'Chill ... 'choud ... I'ce.* Edgar falls into the stage rustic (South-Western) of the time, in which 'I' is represented by 'Che' or 'Ich', so that 'I will' becomes *'Chill*; 'I should' becomes *'choud*; and 'I shall' becomes *I'ce*.

235 *vurther 'cagion* further occasion (in the sense of 'better cause'). *'Cagion* is stage rustic for 'occasion'; the F spelling 'casion' has some advantage for the mere reader, but the Q form may well preserve the noise made on Shakespeare's stage.

237 *go your gate* go your way

238 *And 'choud ha' bin zwaggered out of my life* if fancy talk had been capable of killing me

240 *che vor' ye* I warrant you

241 *costard* (literally, 'apple') head

ballow cudgel. The uncorrected form in Q is 'battero', which the corrector, obviously relying on native sense rather than authority, changed to 'bat'. F reads 'Ballow', from which word the uncorrected Q form must derive. 'Ballow' is not common, but J. Wright in his *English Dialect Dictionary* (6 volumes, 1898–1905) seems to have found some examples.

244 *'Chill pick your teeth.* This suggests that Edgar has now a sword or dagger in his possession. If so he must have acquired it from Oswald – who has still a rapier with which he makes *foins*. Perhaps in a first bout (at line 242) Edgar has his ballow, Oswald his sword and dagger; Edgar beats down Oswald's dagger and seizes it.

245 *foins* rapier thrusts (in the new Continental style)

248, *letters.* Two letters may be meant: (1) the one from
256 Gonerill read out below; (2) one from Regan, perhaps

given at IV.5.33 (see the note). However, only one
letter is mentioned below; and 'letters' can be used
in the plural with only singular meaning.

258   *deathsman* executioner

259   *Leave* grant us your leave

261   *Their papers* to rip their papers

263   *want* lack

264   *fruitfully offered* organized (by Gonerill) so that there
will be results

       There is nothing done. The victory will be meaningless.

267   *for your labour* (1) as a recompense for your labour;
(2) as a place for your (amorous) labours

268   *servant.* This is usually glossed as 'lover', but it may
be nothing more than conventional politeness. The
strange addition of Q, 'and for you her owne for
Venter', has not been explained, and seems best left
out of the text.

270   *indistinguished space of woman's will!* how far beyond
apprehension is the range of woman's lust!

272–3 *Here in the sands | Thee I'll rake up.* It is not clear how
this shallow burial of Oswald was accomplished on
Shakespeare's stage. Presumably Edgar had to drag
the body out of sight, either now (line 277) or at the
end of the scene.

273   *unsanctified* (a curious way of saying 'wicked', suggested presumably by the thought that the sands in
which he is proposing to bury Oswald – unsanctified
ground – are appropriate to the character of the man
buried)

274   *in the mature time* when the time is ripe

275   *ungracious paper* wicked letter

276   *the death-practised Duke* (Albany, whose death is being
practised or plotted)

278   *how stiff is my vile sense* how unresponsive and unpliant
my feelings are, *vile* (basely physical) in this very
incapacity to give way before *huge sorrows*

       vile. See the note on III.2.71.

279   *ingenious* fully conscious

282–3 *woes by wrong imaginations lose | The knowledge of themselves* woes would cease to know their own pain by entering into the illusions of the insane

IV.7   The reunion of Cordelia and Kent prepares the way for the reunion of Cordelia and Lear. The sense of awaking out of a nightmare of cruelty into a world of natural kindness makes this scene an island of paradisal calm in a maelstrom of horror.

3   *every measure fail me* no matter how much I try to do, I will not be able to do enough to recompense you. Cordelia and Kent pick up the arithmetical ideas about desert which prevailed in I.1.

5   *All my reports go with the modest truth* let not what you say of me be excessive but merely report the truth

6   *Nor more, nor clipped, but so* neither exaggerated, nor cut short, but just as they happened. The word *clipped* picks up the coinage idea implicit in *paid* above (line 4).

    suited clothed. Kent still wears the servant's livery he wore as Caius.

7   *weeds* clothes

9   *Yet to be known shortens my made intent* to reveal myself now would anticipate the plan I have made. It is not clear what Kent's *intent* could be – perhaps a last-minute climactic revelation. But it must be confessed that this suits Shakespeare's interests more obviously than Kent's. It is a regular characteristic of Shakespeare's dramatic art that he delays the penetration of disguise till the final denouement.

10   *My boon I make it* the favour I beg is

16   *Th'untuned and jarring senses O wind up.* The slackened strings of his mind no longer yield sense or harmony (true relationships) but jar against one another. He needs the pegs screwed up and the harmony restored.

17   *child-changèd* (1) changed (to madness) by the cruelties of his children; (2) (less probably) changed into second childishness

21, 23   DOCTOR ... GENTLEMAN. These are the speech prefixes given by Q. As F omits the Doctor from this scene, it allots both speeches to the Gentleman. All previous editors transpose the speeches, giving the first to the Gentleman and the second to the Doctor. See the next note.

22   (stage direction) *Enter Gentleman.* F has an entry for the Gentleman at the beginning of the scene (substituting for the Doctor); Q has no entry for him, but gives lines 23–4 as his first speech. The addition of his entry here restores Q's opening of the scene and its distribution of speeches at lines 21 and 23; and it explains why, at line 91 below, the Gentleman knows nothing of Kent's identity.

Enter ... Lear in a chair. This is the F reading; Q has no entry for Lear. In spite of some awkwardness there can be little doubt that F is correct. It restores Lear to his 'throne'; it makes his falling to his knees a plausible action, which 'discovery' in a bed (as indicated in many editions) does not. The entry at this point might seem too early; since Cordelia is asked to *Be by* in the next line it might be taken that her father is not present. I suggest, however, that, when Lear is carried on, Cordelia falls to her knees, at that point of the stage where she is standing. The Gentleman says *Be by* and prepares to wake him; Cordelia's *Very well* is not, however, followed by any immediate movement. The Doctor repeats the request in a less indirect form: *Please you draw near*, and only now does Cordelia move forward and kneel again by Lear's chair.

24   *temperance* calm behaviour

(stage direction) Shakespeare and his contemporaries often use music as part of a process of mental healing, or to represent dramatically the magic power or healing force of nature. Compare *Pericles*, III.2.93, *The Tempest*, I.2.392–4, and *Henry VIII*, III.1.2–14.

30   *white flakes* snow-white hair

31   *challenge* demand

33   *deep dread-bolted thunder* thunder with the thunderbolt that causes deep dread

35   *cross lightning* zigzag (fork) lightning
      perdu. A '*sentinelle perdue*' was an especially daring soldier who was placed (as a spy or a scout) so close to the enemy that he was considered virtually lost.

36   *this thin helm* (the thin hair of old age)

38   *fain* glad

39   *rogues forlorn* abandoned vagrants

40   *short and musty straw.* Long dry straw would make the best bed; short, broken-up straw, damp or mouldy, would not protect from the cold and wet.

42   *concluded all* come to an end altogether
      Speak to him. Cordelia's sense of shame and guilt, together with her temperament, so notably reticent in I.1, prompts her to retreat behind the Doctor.

45–8 *out o'the grave ... molten lead.* Lear supposes that he is experiencing the life after death (as in some sense he is). He takes it that Cordelia is in heaven and that he is in hell. The *wheel of fire* was a common apocryphal appurtenance of the Christian hell (as was *molten lead*). But these images may have more force today as expressions of the psychological torments of guilt.

47   *that* so that

53   *abused* 'in a strange mist of uncertainty' (Dr Johnson)

54   *thus* (thus bewildered and lost)

60   *fond* silly

64   *this man* (Kent)

65   *mainly* very much

71   *Be your tears wet?* (are your tears real, or am I still snared in illusion?)

76   *your own kingdom* the kingdom which is (still) yours

80   *even o'er the time* fill up the gap in time (by reliving the experience he has passed through)

82   *Till further settling* till he is better settled in his mind

83   *You must bear with me.* Presumably he leans on her as he leaves, so that the verb has both a physical and a mental reference.

85   *Holds it true* does it continue to be accepted as true

92   *look about* be wary

92–3   *The powers of the kingdom* the British forces (as against Cordelia's French ones)

94   *arbitrament* deciding of the dispute

96–7   *My point and period will be throughly wrought, | Or well or ill* the sentence of my life and my purpose will be brought to a fully worked-out conclusion or full stop, and it will be clear whether it has been for good or for ill

96   *throughly*. This, the Q reading – F omits the passage – is a common Elizabethan alternative for 'thoroughly'.

V.1   The snare of jealous lust draws more tightly around Regan, Gonerill, and Edmund. Meantime the preparations for the battle go ahead; but a further reckoning, beyond the battle, is prepared for.

1   *his last purpose* (to fight with Regan and Edmund against Cordelia)

4   *constant pleasure* settled resolution

5   *Our sister's man is certainly miscarried.* When Regan parted with Oswald (in IV.5) he was on his way to Edmund. She assumes that something has happened to him.

6   *doubted* feared

9   *In honoured love* in an honourable way. Edmund has become a (verbal) devotee to the idea of honour.

10–11   *found my brother's way | To the forfended place* played her husband's role in that part of her body *forfended*

299

('forbidden') to you (by the commandment against adultery)

12-13   *conjunct | And bosomed with her, as far as we call hers* coupled and intimate with her, to the fullest extent

15   *I never shall endure her* (that is, if the two of you become too intimate)

16   *familiar* unduly intimate

22   *the rigour of our state* the harshness of our administration

25-7   *It touches us . . . oppose* I am moved (to be *valiant* and fight) because this is a French invasion of Britain; but in so far as France's purpose is to embolden the King (and others with just cause of complaint) I am not touched. Albany's language is excessively harsh; the fact that Q is our only text at this point makes corruption a real possibility.

28   *you speak nobly.* See the note on line 9.
     Why is this reasoned? (what is the point of this academic talk about reasons for fighting? The important thing is to fight.)

30   *domestic and particular broils* family and individual quarrels

32   *th'ancient of war* the most experienced warriors

33   *presently* immediately

37   *the riddle.* Gonerill detects behind Regan's words the fear of leaving her with Edmund while she goes with Albany to the council of war.

40   *this letter* (the letter from Gonerill to Edmund which Edgar took from Oswald's dead body)

44   *avouchèd* guaranteed

46   *machination* (the plots and counter-plots that belong to the *business of the world*)

47   *I was forbid it* (by Shakespeare, who does not wish any anticipation here of the denouement in V.3)

52   *Here.* Edmund hands Albany a paper.

53   *diligent discovery* careful reconnaissance

54   *greet the time* go forward to welcome the occasion

56   *jealous* suspicious, watchful

61–2   *And hardly shall I carry out my side, | Her husband being alive.* The emphasis falls on *Her*. He is now talking about *enjoying* Gonerill. He cannot *take* Regan because of Gonerill's opposition; it is difficult to fulfil his side of the bargain with Gonerill (that is, satisfy her lust) because her husband is alive.

62   *Now then* let me see, let me think it out

63   *countenance for the battle* authority, support, while the battle is in progress

65   *taking off* killing

68   *Shall* they shall

69   *Stands* depends

V.2   Gloucester, still guided by Edgar, waits while Lear and Cordelia lose the battle.

1   *father* (as at IV.6.72, a general word of respect rather than a revelation of the particular relationship)

2   *host* shelterer

4   (stage direction) *Alarum and retreat within.* The climactic battle of *King Lear* is treated very cursorily. Shakespeare is interested in motives and in results, but the actual process of the battle is unimportant to him. The real battle between good and evil must be fought out elsewhere.

9–10   *Men must endure | Their going hence even as their coming hither* just as childbirth involves pain and trouble, so death is not just a matter of sitting and rotting, but a painful process that has to be struggled through till it be granted from above

11   *Ripeness is all* (man's duty is not to wait to *rot*, but to await the time of *Ripeness*, which is the time appointed for death. That is all that matters.)

V.3 In the chaos following the battle a still moment of resignation is achieved by the captive Lear and Cordelia. Albany strives to organize justice, and Edgar appears like a *deus ex machina* to defeat Edmund. The lust of the sisters destroys both of them. But the turn towards justice, which seems to be confirmed by the deaths of the wicked, is suddenly halted and even reversed by the entry of Lear with Cordelia dead from prison. His own death follows as a corollary on this; Albany and Edgar are left to bear *The weight of this sad time*.

1 *Good guard* keep a strict guard on them

2–3 *their greater pleasures ... That* the more explicit decisions of those who

16 *take upon's* assume the burden of

17 *God's.* I assume that only one God is meant, even though this requires a monotheistic faith from the pagan Lear.

wear out survive beyond

22–3 *He that parts us shall bring a brand from heaven | And fire us hence like foxes.* Foxes are driven out of their holes by fire and smoke (and then killed). But the fire that parts Lear and Cordelia will have to be more than human. Perhaps Lear is thinking of the final conflagration, at the Last Judgement.

24 *The good-years shall devour them.* It is not clear what kind of bogey-men are meant by *The good-years*. But the tone of the statement seems to be that of a father's homely reassurance to a frightened child.

fell skin

30–31 *make thy way | To noble fortunes* become a nobleman

31–2 *men | Are as the time is* moral principles change according to circumstances

33 *Does not become a sword* is not appropriate for a soldier

36 *write happy* call yourself a fortunate man

37 *carry it* arrange it

41   *your valiant strain* the valour that you have derived
      from your ancestors. Note the implicit denial, in this,
      of Edmund's bastardy speech, I.2.1–22.

46   *equally* with justice

49   *title* (1) kingship; (2) legal right to the possession of
      the land

51   *impressed lances* conscript pikemen (but the reverbera-
      tions of the strongly physical side of the image should
      also be noted: common humanity might turn back on
      us, and press their points into the very eyeballs which
      should control them in a commanding vision of how
      things must be)

57–8 *And the best quarrels in the heat are cursed | By those
      that feel their sharpness* even good arguments are hate-
      ful at this moment of passionate involvement, when
      we are all suffering the pains and losses of battle.
      Edmund stalls for time to get Lear and Cordelia
      killed, pretending that they would not, at the moment,
      get a fair hearing at their trial.

62   *we.* Regan has assumed the plural of royalty.

66   *immediacy* the condition of being 'immediate' to my
      sovereignty, next in line

69   *your addition* the title you have given him

70   *compeers* equals

75–9 *General . . . master.* Regan creates Edmund *General* of
      the city (herself) which she surrenders. He has con-
      quered her *walls* (her 'resistance') and now has the
      right to dispose of her soldiers etc. She gives in uncon-
      ditionally.

79   *enjoy him.* By linguistic convention, men 'enjoy'
      women, not vice versa. The application to Regan marks
      her masculine and commanding nature.

80   *The let-alone lies not in your good will* the power to
      hinder it does not lie within the scope of your consent

83   *hear reason.* Albany does not seem to be arguing for
      talk rather than action, since almost immediately he
      calls for the trumpet to sound. His speech contains

the details of the complex situation, the 'reasons' which will be needed to *prove title*.

84–5   *and, in thy attaint, | This gilded serpent* and I also arrest Gonerill who has provided the *attaint* or accusation against you. The F word, 'arrest', is clearly a mistaken repetition of the word in the line above. Note the style of this whole speech: Albany slips into the quasi-legal formality and paradox of the *deus ex machina*.

85   *sister* sister-in-law

87   *sub-contracted* (only *sub*-contracted because she is already contracted to Albany)

89   *If you will marry, make your loves to me.* If Gonerill and Edmund are contracted to one another, then Albany is the only man free to enter into a new relationship.

90   *An interlude!* what an old-fashioned little farce! 'Interludes' were short, often humorous, plays of the pre-Shakespearian period.

94   *make it* (perhaps equivalent to 'make it good', fulfil it)

95   *in nothing* in no point

97   *medicine* poison

98–9   *What in the world he is | That* whatever the rank of the person who

99   *villain-like* like a slave

103   *thy single virtue* your unaided valour

108–15   (stage directions) *A trumpet sounds.* . . . Considerable textual confusion surrounds this heraldic occasion. The text (line 112) speaks of three trumpet calls. F in fact has four, one before the reading of the challenge and three after; Albany commands the first and the Herald the other three. Q has three trumpet calls, the first commanded by a *Captain*, the second and the third by *Bastard* (that is, Edmund). Editors often try to compromise between the two versions, but since they are alternative organizations of the same thing it seems best to stick to one – F's in this case.

115 (stage direction) *a trumpet* a trumpeter

120 *canker-bit* worm-eaten

122 *cope* match

127–8 *Behold; it is the privilege of mine honours, | My oath, and my profession* see my sword; the right to draw it is the privilege conferred on me by my honour, by my oath of knighthood, and my religious vows (*professions*)

129 *Maugre* in spite of

130 *thy ... fire-new fortune* your new-minted rank as military leader and earl

134 *extremest upward* topmost part

136 *toad-spotted traitor* spotted (stained) with treason as the toad is spotted (allegedly with venom)

141 *thy tongue some 'say of breeding breathes* the way you speak gives some *assay* or proof of the quality of your upbringing. But perhaps F's 'say' only means 'speech'.

142 *nicely* by being meticulous

145 *the hell-hated lie* the lie (that I am a traitor) which I hate as I hate hell

146–8 *Which, for they yet ... rest for ever* the mere return of accusations to your head and heart glances off your armour; but my sword will push them straight into your heart, and there they will remain. *Which* probably refers back both to *treasons* and to *heart* ('into which').

146 *for* because

148, (stage directions) *Edmund falls. . . . to Edgar, about to*
149 *kill Edmund.* I have inserted these stage directions to explain Albany's words, which are not clearly directed in the text. Some have supposed that it is Gonerill who says *Save him, save him!*, which solves the problem in another way.

149 *practice* plotting

152 *cozened and beguiled* tricked and deceived

153 *this paper* (the letter from Gonerill to Edmund which passed through the hands of Oswald and Edgar. It is not clear if the 'stopping' is to be physical or mental.) *Hold, sir!* It is not clear to whom this is addressed.

Perhaps it is to Edgar, with his sword once again at Edmund's throat.

156   *the laws are mine, not thine* (presumably because she is the daughter of the sovereign (the source of legality), and Albany only the consort)

157   *Who can arraign me* (as sovereign she cannot be brought to trial)

159   *desperate* (in the state of despair, theologically defined as 'having lost any sense of Divine Grace', and therefore liable to commit suicide. This is why she has to be 'governed' or restrained.)

163   *noble* of good breeding. The same idea is picked up in Edgar's *no less in blood* ('of no worse breeding') in line 165. Edmund has relapsed from the revolutionary posture of his I.2 soliloquy into traditional conceptions of nobility and breeding.

166   *If more* if legitimacy confers more nobility than illegitimacy does

168   *our pleasant vices* the vicious acts which give us pleasure

170–71   *The dark and vicious place where thee he got | Cost him his eyes* (the darkness of sin resulted in the physical darkness of his blind state)

171–2   *'Tis true. | The wheel is come full circle.* Edmund picks up Edgar's point about the poetic justice of Destiny (*'Tis true*), and applies it to himself. He made Edgar his enemy, he embraced force and deceit as methods; and now the disguised Edgar has conquered him by force. We should remember how he alleged Edgar's sword had wounded him in II.1. Now he is killed by the method he used to start his career.

181–97   *The bloody proclamation ... Burst smilingly.* The narrative of important and moving events off-stage, told by a messenger, traditionally makes its effect by a more rhetorical, more statuesque mode than is usual in dramatic poetry. The example here (properly called a *period* – a classical paragraph – in line 202) involves continuously suspended syntax carrying the narration forward without a single full-stop.

181   *The bloody proclamation* (the proclamation (see II.3.1) that he should be put to death if found)

183–4   *we the pain of death would hourly die | Rather than die at once* we prefer to suffer the pain of death every hour of our life rather than die quickly and get it over with

194,   *his flawed heart . . . smilingly* his cracked (*flawed*) heart
196–7   burst under the contrary pressures of joy and grief; but this was not a death in despair; at the moment of death he knew joy

201   *dissolve* weep myself into liquid

202   *a period* a complete sentence, with its own consummation and final point of punctuation

203–5   *but another . . . And top extremity.* The first *period* was an 'amplification' (in the language of rhetoric) of one sorrow (Gloucester's); to amplify another sorrow (Kent's) in the same way would take one beyond the *period* (limit) of what one can stand. Kent's *period* is in fact shorter than Gloucester's.

206   *big* ready to burst forth

207   *worst estate* poorest condition (when he was Poor Tom)

209   *so endured* lived as Poor Tom

211   *threw him on my father* threw himself on the body of the dead Gloucester

214   *puissant* overpowering
       the strings of life the heart-strings (but I think the vocal cords are also in Shakespeare's mind: the violence of his outcry cracked both vocal cords and heart-strings)

216   *tranced* in a trance, unconscious

218   *his enemy king* (King Lear, who had (I.1.178) declared himself his enemy)

221   *smokes* steams

222   *from the heart of –.* The failure to complete the statement allows the *coup de théâtre* of suggesting for a moment that it is Cordelia who is killed.

227   *marry* join together

231–2   *the compliment | Which very manners urges* the formal
courtesies which good manners alone would cause us
to observe

233   *aye good night* farewell for ever. We are not told, and
need not know, whether Kent has a premonition of
Lear's death or assumes that his own death is immi-
nent, as may be suggested by *the strings of life | Began
to crack* (lines 214–15). In either case, his dramatic
task is done.

235   (stage direction) *brought out. Out*, in the theatrical
sense being used here, means 'out, on to the stage'; in
these terms 'in' means 'inside the stage-façade,
behind the stage'. F's '*brought out*' implies a theatrical
origin for the 'copy' behind it, just as Q's '*brought in*'
implies a literary 'copy' not used for stage purposes.
The dead daughters are all brought back on to the
stage to reassemble there the cast of I.1.

236   *object* spectacle of pity or horror

243   *brief* quick

249   EDGAR *Haste thee for thy life*. I follow F here (Q,
followed by many editors, gives the speech to '*Duke*' –
that is, Albany – and makes Edgar exit, bringing him
on stage again with Lear). Edgar must be placed on
the stage beside Edmund; he takes the sword from
him and gives it, with his instructions, to the Officer.

252–3   *blame upon her own despair, | That she fordid herself*. If
we compare the language applied in lines 289–90 to
the deaths of Gonerill and Regan (*fordone themselves, |
And desperately are dead*) we can see the ironic repetition of the first Act here: there is an attempt to make
Cordelia seem to behave in the same way as her sisters,
but it does not succeed.

254   *The gods defend her*. A. C. Bradley and others have
seen an ironic relationship between this and the stage
direction immediately following: *Enter Lear with
Cordelia in his arms*.

255   *O, you are men of stones.* I think that the primary idea
      here is of statues, silent, frozen-still (in horror), and
      impermeable by grief. The over-all image governing
      the following lines may be that of a funerary chapel or
      pantheon with statues and a vault: but as this is
      heaven's vault an intentional confusion between the
      living and the dead is created.

256   *Had I your tongues and eyes.* It is not clear how they
      could use their *eyes* to make *heaven's vault crack*,
      except that tongues used for outcry and eyes used for
      weeping come irresistibly together. Perhaps the only
      point made is that Lear's eyes are failing him (as in
      line 280). *Tongues* and *eyes* represent within the human
      microcosm the sources of thunder and lightning in
      the macrocosm – the vault of heaven. Thus the tempest
      is recalled.

260   *stone* mirror (perhaps short for 'specular stone', a
      species of mica, selenite, or talc)

261   *the promised end* the end of the world (as foretold in
      Mark 13). Kent may also mean 'the end that Lear
      promised himself when he divided the kingdom'.

262   *image* representation. Similarly, Macduff calls the
      death of Duncan 'The Great Doom's image' (*Mac-
      beth*, II.3.75).
      Fall and cease let the heavens fall and life on earth
      cease

269   *stay a little.* We should notice the ironic relation of
      this second (permanent) exile to the first.

272   *I killed the slave.* So much for the *noble fortunes*
      promised at line 31.

274   *falchion* (an old-fashioned word for sword, appropriate
      to the memory of Lear's youth, as is the 'long sword'
      that Justice Shallow (in *The Merry Wives of Windsor*,
      II.1.203) remembers from *his* youth)

275   *him.* This is F's reading; Q has 'them'. In meaning
      they seem to be indifferent – which gives F, the better
      text, the preference.

276 *these same crosses spoil me* these troubles of my old age have spoiled me (as a swordsman)

278-9 *If Fortune brag of two she loved and hated | One of them we behold.* The two people are clearly Lear and Kent, both fortunate and unfortunate in extreme degrees. Each beholds *One* – they are looking at one another.

280 *This is a dull sight* (often thought to be a complaint about his fading eyesight rather than a comment on what he sees before him)

285 *I'll see that straight* I'll attend to that immediately. Lear copes with the tedium of people who try to distract him from Cordelia by promising to attend to them later.

286 *your first of difference and decay* from the beginning of your change and decline of fortune

288 *Nor no man else.* This completes his preceding sentence (*I am the very man . . . Nor no man else*), but also begins his reply to Lear's *welcome* ('I am not welcome, nor is anyone else – *All's . . . deadly*').
 deadly death-like

289 *fordone themselves* destroyed themselves

290 *desperately are dead* have died in a state of despair. This suggests an assumption that they both committed suicide (even though we know that Regan was poisoned by Gonerill), thus bringing the moral pattern to a neat conclusion.

291 *He knows not what he sees.* The point seems to be that Lear's *sight*, rather than his utterance, has become imperfect. This ties in with *present us to him* in the next line and with the references above to failing sight (lines 256 and 280) – which do not fit with F's 'He knowes not what he saies'.

292 *bootless* useless, profitless

295 *this great decay* (Lear himself, and the situation which surrounds him)

296 *us, we.* Albany, as sovereign ruler of Britain, assumes the royal plural.

299   *With boot, and ... addition* with something extra (presumably new titles of honour)

302   *O, see, see!* What exactly draws their attention is not clear, but it must be some new posture of Lear as he cradles Cordelia in his arms, or picks her up again, or kneels at her side.

303   *my poor fool.* Presumably Cordelia is meant (since she is the centre of his attention, and was hanged), 'poor fool' being a common Shakespearian form of parental endearment. It is impossible to know if the reminiscence of the Fool's title is accidental or intentional. It has been suggested that the same boy actor played both parts; but the Fool is likely to have been played by Robert Armin (see Introduction, page 11).

    no life. I take it that Lear is making a general point ('Let all life cease') rather than the particular one: 'There is no life left in Cordelia'.

307   *this button* (presumably the button at his own throat, which seems to be causing his feeling of suffocation. But it could equally well be a button on Cordelia's garment.)

308   *Do you see this? Look on her! Look, her lips!* Clearly Lear imagines he sees Cordelia coming to life again. Whether this means that 'Lear dies of joy' (as A. C. Bradley suggested) or that he is in a mere delirium is more doubtful, and not very important for the play as a whole. It would be difficult for any actor to project a precise interpretation.

312   *the rack of this tough world* the torture-machine that stretches a man between hope and despair. The *tough* suggests that it is the body that is referred to, as the rack of the spirit.

321–4   *The weight ... live so long.* Q gives the final speech to Albany ('Duke'). Tragedies commonly end with a generalizing speech from the most senior survivor, and this may have been in the Q pirates' minds. F corrects to '*Edgar*', and certainly the *we that are young* sounds better in the mouth of Edgar. We may also notice that Albany in line 317 addresses both Kent and Edgar, and that (apart from this speech) Edgar has no reply.

321 *weight* sadness. The use of the word may imply that Edgar is already carrying Lear (or Cordelia) from the stage.

322 *Speak what we feel, not what we ought to say*. Regal formality has broken down into individual feelings. There may be in this an element of apology for taking the last speech from Albany.

AN ACCOUNT OF THE TEXT

The great difficulty in establishing an acceptable text for *King Lear* arises from the duplication of evidence, an embarrassment of witnesses whose credentials can be investigated but not finally tested. The text appears in two separate definitive editions, in the First Folio (1623) of Shakespeare's plays and in a quarto (small format) text of 1608: *M. William Shakespeare his True Chronicle History of the life and death of King Lear and his three daughters. With the unfortunate life of Edgar, son and heir to the Earl of Gloucester, and his sullen and assumed humour of Tom of Bedlam.* The title-page goes on to tell us that it is printed 'as it was played before the King's Majesty at Whitehall upon S. Stephen's night in Christmas holidays' – that is, on 26 December. The year must have been 1606, for the text was entered in the Register of the Stationers' Company on 26 November 1607, with the same title as above, and naming the same occasion of performance.

The entry may have been official but the consensus view among textual critics has been, for most of this century, that the 1608 quarto is in some sense a 'bad' quarto – one of those texts not supplied to the publisher by the acting company but obtained for publication by some more oblique method. In this sense it can be counted as one of the 'divers stolen and surreptitious copies' against which the editors of the First Folio warned their readers '. . . where before you were abused with divers stolen and surreptitious copies, maimed and deformed by the frauds and stealths of injurious imposters that exposed them, even those are now offered to your view cured and perfect of their limbs, and all the rest absolute in their numbers [that is, versification] as he conceived them'. This is, of course, advertising copy rather than fact, but (as in the best advertising copy) there is a grain of truth in it. The theatrical companies were always anxious to avoid premature publication of works whose value was enhanced by the theatres' monopoly. After about 1600 Shakespeare's company seems to have been very effective in preventing good copies of his plays from reaching print. The printers, however, retained their appetite for Shakespearian texts, and a small number of these (five in total) reached print. In all these cases it looks as if the route to the printing house was an illicit one. But that is not in itself a reason to suppose that a text so printed lacks authenticity.

Certainly, at a first glance, the 1608 *King Lear* seems to show signs of the deterioration one would associate with underhand procurement: lines cobbled together clumsily, verse collapsed into prose, prose turned into verse, sharp phrasings rendered as commonplace ones. An extreme example of the difference between Quarto and Folio can be seen in the last lines that Lear speaks in the play. These are printed in the Folio as

> Do you see this? Looke on her? Looke her lips
> Looke there, looke there

The same moment is represented in the Quarto more simply, as

> O,o,o,o.

Yet it would be easy to exaggerate the badness of this Quarto. It cannot be regarded simply as a botched version of the F text: it contains some 300 lines not in the Folio (and the Folio in turn contains some hundred lines not in the Quarto). The explanatory hypothesis that is needed is one that will account for both its 'badness' and its 'goodness', both its importance as a source of apparently genuine Shakespearian readings and the presence of the film of corruption that so obviously distorts what it presents. The first serious attempt to deal with this issue in terms of Elizabethan theatrical practice derived from work by

W. W. Greg and other members of 'The New Bibliography' movement (see F. P. Wilson, *Shakespeare and the New Bibliography* (1970)). These men found theatrical manuscripts subject to degeneration when the actors (for one reason or another) sought to supply the text of a play whose promptbook was not available; among the corruptions were some that seemed to derive from mishearings rather than misreadings, as if based on the memories of actors rather than a sight of the script. Since this characteristic appears also in Q *King Lear* – 'in sight' for 'insight', 'have' for 'of', 'dogge so bade' for 'dog's obeyed' – there is an initial presumption that this also is a text in which hearing has played a part in the transmission. If it was the actors who supplied the publishers with a text reconstructed in this way, it could hardly have been the main actors, the patented shareholders, for they were the very people with the greatest interest in retaining copyright. It has been pointed out that the errors that seem to derive from memory rather than misreading in the 1608 *King Lear* are concentrated on a small number of scenes; other scenes (for example, III.4, 5, 6) are too accurate to be the result of mere memory. Dr Alice Walker suggests that the two boy actors who played Gonerill and Regan were (appropriately enough) the agents who betrayed the text to the mutilations of the printer. They did this, it is suggested, by reciting the scenes in which they appeared, and by copying the rest from the author's rough draft or 'foul papers' at such times as they could catch a glimpse of them. There is evidence that these 'foul papers' were preserved, probably as second copies, in case the promptbook should be lost. The disadvantage of this view is that it requires the invention of two unprovable hypotheses, thus squaring the difficulty.

The version of the play produced by this or some other method seems to have created grave problems for the printer who set it up in type. The manuscript must have been difficult to read, imposing a continuous struggle to get the readings right, or even plausible, and eventually there had to be wholesale resettings. The first sheet (eight pages) is, in the twelve surviving copies, without corrections (though not without errors). But thereafter the quarto shows a scattering of about 146 substantive variant readings. Most of these were corrections made, it should be noted, while the press continued in operation, so that corrected pages on one side of the sheet are (in about half of the cases) matched with uncorrected pages on the other side. This leaves modern scholarship with the task of discriminating those words that reflect a re-reading of the manuscript from those that reflect the common sense of the printer, his desire to do no more than turn out a neat and intelligible piece of work. Of the 146 substantive 'corrections' that Greg discusses in his account of the variants, some certainly show the printer returning to the manuscript. The uncorrected version of II.4.126 reads

> I would deuose me from thy mothers fruit

The corrector turns this into

> I would diuorse me from thy mothers tombe,

which obviously derives from something more than a clever guess.

On the other hand, the corrector often indulged in mere guesswork, as when he changed 'deptoued' (II.4.132) to 'depriued' instead of the obviously authentic reading, 'deprau'd', found in the Folio, or when he curtailed the meaningless 'battero' to 'bat' instead of going to the manuscript and discovering the strange word 'ballow' (as printed in the Folio). It should be noted that the practice of the time makes it very improbable that Shakespeare himself had anything to do with the printing process.

However depraved the 1608 Quarto might be from a company point of view, the company-backed printers of the First Folio still found it convenient to use the Quarto as the basis for the new version they were offering to the public as 'cured and perfect of [its] limbs'. (In fact it now seems probable that the basic copy was a second quarto, reprinted from the First, and also dated 1608 but actually printed in 1619, as part of an effort to make an unauthorised collection of Shakespeare's plays). Before it got to the printer's shop this copy must have been annotated with corrections, taken, no doubt, from the playhouse originals. The company thus fulfilled their duty to 'our Shakespeare', without losing control of the official prompt copy, bearing the licence to perform.

There can be no argument that the new material incorporated in the Folio text greatly improved its intelligibility: prose was reassembled as verse and nonsense as sense. One's pleasure in the restoration is, however, limited by a number of factors. The text which supplied the corrections was presumably that in current theatrical use in 1622. That may have been the same one as was used in 1605, or it may have been affected by theatrical modifications. We know that plays were revised to keep up with shifts in theatrical fashion, but it is hard to align the changes between Q and F with any such movement. One whole scene (IV.3) is missing in F. There is recurrent evidence of a desire to simplify the staging. In IV.7 both the music and the doctor are gone, the latter replaced (as in IV.7) by an easier-to-use 'Gentleman'. The invasion of Britain by France is largely concealed, though this may reflect censorship rather than theatrical cutting. Censorship may be suspected on two other occasions, in the removal of I.2.143–9 – the account of prophecies to be fulfilled (including maledictions against king and nobles) – and of I.4.138–53, in which the king is called a 'fool' and reference is made to the greed of 'great men' for monopolies. Many cuts seem designed only to make the play shorter. Passages like II.vi.100–113 and V.3.202–19, may seem indispensable to the modern reader, but the play as a theatrical structure will hang together perfectly well without them.

Another reason for reserve about the Folio text derives from the fact that it was set up by two of the more incompetent compositors in the printing house, one an apprentice and the other a careless journeyman. There is evidence of their eyes and their minds wandering from the line in hand. Thus 'pregnant and potential spurs' (II.1.75) is misprinted in the Folio 'pregnant and potentiall spirits', probably because the compositor's eye caught the '-its' ending of 'profits' in the line before.

Lastly, in *King Lear* as throughout its length, the Folio is concerned to express its material in up-to-date and 'correct' English, or even in that kind of English that the individual compositor preferred. A number of the new readings in the Folio may be attributed to this rather than to the recovery of truly Shakespearian readings. The substitution of 'squints' (III.4.112) for 'squenies' (printed as 'squemes' in the Quarto) may well be of this kind, like 'sticke' for 'rash' at III.7.57 or 'sterne' for 'dern' at III.7.62. In smaller things moderniza- tion is probably commoner and more difficult to detect, but examples I assume are 'yond' for 'yon' (IV.6.18, 118, and 152) and 'if' for 'and' (II.2.42).

The Quarto is quite without indications of Act and scene divisions. In this it follows the common form of early play publication. The Folio, on the other hand, sets out the enumeration of Acts and scenes with great clarity and exactitude. It need not be supposed that the enumeration reflects Shakespeare's precise intention; it is rather part of the later literary and even classical polish applied to the plays. But it is a rational convenience, and like all modern editors I follow the Folio except in three instances. In Act II of the *Actus Secundus*, *Scena Prima* is marked, and then *Scena Secunda*, but the third and fourth scenes of Act II in the modern division are not marked. It could be argued that Kent is present on the stage (in the stocks) continuously from II.2 to II.4 and that the Folio recognizes this in its scene division – it does not give Kent an exit at II.2.171. This is possible, but it does not correspond with normal Elizabethan dramaturgy. Act II, scene 3 is delocalized and separate, whether Kent is on the stage or not. The other place where the Folio misleads is in Act IV, where the F text omits IV.3. It follows that scenes 4, 5 and 6 of this Act are misnumbered as 3, 4 and 5. Act IV, scene 7 is, however, correctly described ('*Scena Septima*'); this suggests that someone discovered the error during the printing of the Folio, avoided a continuation of it, but did not correct the instances already perpetrated.

The present text is based on the Folio; but all the variants to be discovered in the Quarto (corrected and uncorrected) have been considered, and have been admitted if a good enough argument for their superiority could be discovered. Where the Folio has been printed from the uncorrected state of the Quarto, I have treated the corrected readings (where these are not duplicated by the Folio corrector) as primary authority. A list of the places where the Quarto has been preferred to the Folio is given below (list 1.) I also give a list of places where neither Q nor F is accepted (stage directions excluded).The third list is of stage directions. It should be noted that I have assumed a higher degree of authority for the Quarto in stage directions than in text. If Q represents memories of a theatrical performance, then it is likely to be more accurate in describing what happened on the stage than in giving the detail of what was spoken. The two texts often differ in the kind of directions they give. F, as a company text, is not interested in stage directions except where props (the stocks, the thunder machine, trumpets) are concerned, or where persons are to be got on and off the stage. Q on the other hand is more concerned with description and less with business, but only at two points – the fall at 'Dover Cliff', and the fight between Edgar and Oswald – is substantive stage action described which is wholly omitted by the Folio. Both texts leave many important and significant stage actions undescribed, and so I have been fairly free with additional directions, as collation list 3 will show. I assume that this is a play in which the physical relationship of person to person and the range of significant gesture are very important, and often (especially in the scenes of folly and madness) far from obvious. In the elaborately scored scenes in the middle of the play it is sometimes difficult to discover which person is being addressed, and I have sought to clarify this in the stage directions.

The last collation lists 'rejected readings' and will enable the reader to see some ways in which the present text differs from others. It will be seen that it follows the Folio in more places than its contemporaries. The history of modern texts of *King Lear* is (with some exceptions) a history of drift from Quarto to Folio. (But in the 1980s and 1990s this current seems to be reversing itself. Peter Blayney, *The Texts of 'King Lear' and their Origins*, is expected to produce in Vol. II an elaborate argument for Shakespeare's foul papers as the source of the Quarto, which, if it is accepted, will tilt the balance still further in this direction.) The old 'Cambridge' text of Clark and Wright (1891), the foundation of modern textual scholarship, differs from the present text in over 260 substantive readings (not including lineation and stage directions). Most of these variants derive from the substitution of Folio for Quarto readings; the greater obviousness of the former's vocabulary often makes it seem 'safer' or 'more probable', especially in the absence of a general theory of the relationship of the texts. Readings that appear to be unusual if not unique among modern texts appear at I.1.5 and 70, I.5.46, II.1.8 and 119, III.6.22, IV.1.10, IV.3.20, IV.7.21, 23 and 53, V.1.16, V.3.158 and 275.

In the text I have normalized the speech prefixes, preferring 'Edmund' to 'Bastard' (the commoner form in Q and F) and 'Oswald' to 'Steward' (the standard form in Q and F). I have kept the F form 'Gonerill' (Q has 'Gonorill') since I know of no relevant authority by which to correct it. I have also preferred F's 'Albany' and 'Corn[e]wall' to Q's 'Duke', and F's 'Gloucester' to Q's 'Gloster', though I accept that 'Gloucester' may reflect only Folio modernization.

COLLATIONS

Quotations from Q and F are given in the original spelling, except that 'long s' (ſ) has been replaced by 's'.

I

Readings accepted from Q , with substantive alternatives from
F which have been rejected (given as the final element in
each entry).

I.1.	35	liege] Lord
	74	possesses] professes
	104	To love my father all] *omitted*
	149	stoops] falls
	155	a pawn] pawne
	156	nor fear] nere feare
	168	vow] vowes
	188	GLOUCESTER] (*Glost.*); *Cor.*
	214	best object] obiect
	225	well] will
	241	Lear] King
	289	not been] beene
	302	hit] sit
I.2.	41–2	*prose*] *verse* (. . . it: | . . . them, | . . . blame. |)
	55	waked] wake
	95–7	EDMUND Nor is . . . earth] *omitted*
	127	disposition to] disposition on
	130	Fut] *omitted*
	132	Edgar] *omitted*
	143–9	as of . . . astronomical] *omitted*
I.3.	17–21	Not to . . . abused] (*prose in* Q); *omitted*
	25–6	I would . . . speak] (*prose in* Q); *omitted*
	27	very] *omitted*
I.4.	98	KENT Why, Fool] *Lear.* Why my Boy
	138–53	That lord . . . snatching] *omitted*
	158	thy crown] thy Crownes
	174	fools] Foole
	193	crust nor] crust, not
	228–31	LEAR I would . . . father] *omitted*
	254	O . . . come] *omitted*
	301	Yea . . . this] *omitted*

II.1.   2–4   *prose*] *verse* (... bin | ... notice | ... Duchesse | ... night. |)
            2   you] your
        10–11   *prose*] *verse* (... toward, | ...*Albany?* |)
           52   But] And
           69   I should] should I
           70   ay, though] though
           75   spurs] spirits
           77   I never got him] *omitted*
II.1.   78   why] wher
           86   strange news] strangenesse
          119   price] (*uncorrected*: prise; *corrected*: poyse); prize
II.2.   42   and] if
           76   Renege] Reuenge
          128   respect] respects
       139–43   His fault ... with] *omitted*
          143   The King] The King his Master, needs
          148   For ... legs] *omitted*
          149   Come] *Corn.* Come
II.3.   15   mortified bare arms] mortified Armes
II.4.   18–19   LEAR No, no ... have] *omitted*
           30   panting] painting
           33   whose] those
          181   fickle] fickly
          295   bleak] high
III.1.   7–15   tears ... take all] *omitted*
         30–42   But true ... to you] *omitted*
III.2.   3   drowned] drown
III.4.   12   this] (*corrected*; *uncorrected*: the); the
           51   ford] Sword
           87   I deeply] I deerely
          110   foul fiend] foule
          111   till the first] at first
          128   stock-punished] stockt, punish'd
          129   hath had] hath
III.5.   9   letter he] Letter which hee

III.5.   24 dearer] deere
III.6. 17–55 EDGAR The foul ... 'scape] *omitted*
          69 tike] tight
          76 makes] make
        95–9 KENT Oppressèd ... behind. GLOUCESTER]
             omitted
     100–113 EDGAR When we ... lurk] *omitted*
III.7.   57 rash] sticke
          62 dern] sterne
      98–106 SECOND SERVANT I'll never ... help him]
             omitted
IV.1.   10 parti-eyed] (*corrected*; *uncorrected*: poorlie,
             leed); poorely led
          41 Then prithee] *omitted*
       57–62 Five fiends ... master] *omitted*
IV.2.   17 arms] names
          28 A fool] (*corrected*; *uncorrected*: My foote); My
             Foole
             bed] (*corrected*; *uncorrected*: body); body
          29 whistling] (*corrected*; *uncorrected*: whistle);
             whistle
       31–50 I fear ... deep] *omitted*
        53–9 that not ... he so] *omitted*
          60 shows] (*corrected*; *uncorrected*: seemes); seemes
        62–9 ALBANY Thou ... news] *omitted*
          75 threat] threat
          79 justicers] (*corrected*; *uncorrected*: Iustices); Ius-
             tices
IV.3.   1–55 KENT Why ... me] *omitted*
IV.4.   11 DOCTOR] *Gent.*
          18 distress] desires
IV.5.   39 meet him] meet
IV.6. 18, 118, 152   yon] yond
          71 enridgèd] enraged
          83 coining] crying
         134 *prose*] *two lines* (... first, | ... Mortality. |)
         198 Ay ... dust] *omitted*

IV.6. 205 one] a

IV.7. 13, 17, 21, 43, 51, 78 DOCTOR] *Gent.* (or *Gen.*)

    23 GENTLEMAN] *omitted*

    24 doubt not] doubt

    24–5 Very . . . there] *omitted*

    33–6 To stand . . . helm] *omitted*

    59 No, sir,] *omitted*

    79–80 and yet . . . lost] (*prose in* Q); *omitted*

    85–97 GENTLEMAN Holds . . . fought] *omitted*

V.1. 11–13 EDMUND That . . . hers] *omitted*

    18–19 GONERILL I had . . . me] (*prose in* Q); *omitted*

    23–8 Where . . . nobly] *omitted*

    33 EDMUND I shall . . . tent] *omitted*

    46 love] loues

V.3. 39–40 CAPTAIN I cannot . . . do't] *omitted*

    48 and appointed guard] (*corrected*; *uncorrected omits*); *omitted*

    55–60 At this time . . . place] *omitted*

    84 attaint] arrest

    127 it is the privilege] it is my priuiledge, | The priuiledge

    194 my] our

    202–19 EDGAR This would . . . slave] *omitted*

    291 sees] saies

2

Emendations incorporated in the present text (not including stage directions, or variants judged to derive from spelling rather than meaning, or from the obvious correction of obvious error).

THE CHARACTERS IN THE PLAY] *not in* Q , F

I.1. 110 mysteries] mistresse Q ; miseries F

    283–5 *verse in* Q, F (. . . say, | . . . both, | . . . to night. |)

I.2. 21 top the] tooth' Q ; to'th' F

I.3   23–7   *prose in* Q, F

I.4   211–13 *prose in* Q, F

      252–3   *prose in* Q, F

      302   Let] Ha ? Let F; (*not in* Q)

      340   a-taxed for] alapt Q *uncorrected*; attaskt for Q
             corrected; at task for F

I.5.   44–5   *prose in* Q, F

       46   KNIGHT] *Gent.* F; *Seruant.* Q

II.2. 45–6   *prose in* Q, F

      141   contemned'st] contaned Q *uncorrected*; temnest
             Q *corrected*; (*not in* F)

II.4.   55   Hysterica] *Historica* Q , F

       73   ha' . . . use] haue . . . follow Q ; hause . . .
             follow F

III.1. 10   out-storm] outscorne Q ; (*not in* F)

III.2. 85–6   Then shall . . . confusion] *placed after* 'build'
             (*line* 92) *in* F; (*not in* Q)

III.4. 45   *prose in* Q, F
             blow the cold winds] blowes the cold wind Q ;
             blow the windes F

       60   What, has his] What, his Q ; Ha's his F

       73   *prose in* Q, F

      95–6   *prose in* Q, F

      112   squenies] queues Q *uncorrected*; squemes Q
             corrected; squints F

      138–9 *prose in* Q, F

III.6. 21   justicer] Iustice Q ; (*not in* F)

       24–5 madam? | Come . . . me] madam come . . . mee
             Q ; (*not in* F)

       25   burn] broome Q ; (*not in* F)

       33–4 *prose in* Q ; (*not in* F)

       47   she kicked] kickt Q ; (*not in* F)

       68   lym] him Q ; Hym F

      99–101 *prose in* Q ; (*not in* F)

III.7 44–5   *prose in* Q, F

      99–101 *prose in* Q ; (*not in* F)

      105–6 *prose in* Q ; (*not in* F)

IV.1.   60 Flibberdigibbet] *Stiberdigebit* Q ; (*not in* F)

IV.2.   32 its origin] it origin Q *uncorrected*; ith origin
          Q *corrected*; (*not in* F)

        47 these] the Q *uncorrected*; this Q *corrected*; (*not
          in* F)

        57 begins to threat] begin threats Q *uncorrected*;
          begins thereat Q *corrected*; (*not in* F)

IV.3.   11 Ay, sir] I say Q ; (*not in* F)

        16 strove] streme Q ; (*not in* F)

IV.3.   31 moistened] moystened her Q ; (*not in* F)

IV.6. 118–27 *prose in* Q , F

      161–74 *prose in* Q , F

        166 Plate] Place F ; (*not in* Q)

        184 This's a] This a Q , F

V.1. 12–13 *prose in* Q ; (*not in* F)

V.3.   211 him] me Q ; (*not in* F)

      221–2 *prose in* Q , F

        273 SECOND OFFICER] *Cap.* Q ; *Gent.* F

3

The following list of stage directions concerns itself only with
those added to, or considerably adapted from, the substantive
texts, Q and F, where the editor's interpretation of requirements has been involved. Provision of exits, where these are
clearly demanded by the context, is not recorded; nor is the
common slight adjustment of the point at which entries and
exits are mentioned; these are often a line or two early in F.
Asides and other indicators of the mode of utterance ('*aloud*',
'*sings*', etc.) are always editorial, as are indicators of the person
addressed, and these are not collated.

I.1.   35 *Exeunt Gloucester and Edmund*] *Exit.* F

      161 *not in* Q , F

      266 *Flourish. Exeunt Lear, Burgundy, Cornwall,
          Albany, Gloucester, and attendants*] *Flourish.
          Exeunt.* F ; *Exit Lear and Burgundie.* Q

I.4.   o *Enter Kent in disguise*] *Enter Kent.* Q , F

I.4. 7 *Enter Lear and Knights*] *Enter Lear and Attendants.* F

    8 *not in* Q , F

   43 *Exit Second Knight*] *not in* Q, F

   46 *not in* Q , F

   47 *not in* Q , F

   75 *not in* Q , F

   76 *not in* Q , F

   83 *not in* Q , F

   85 *not in* Q , F

   91 *not in* Q , F

   94 *He gives him money*] *not in* Q , F

   194 *not in* Q, F

   268 *not in* Q, F

   269 *not in* Q, F

   271 *not in* Q, F

I.5. 0 *Enter Lear, Kent, Knight, and the Fool*] *Enter Lear, Kent, Gentleman, and Foole.* F

II.1. 0 *...by opposite doors*] *Enter ... seuerally.* F

   35 *not in* Q , F

   42 *not in* Q , F

II.2. 0 *Enter Kent and Oswald by opposite doors*] *Enter Kent, and Steward seuerally.* F

   30 *not in* Q , F

   38 *not in* Q , F

   39 *not in* Q , F

   148 *not in* Q , F

II.4. 0 *Kent still in the stocks*] *not in* Q , F

   130 *not in* Q , F

   148 *not in* Q , F

   153 *not in* Q , F

   212 *not in* Q , F

   281 *Exeunt Lear, Gloucester, Kent, the Fool, and Gentleman*] *Exeunt Lear, Leister, Kent, and Foole.* Q ; *Exeunt.* F

III.1. 0 *...by opposite doors*] *..., seuerally.* F

   55 *Exeunt by opposite doors*] *Exeunt.* Q , F

III.4.   37, 43   *Enter the Fool from the hovel ... Enter Edgar*
                 disguised as Poor Tom] Enter Edgar, and Foole.
                 F (after line 36)

         105   *not in Q, F*

         153   *not in Q, F*

III.6.   99   *Exeunt Kent, Gloucester, and the Fool, bearing*
              off the King] Exeunt F

III.7.   20   *not in Q, F*

         23   *not in Q, F*

         32   *not in Q, F*

III.7.   34   *not in Q, F*

      76, 77, *Cornwall draws his sword ... He lunges at him*
         78   *... drawing his sword ... He wounds Cornwall]*
              draw and fight. Q (after line 77)

         81   *not in Q, F*

         97   *Exit Cornwall, supported by Regan] Exeunt, F*

        106   *Exeunt by opposite doors] Exit. Q*

IV.2.   21   *not in Q, F*

IV.4.   0   *Enter, with drum and colours, Cordelia, Doctor,*
              and soldiers] Enter with Drum and Colours,
              Cordelia, Gentlemen, and Souldiours. F; Enter
              Cordelia, Docter and others. Q

IV.6.   0   *Enter Gloucester and Edgar in peasant's clothes]*
              Enter Gloucester, and Edgar. F

         41   *Gloucester throws himself forward] He fals. Q*

         80   *Enter Lear fantastically dressed with wild*
              flowers] Enter Lear mad. Q

         95   *not in Q, F*

        132   *not in Q, F*

        170   *not in Q, F*

        181   *not in Q, F*

        188   *He throws down his flowers and stamps on them]*
              not in Q, F
              Enter a Gentleman and two attendants. Gloucester
              and Edgar draw back] Enter three Gentlemen. Q

        203   *Exit running, followed by attendants] Exit King*
              running. Q

IV.6.   208 *not in* Q, F

          217 *not in* Q, F

          231 *not in* Q, F

IV.7.   22 *Enter Gentleman ushering Lear in a chair carried by servants. All fall to their knees*] *Enter Lear in a chaire carried by Seruants* F

          24 *not in* Q, F

          26 *not in* Q, F

          58 *not in* Q, F

          70 *not in* Q, F

          95 *not in* Q, F

V.1.   37 *As Albany is going out, enter Edgar*] *Enter Edgar* Q, F

V.3.   21 *not in* Q, F

          26 *Exeunt Lear and Cordelia, guarded*] *Exit.* F

          84 *not in* Q, F

          94 *not in* Q, F

          98 *not in* Q, F

          106 *not in* Q, F

          115 *Trumpet answers within. Enter Edgar armed, a trumpet before him*] *Trumpet answers within. Enter Edgar armed.* F; *Enter Edgar at the third sound, a trumpet before him.* Q

          126 *not in* Q, F

          148 *Alarums. Fights. Edmund falls*] *Alarums. Fights.* F (after 'save him!')

          149 *to Edgar, about to kill Edmund*] *not in* Q, F

          159 *not in* Q, F

          219 *Enter a Gentleman with a bloody knife*] *Enter a Gentleman.* F; *Enter one with a bloudie knife,* Q

          228 *not in* Q, F

          249 *not in* Q, F

          254 *Edmund is borne off*] *not in* Q, F

              followed by Second Officer and others] *not in* Q, F

4

This list sets against the readings of the present text (printed to the left of the square bracket) substantive readings of other modern editions – in particular those of Peter Alexander (1951), Kenneth Muir (1952), Dover Wilson and Duthie (1960) – which have been considered and rejected. Similar readings can, of course, be found in many other editions. The reading cited from the present text can be understood to derive from F except where an asterisk directs attention to collation-list 1 above (in which case the reading derives from Q) or where it is an emendation recorded above in list 2. In most cases the rejected readings derive from editors' preference for Q, and in such cases '(Q)' indicates the source. In the same way '(F)' is used to indicate derivation from the Folio. Sometimes the rejected reading is an emendation – often to be traced back to the eighteenth-century editors – and in such cases the Q reading if variant) is supplied before the rejected reading.

I.1.	5	qualities] equalities (Q)
	74	square] spirit (Q)
	128	the third] this third (Q)
	163	Kill] Do. | Kill (Q)
		thy fee] the fee (Q)
	*168	vow] vows (F)
	206	up in] up on (Q)
	237	intends to do] intends (Q)
	239	stands] stand (Q)
	248	and fortunes] of fortune (Q)
	281	covers] (F, Q); covert
I.2.	133	pat] and pat (Q)
I.4.	21	he's] he is (Q)
	40–41	me if . . . dinner. I] me. If . . . dinner I
	111	the Lady Brach] (Ladie oth'e brach Q); Lady the Brach; the Lady's brach
	199	Sir] (F, Q); *omitted*

330

I.4. 212 it's] it (Q)
      *254 sir] *omitted*
      *301 Yea] Ha (F)
       302 Let] Ha! Let (F). *See Commentary*
I.5.   1 Gloucester] (F, Q); Cornwall
       44 *most editors add the direction* Enter a Gentleman
       46 KNIGHT] (*Seruant.* Q); GENTLEMAN (F)
II.1.   8 kissing] bussing (Q)
       39 stand] stand's (Q)
       45 the thunder] their thunder (Q)
       51 latched] lanch'd (Q)
      *52 But] And (F)
       76 O strange] strong (Q)
       77 letter, said he] letter (Q)
      119 price] poise (Q); prize. *See Commentary*
II.2.   55 A tailor] Ay, a tailor (Q)
       75 Being] Bring (Q)
           the] their (Q)
       80 Smile] Smoile (F, Q)
      149 my lord] my good lord (Q)
II.3.   19 Sometimes . . . sometime] Sometimes . . . sometimes (Q)
II.4.   2 messengers] messenger (Q)
      *19 Yes] Yes, yes
       52 for thy] (*not in* Q); from thy
       73 ha' . . . use] have . . . follow (Q). *See Commentary*
       97 commands, tends, service] commands her service (Q); commands their service
      143 his] her (Q)
      163 blister] blast her pride (Q); blister her
      164 rash mood is on] rash mood (Q)
      *181 fickle] sickly (F)
      261 needs –] (needs: F); needs, (Q)
      266 that patience] (F, Q); patience
III.1. 10 out-storm] out-scorn (Q)

III.1.   20 is] be (Q)
          48 that] your (Q)
III.2.   9 makes] make (Q)
          54 simular] simular man (Q)
          57 Has] Hast (Q)
          71 And] That (Q)
          78 boy] my good boy (Q)
        85–6 Then shall . . . confusion] *placed after line* 92 (F)
III.4.   45 cold winds] cold wind (Q); winds (F)
          46 thy bed] thy cold bed (Q)
          78 word's justice] words justly (Q); word justly
III.4.   96 mun, nonny] (hay no on ny Q); mun, hey no
              nonny; mun, hey, nonny, nonny
III.6.   *22 No] Now
          *53 store] stone
III.7.   52 answer] first answer (Q)
          58 bare] loved (Q)
          76 What] (F, Q); REGAN What
IV.1.   *10 parti-eyed] poorly led (F); poorly eyed
          38 fool] the fool (Q)
          *60 mopping] mocking
IV.2.   *28 A fool usurps my bed] My Fool usurps my
              body (F)
          *29 whistling] whistle (F)
          *32 its] (ith Q *corrected*); it (Q *uncorrected*)
IV.3.   *20 seem] seemed
          *29 be believed] believe it
          *31 And clamour] That clamour
IV.6.   15 sampire] (F, Q); samphire
*18, 118, 152 yon] yond (F)
          97 the white] white (Q)
       128–32 (*prose*)] (F, Q); *verse*
       130–31 civet; good apothecary, sweeten] civet, good
              apothecary, to sweeten (Q)
       158–60 (*prose*)] (F, Q); *verse*
          165 great] small (Q)
          184 This's] This (F, Q); This'

IV.6.   202 Come] Nay (Q)

          250 English] British (Q)

          260 we] we'ld (Q)

IV.7.   *21 DOCTOR] GENTLEMAN (F)

     *23 GENTLEMAN] DOCTOR

      32 jarring] warring (Q)

      49 Where] when (Q)

      53 even] (eu'n F); e'en (Q)

      58 hand] hands (Q)

V.1.   16 Fear not] Fear me not (Q)

      21 heard] hear (Q)

      36 Pray] pray you (Q)

V.3.   5 I am] am I (Q)

      77 is] (*not in* Q); are

    100 the] thy (Q)

    102 ho!] ho! | EDMUND A herald, ho, a herald (Q)

               Enter a Herald] (F (*after* 'firmly'.')); *most editors place after line* 106

    108 this.] this. | OFFICER Sound, trumpet! (Q)

    113 *defence.*] defence. | EDMUND Sound (Q); defence. | EDMUND Sound trumpet

    129 place, youth] youth, place (Q)

    153 stop] stople (Q)

    158 EDMUND] GONERIL (Q)

    273 SECOND OFFICER] CAPTAIN (Q); OFFICER

    275 him] them (Q)

  *291 sees] says (F)

ADDITIONAL NOTE (1996)

The account of the relation between the Quarto and Folio texts of *King Lear* given above has been challenged in the last fifteen years or so by an alternative explanation of the evidence. The classic statement of the new theory is to be found in Michael Warren's 'Quarto and Folio *King Lear*' published in *Shakespeare, Pattern of Excelling Nature*, ed. Bevington and Halio (1978), but the textual impulse can be traced back to E. A. J. Honigmann's *The Stability of*

Shakespeare's Text (1965). The members of this movement (whose contiguous points of view are conveniently set out in *The Division of the Kingdoms: Shakespeare's Two Versions of 'King Lear'*, ed. Michael Warren and Gary Taylor (1983)) argue that Q and F are not complementarily imperfect versions of one play (as suggested above) but two distinct Shakespearian plays – a first version of 1605–6 and a revised version of 1610. The arguments advanced to make this point are partly bibliographical and partly literary-critical.

The new theory derives its main impulse from dissatisfaction with those that preceded it, which clearly failed to solve all the contradictions that lie between Q and F, and which often showed an improper lack of tentativeness in expression. The idea of revision (even if not authorial revision) is well attested in Elizabethan playhouse practice; and F has often been thought to reflect a tidying-up of the (complete) play, so that it would be easier to handle on the stage. The new argument has certainly opened up what could be seen as a bibliographical closed shop; but we should notice that mere textual evidence is seldom susceptible of only one explanation: and clearly it cannot *require* us to believe either that F is a revision or that Q and F are both derived from a single original. The scholar, if he is to convince, is obliged to venture beyond facts into speculations why the variants occur, and these speculations have a tendency to derive from the merely personal taste which calls some readings misprints and others defensible Shakespearian locutions, or from undiscussed *a priori* positions – see Marion Trousdale, 'A Trip Through the Divided Kingdom', *Shakespeare Quarterly* 37 (1986), 218–23.

The basic given of the literary defence is the fact that the final speech in the play is assigned to Edgar in F and to Albany in Q. Any number of printing-house accidents could have produced this variation, or it may reflect an uncoordinated piece of playhouse revision. Michael Warren argues that it points us to a whole pattern of changes – and in this he is followed by all other members of the movement –

changes designed to make Albany look like the 'stronger' character in Q, and the 'weaker' one in F. To sustain this argument many individual passages in both texts have to be read from the angle of a presumed authorial *intention*. And such angles are easily available to an accomplished literary critic (or director) reading through the poetically open and evasive words; and it would not be difficult for a method actor to discover in these any number of secret biographies which he could draw on to depict either 'weakness' or 'strength'. The basic problem lies indeed in the very easiness of this kind of interpretation.

The text presented in this present volume is a unified 'conflated' text – one drawing on readings from both Q and F, and so, as is said, a modern fabrication perhaps never performed on any Elizabethan stage, and never seen in print before the eighteenth century. For this reason both current 'Oxford' and 'Cambridge' series print separate texts of Q and F *King Lear*. But that solution of the problem is not acceptable here. The rigidity (and indeed old-fashionedness) of the conceptions used (two artefacts, each having the status of a literary classic, each to be protected from addition or subtraction) bears little relation to the status of unprinted theatrical texts, present in the playhouse as open resources from which different performances could be drawn for different occasions (such as performances at court, or in the country). When neither variant text can be given a clear claim to total truth it seems only proper to replicate that open resourcefulness. Moreover, when theoretical clarity fails it seems right to give weight to practical matters. If the additions found in both Q and F are entirely or mostly by Shakespeare (and there is little argument about this), then it is right to allow readers (and these, not textual scholars, are the audience aimed at) to enjoy all the poetry Shakespeare wrote; and to enjoy it in a form whose general coherence (within the limits common to Elizabethan drama) has stirred only occasional and uncoordinated objections among the generations who have been moved and inspired by its existence.

WORDS FOR MUSIC IN 'KING LEAR'

THE traditional expressions of socially accepted madness in the snatches of court Fool and Bedlam beggar in *King Lear* involve the idea of music, and probably were given, in Elizabethan performance, the reality of music. We may take it that the roles of Edgar and the Fool were played by two of the singing actors in the company. Neither the Quarto nor the Folio, however, has any stage directions indicating singing. It has been left to editors to imagine what music was used. Dr F. W. Sternfeld, to whose work I am indebted, has listed eighteen places in the play where one might expect singing (*Music in Shakespearean Tragedy* (1963), pages 174-5). His list is valuable; but it cannot be accepted just as it stands. It includes one item which does not seem to be a lyric – the Fool's 'prophecy' at the end of Act III, scene 2: fourteen lines which can be rearranged as two stanzas, but still lack the regularity of strophic composition. There are also four passages (items 7, 13, 14, and 15 below) which might have been sung but are not included by Dr Sternfeld. My list therefore contains twenty-one items.

It will be seen that these passages all occur in five scenes in the first three Acts of the play; and that the singing role of the Fool is abandoned in III.4 when Poor Tom joins the group on stage – except that 'Come o'er the burn, Bessy' is shared between the two singing actors.

Three of the passages (items 4, 12, and 19) seem to be from ballads with a wide currency; for two of these (4 and 19) music of the early seventeenth century survives, and is transcribed on page 344. Item 12 ('He that has and a little tiny wit') is related, of course, to the last song of *Twelfth Night*, but no music earlier than the eighteenth century has survived. A transcription is printed in the New Penguin edition of *Twelfth Night*.

For the rest, no tunes with any likelihood of authenticity
survive. One can only guess from the subject-matter and the
metrical form whether these are traditional words using traditional music; brief comments on these probabilities are given
in the list. At least ten of the passages seem unlikely to have
been associated with traditional tunes.

Below I indicate the metrical form of each passage, listing the
number of stresses in each line aligned above the rhyme scheme
(represented by letters); the line division and possible stanzaic
structure are indicated by commas and semi-colons.

1. I.4.117–26 (FOOL Have more than thou showest)

$$2 \ 2 \ 2 \ 2 \ 2 \ 2 \ 2 \ 2 \ 2 \ 2$$
a, a, a, a, a, a, b, b, b, b

The repetition of the (anapaestic) rhythmic structure and
of the same rhyme suggests an attempt to create an effect of
incantation through words alone, making music superfluous.

2. I.4.138–45 (FOOL That lord that counselled thee)

$$3 \ 3 \ 3 \ 3 \quad 3 \ 3 \ 3 \ 3$$
a, b, a, b; c, d, d, d

The form is strophically accurate. But the subject-matter is
so germane to *King Lear* that if the passage does have a ballad
origin the words must have been much modified. There is an
obvious parallel with traditional 'counting-out' songs.

3. I.4.163–6 (FOOL Fools had ne'er less grace in a year)

$$4 \ 3 \ 4 \ 3$$
a, b, a, b

The form is apt for music, but these words cannot be traditional.

4. I.4.171–4 (FOOL Then they for sudden joy did weep)

4 3 4 3
a, b, a, b

Lines three and four are obviously Shakespeare's invention, but the first two lines appear (with variations) in several ballad scraps and adaptations of the period. One of these supplies the music cited on page 344; it was written in manuscript in a printed book of 1609 (Thomas Ravenscroft's *Pammelia*) now in the British Museum, with the following words:

> Late as I waked out of sleep
> I heard a pretty thing:
> Some men for sudden joy do weep,
> And some for sorrow sing.

In the transcription below, Shakespeare's words are fitted to the same tune. The words may be sung as a round, the second and third voices entering at the eighth and fifteenth bars; but of course no such effect was sought in *King Lear*.

5. I.4.192–4 (FOOL Mum, mum! | He that keeps nor crust nor crumb)

2 4 4
a, a, a

On the repeated rhyme see under item 1. The tone is more that of a proverb than a song.

6. I.4.211–12 (FOOL The hedge-sparrow fed the cuckoo so long)

4 4
a, a

Again, more a proverb than a song.

7. I.4.221 (FOOL Whoop, Jug, I love thee!)

3
a

Sounds like a ballad-refrain, but not otherwise known.

339

8. I.4.314–18 (FOOL A fox, when one has caught her)

3 2 2 3 2
a, a, a, a, a

Sounds like a comic exercise in rhyming words notoriously difficult to pronounce.

9. II.4.46–51 (FOOL Fathers that wear rags)

3 3 3 3 3 3
a, b, a, b, c, c

Does not sound like traditional ballad material.

10. II.4.74–81 (FOOL That sir which serves and seeks for gain)

4 3 4 3 4 3 4 3
a, b, a, b; c, d, c, d

There is no reason why this should not be a ballad; but there is no evidence to connect it with one.

11. III.2.27–34 (FOOL The cod-piece that will house)

3 3 3 3 3 3 3 3
a, b, a, b; c, d, c, d

The compression and obliquity of language makes this unsuitable for music.

12. III.2.74–7 (FOOL He that has and a little tiny wit)

4 4 4 4
a, b, a, c

The stage direction in the Folio printing of *Twelfth Night* ('*Clowne sings*') tells us that this was a song in Shakespeare's day; but no music of that period has survived.

13. III.4.45 (POOR TOM Through the sharp hawthorn blow the cold winds)

4

a

The phrase is obviously related to Edgar's nakedness; but it would have most effect if derived from traditional material.

14. III.4.73 (POOR TOM Pillicock sat on Pillicock Hill)

4

a

Sounds like a ballad-refrain, but not otherwise known. I have assumed that 'Alow, alow, loo, loo!' – the line following – is an imitation of the huntsman's cry and is not part of a traditional song.

15. III.4.95–6 (POOR TOM Still through the hawthorn blows the cold wind)

4 3

a, b

See under item 13. Line 96 *may* be connected with line 95, and I have so printed it; but it may be a quite disparate remark.

16. III.4.115–18 (POOR TOM S'Withold footed thrice the 'old)

4 4 4 4

a, a, bb, c

Form and content suggest incantation rather than song.

17. III.4.131–3 (POOR TOM Horse to ride and weapon to wear)

4 4 4

a, a, a

The source in *Bevis of Hampton* makes music unlikely.

341

18. III.4.176–8 (POOR TOM Child Roland to the dark tower came)

4 4 4

a, a, a

The material is, in part at least, traditional. But these do not sound like words for music.

19. III.6.25–8 (POOR TOM *and* FOOL Come o'er the burn, Bessy, to me)

3 2 2 3

a, b, b, a

Various pieces of music with this title have survived. They raise the question whether Tom should sing the full three lines of the original –

> Come o'er the burn, Bessy,
> Thou little pretty Bessy,
> Come o'er the burn, Bessy, to me –

or merely the shortened version. For the transcription on page 344 I have assumed the latter. The first line is, I take it, merely a cue, used to suggest the song to the audience, to provide a basis on which the Fool can embroider his parody.

The transcription gives the refrain sections of the tune with this heading found in a Cambridge lute manuscript (MS. Dd. 2. 11, fol. 80ᵛ). This seems more appropriate than any tune extracted from the elaborate contrapuntal setting in a British Museum manuscript (Additional MS. 5665, fols. 143–4). I have placed inside square brackets the part of the refrain which is not printed in Shakespeare's text.

20. III.6.41–4 (POOR TOM Sleepest or wakest thou, jolly shepherd?)

4 3 4 3

a, b, c, b

Form and content would make a ballad source quite plausible.

21. III.6.65–72 (POOR TOM Be thy mouth or black or white)

4 4 4 4 4 4 4 4
a, a, b, b, c, c, d, d

These trochaic octosyllabics suggest incantation rather than song. They are strongly reminiscent of the witches' incantations in *Macbeth*.

4. I.4.171–4 (Then they for sudden joy did weep)

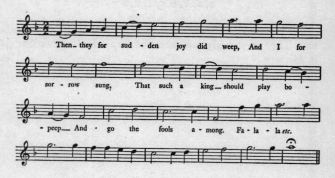

Then they for sud-den joy did weep, And I for sor-row sung, That such a king should play bo-peep And go the fools a-mong. Fa-la-la *etc.*

19. III.6.25–8 (Come o'er the burn, Bessy, to me)

Come o'er the burn, Bes-sy, Thou lit-tle pret-ty Bes-sy, Come o'er the burn, Bes-sy, to me. Her boat hath a leak And she must not speak Why she dares not come o-ver to thee.

READ MORE IN PENGUIN

In every corner of the world, on every subject under the sun, Penguin represents quality and variety – the very best in publishing today.

For complete information about books available from Penguin – including Puffins, Penguin Classics and Arkana – and how to order them, write to us at the appropriate address below. Please note that for copyright reasons the selection of books varies from country to country.

In the United Kingdom: Please write to *Dept. EP, Penguin Books Ltd, Bath Road, Harmondsworth, West Drayton, Middlesex UB7 0DA*

In the United States: Please write to *Consumer Sales, Penguin Putnam Inc., P.O. Box 12289 Dept. B, Newark, New Jersey 07101-5289*. VISA and MasterCard holders call 1-800-788-6262 to order Penguin titles

In Canada: Please write to *Penguin Books Canada Ltd, 10 Alcorn Avenue, Suite 300, Toronto, Ontario M4V 3B2*

In Australia: Please write to *Penguin Books Australia Ltd, P.O. Box 257, Ringwood, Victoria 3134*

In New Zealand: Please write to *Penguin Books (NZ) Ltd, Private Bag 102902, North Shore Mail Centre, Auckland 10*

In India: Please write to *Penguin Books India Pvt Ltd, 11 Community Centre, Panchsheel Park, New Delhi 110017*

In the Netherlands: Please write to *Penguin Books Netherlands bv, Postbus 3507, NL-1001 AH Amsterdam*

In Germany: Please write to *Penguin Books Deutschland GmbH, Metzlerstrasse 26, 60594 Frankfurt am Main*

In Spain: Please write to *Penguin Books S. A., Bravo Murillo 19, 1° B, 28015 Madrid*

In Italy: Please write to *Penguin Italia s.r.l., Via Benedetto Croce 2, 20094 Corsico, Milano*

In France: Please write to *Penguin France, Le Carré Wilson, 62 rue Benjamin Baillaud, 31500 Toulouse*

In Japan: Please write to *Penguin Books Japan Ltd, Kaneko Building, 2-3-25 Koraku, Bunkyo-Ku, Tokyo 112*

In South Africa: Please write to *Penguin Books South Africa (Pty) Ltd, Private Bag X14, Parkview, 2122 Johannesburg*

ROYAL SHAKESPEARE COMPANY

The Royal Shakespeare Company today is probably one of the best-known theatre companies in the world, playing regularly to audiences of more than a million people a year. The RSC has three theatres in Stratford-upon-Avon, the Royal Shakespeare Theatre, the Swan Theatre and The Other Place, and two theatres in London's Barbican Centre, the Barbican Theatre and The Pit. The Company also has an annual season in Newcastle-upon-Tyne and regularly undertakes tours throughout the UK and overseas.

Find out more about the RSC and its current repertoire by joining the Company's mailing list. Not only will you receive advance information of all the Company's activities, but also priority booking, special ticket offers, copies of the RSC Magazine and special offers on RSC publications and merchandise.

If you would like to receive details of the Company's work and an application form for the mailing list please write to:

RSC Membership Office
Royal Shakespeare Theatre
FREEPOST
Stratford-upon-Avon
CV37 6BR

or telephone: 01789 205301

A SELECTION OF PLAYS

Edward Albee	**Who's Afraid of Virginia Woolf?**
Alan Ayckbourn	**Joking Apart and Other Plays**
James Baldwin	**The Amen Corner**
Bertolt Brecht	**Parables for the Theatre**
Albert Camus	**Caligula and Other Plays**
Anton Chekhov	**Plays (The Cherry Orchard/Three Sisters/ Ivanov/The Seagull/Uncle Vanya)**
Euripides	**Andromache/Electra/Hecabe/Suppliant Women/Trojan Women**
Henrik Ibsen	**A Doll's House/League of Youth/Lady from the Sea**
	Brand
Ben Jonson	**Every Man in his Humour/Sejanus, His Fall/ Volpone/Epicoene**
Thomas Kyd	**The Spanish Tragedie**
Mike Leigh	**Abigail's Party/Goose-Pimples**
Arthur Miller	**The Crucible**
	Death of a Salesman
Jean-Paul Sartre	**In Camera/The Respectable Prostitute/ Lucifer and the Lord**
Peter Shaffer	**Lettice and Lovage/Yonadab**
	The Royal Hunt of the Sun
	Equus
Bernard Shaw	**Plays Pleasant**
	Pygmalion
	John Bull's Other Island
Arnold Wesker	**Plays, Volumes 1-7**
Oscar Wilde	**The Importance of Being Earnest and Other Plays**
Thornton Wilder	**Our Town/The Skin of Our Teeth/The Matchmaker**
Tennessee Williams	**Cat on a Hot Tin Roof/The Milk Train Doesn't Stop Here Anymore/The Night of the Iguana**
August Wilson	**The Piano Lesson/Joe Turner's Come and Gone**

READ MORE IN PENGUIN

CRITICAL STUDIES

Described by *The Times Educational Supplement* as 'admirable' and 'superb', Penguin Critical Studies is a specially developed series of critical essays on the major works of literature for use by students in universities, colleges and schools.

Titles published or in preparation include:

The Alchemist
The Poetry of William Blake
Critical Theory
Dickens's Major Novels
Doctor Faustus
Dombey and Son
Frankenstein
Great Expectations
The Great Gatsby
Heart of Darkness
The Poetry of Gerard
  Manley Hopkins
The Poetry of Keats
Mansfield Park
The Mayor of Casterbridge

Middlemarch
Paradise Lost
The Poetry of Alexander Pope
Rosencrantz and Guildenstern
  are Dead
Sense and Sensibility
Sons and Lovers
Tennyson
Tess of the D'Urbervilles
To the Lighthouse
The Waste Land
Wordsworth
Wuthering Heights
The Poetry of W. B. Yeats